Śiva's Demon Devotee

Śiva's Demon Devotee

Kāraikkāl Ammaiyār

ELAINE CRADDOCK

SUNY
PRESS

Cover photo courtesy of The Nelson-Atkins Museum of Art, Kansas City, Missouri. Purchase: William Rockhill Nelson Trust, 33-533. Photograph by E.G. Schempf.

Published by
State University of New York Press, Albany

Printed in the United States of America

For information, contact State University of New York Press, Albany, NY
www.sunypress.edu

Production by Kelli W. LeRoux
Marketing by Michael Campochiaro

Library of Congress Cataloging-in-Publication Data

Craddock, Elaine.
Siva's demon devotee : Karaikkal Ammaiyar / Elaine Craddock.
p. cm.
Includes translations from Tamil.
Includes bibliographical references and index.
ISBN 978-1-4384-3088-1 (pbk. : alk. paper)
ISBN 978-1-4384-3087-4 (hardcover : alk. paper)
1. Karaikkalammai, 6th cent.—Criticism and interpretation. 2. Devotional poetry, Tamil—History and criticism. 3. Saiva Siddhanta in literature. I. Karaikkalammai, 6th cent. Selections. English. II. Title.

PL4758.9.K3732Z633 2010
894.8'118109—dc22 2009033233

10 9 8 7 6 5 4 3 2 1

7-4 (hardcover : alk. paper)

For my father, Lane,
and my mother, Jean (1933–2008),
and for Marsh

Contents

List of Illustrations

Acknowledgments

First and foremost I want to thank Dr. R. Vijayalakshmy, Professor Emeritus at the International Institute of Tamil Studies, with whom I read Kāraikkāl Ammaiyār's poetry. Without her generosity of spirit and willingness to share her vast knowledge of Tamil literature with me, this project would not have been possible. I am eternally grateful to her for opening up this world to me, and for the wonderful memories of sitting on the front porch of her house with her, looking out at her beautiful garden, and discussing Śaiva poetry and Tamil culture.

My field research associate Mr. M. Thavamani accompanied me to the temples, conducted many interviews with key people, attended and documented festivals and events, and assisted with a variety of translations. His enthusiasm, wisdom, insights, and ability to connect with people made working with him not only rewarding but joyful. His contributions have added immeasurably to this work.

Several other people in Tamilnadu were also invaluable to this work. In Tiruvālaṅkāṭu, the temple Gurukkaḷ Śri S. Sabarathina generously gave his time and shared his knowledge of the temple and Śaiva traditions. The temple Ōtuvār Mr. K. Aruḷānantam kindly provided information and sang some of Ammaiyār's songs for us. Mrs. Hema Chandrasekhar extended her gracious hospitality during the festival, and willingly gave important information. It was a privilege to participate in the celebration that her grandmother began. The priest at the Paḻaiyaṉūr Kailāsanātha temple told us helpful information. In Kāraikkāl, I am grateful to Mr. Tirumalai at the Kāraikkāl Ammaiyār temple, and Mr. Kailasanathan, for the important information they shared.

Financial support for this project was provided by Southwestern University, for which I am very grateful. Ginni Ishimatsu, Martha Selby, and Tracy Pintchman read portions of this manuscript and offered insightful comments. I would also like to thank the two anonymous reviewers who made invaluable suggestions for improving this work. I am very grateful to Nancy Ellegate at SUNY Press for her support and kindness. Kelli W. LeRoux provided excellent editorial oversight, and Leonard S. Rosenbaum prepared a draft of the index. My wonderful parents have never wavered in their interest in and support of my work; my mother died before she could see the final product, but her spirit permeates the text. I also appreciate the encouragement my sister Susan and brother-in-law George have given me over the years.

I owe the largest debt of gratitude to my partner, Marsha Russell, without whom I could not have completed this work. She is a perceptive reader and editor, a gifted photographer, and an intrepid adventurer; she also shares the joy in my work, nurtures my spirit, and keeps me going. In short, she makes it all worthwhile.

Portions of this manuscript have been published previously in the following articles and are reproduced here with permission: "Kāraikkāl Ammaiyār: Bridging the Caṅkam and Śaiva Worlds," in *Passages: Relationships between Tamil and Sanskrit*, ed. Kannan M. and Jennifer Clare (Institut Français de Pondichéry; Tamil Chair, Department of South and Southeast Asian Studies, University of California, Berkeley, 2009), 171–196; and "The Anatomy of Devotion: The Life and Poetry of Karaikkal Ammaiyar," in *Women's Lives, Women's Rituals in the Hindu Tradition*, ed. Tracy Pintchman (Oxford: Oxford University Press, 2007), 131–147.

Introduction

Kāraikkāl Ammaiyār, the "Mother from Kāraikkāl," was probably the first poet to write hymns to the god Śiva in Tamil, in approximately the mid-sixth century, when the boundaries between Śiva's devotees and competing groups were just starting to be articulated in a self-conscious way. Speaking to god in one's mother tongue, rather than Sanskrit, was pivotal to the triumph of Hindu devotionalism over the religions of Jainism and Buddhism that reached the apex of their popularity in South India during the fifth and sixth centuries. The Tamil Śaiva tradition considers Kāraikkāl Ammaiyār the author of four works of poetry. Her powerful poetry is what Indira Peterson calls a "rhetoric of immediacy," as it speaks to a particular community defining itself in a context of competing religious allegiances (1999, 165). Along with the hymns of the later saints, her 143 poems envision a world where devotees can dwell in perpetual bliss with Śiva, ridicules those who cannot see that Śiva is the only truth, and points to the sophisticated philosophy that would be systematized as Śaiva Siddhānta centuries later.

In the southernmost Indian state of Tamilnadu, Śaiva Siddhānta developed over many centuries to become the dominant philosophical, theological, and ritual system associated with the god Śiva. The tradition was systematized between the twelfth and fourteenth centuries but draws its devotional perspectives from the stories and hymns of the *nāyaṉmārs*, or "leaders," the sixty-three devotees of Śiva who were canonized as saints in Cēkkiḻār's twelfth-century hagiography, the *Periya Purāṇam*. Seven of these saints wrote poems to Śiva between the sixth and ninth centuries. Along with the Āḻvārs who sang to Viṣṇu, these poets were part of the *bhakti* or devotional movements that began in South India and spread the emotional worship of a personal god throughout the Indian subcontinent.

The devotional movements contained elements of social as well as religious reform, protesting Brahmanical orthodoxy along with the heterodox faiths of Buddhism and Jainism. But this revivalist Hinduism was rooted in the temple, which depended on royal patronage. So, although the devotional ideology undercut caste and gender hierarchies in principle, in practical terms the patriarchal boundaries remained. Statistically, women are not very visible among the Tamil devotional movements: Āṇṭāḷ is the only woman Vaiṣṇava saint, and out of the sixty-three Śaiva *nāyaṉmārs*, only three are women (Ramaswamy 1997, 120–121). However, the life and poetry of Kāraikkāl Ammaiyār, the only woman poet among the *nāyaṉmārs*, reveals a fascinating portrait of the localization of a pan-Indian god and the potential space for women in this emerging tradition.

I first became acquainted with Kāraikkāl Ammaiyār many years ago when I saw Cōḻa bronze images of her in the Nelson-Atkins Museum in Kansas City and the Metropolitan Museum of New York. I was immediately attracted to her: Her beautiful face wore an expression of pure bliss; her mouth was open, singing her praises for Śiva, her Lord. Her enraptured face seemed profoundly at odds with her skeletal, vaguely demonic form. Her striking image led me to read her poetry, and to discover that she indeed had a demon or *pēy* form,[1] in which she lived with Śiva in the cremation ground. As I investigated Kāraikkāl Ammaiyār's life and work, it became clear that there is a continuing tension between the twelfth-century image of her created by Cēkkiḻār and standardized in the ensuing centuries—that of a devoted wife whose love for Śiva finally disrupts her domestic life—and the image she presents of herself in her poetry, a *pēy* happily singing in the cremation ground, enraptured by Śiva's dance. It turns out that the way I became acquainted with Kāraikkāl Ammaiyār is a common pattern even in South India, where most people know at least the outline of her story. Worshipers at temples to Śiva in Tamilnadu see her image among the sixty-three saints recognized by the Śaiva tradition. But not many people are acquainted with her poetry. The divergence between her poetry and her popular life story will be examined in detail in the following chapters.

A Brief Synopsis of Her Story

Chapter 3 explores the story of Kāraikkāl Ammaiyār in detail, but here I provide a brief synopsis of her story:

Kāraikkāl Ammaiyār was born in the sixth century into a well-to-do trading family in the coastal town of Kāraikkāl and originally named Puṉitavati. She was a faithful wife to a rich merchant, as well as an ardent devotee of Śiva. One day her husband brought home two mangoes for his midday meal. But before the meal Puṉitavati gave a Śaiva holy man who came to the door for alms one of the mangoes and some rice. When her husband ate his meal and asked for the second mango, Puṉitavati prayed to Śiva for help; another mango appeared, which she served to her husband. This one was so much more delicious than the first, her husband was suspicious and asked his wife where she'd gotten it. She reluctantly told him, but he doubted her story and asked her to repeat the miracle in his presence. Again Puṉitavati prayed to Śiva, and another mango appeared; her husband was terrified of her power and fled to another city without releasing her from her wifely duties.

Puṉitavati continued to keep up his house and her appearance in anticipation of his return, but eventually her parents found out where he was living with his second wife and daughter. When Puṉitavati learned that her husband didn't want her as a wife anymore, she begged Śiva to take away the beauty she no longer needed and give her a demon form. He granted her wish; she then made a pilgrimage to the Himalayas, walking on her hands so as not to defile god's heavenly abode with her feet. Śiva was so moved by her devotion he called her "Ammai" or mother, and allowed her to perpetually witness his dance at Tiruvālaṅkāṭu, where she lived as his adoring servant.[2]

The ascetic path she embodies and praises in her poetry forms a critique of her previous life as a devoted wife. The beautiful Cōḻa bronzes I saw, along with many other images I have seen since, convey the bliss of Kāraikkāl Ammaiyār's devotion to God, but soften the fierce, demonic form she took when she renounced the world to meditate on Śiva. She is a bridge between the ancient Tamil world, in which ghosts and demons and fierce goddesses inhabited the forests, and the formalization of the devotional tradition that became dominant in the centuries after she lived and composed her poetry. As the Sanskritic god Śiva became localized in Tamilnadu, the fierce female beings integral to the local tradition lost their place of power. Although Kāraikkāl Ammaiyār's poetry portrays a woman who forged her own spiritual path in opposition to cultural norms, her story reveals continuing cultural ambivalence concerning women's renunciation of the domestic life.[3] In the temple dedicated to her in her birthplace, Kāraikkāl, her image is that of an auspicious married woman, and the annual mango festival celebrates her marriage and her devotion to Śiva in the domestic realm. At the temple of Tiruvālaṅkāṭu, where she watched Śiva dance and where she is said to have achieved liberation, she has only relatively recently become part of the temple's annual festival.

Kāraikkāl Ammaiyār's poetry portrays a life lived as a ritual offering to Śiva as the only true life, wherein rituals are not performed to achieve specific goals, as in the domestic sphere, but where goal and ritual merge in perpetual devotion to Śiva alone: Text is practice, and practice is text. This is a central idea of the devotional path. Her poetry contains some of the earliest elements of what would become Śaiva Siddhānta, and provides a striking portrait of a nascent community embracing and localizing a powerful new god.

In the 1982 edition of Karavelane's French translation of Kāraikkāl Ammaiyār's poetry, François Gros wrote a Postface in which he highlights how her story developed apart from her work, and the different fates of each.[4] In this work I attempt to locate the poetry in its sixth-century context separately from the story that develops many centuries later.

Outline of the Book

The goal of this book is to convey a multilayered portrait of Kāraikkāl Ammaiyār through her work, her role in the development of Tamil Śaiva devotionalism, historical and contemporary narratives of her life, and her worship in temples in contemporary Tamilnadu. This portrait reveals divergences between her work and her life narratives, and investigates the religious and cultural themes that emerge.

Chapter 1 sets the historical and literary landscapes for Kāraikkāl Ammaiyār's poetry. Tamil is an ancient language with a rich and complex secular literature dating from before the beginning of the Common Era. The new devotional literature drew language, themes, and structures from the earlier love and praise poetry and fashioned them into powerful hymns to god. This chapter also outlines the beginning of the Tamil *bhakti* or devotional movement, especially as it develops in the hymns of the *Tēvāram* saints who are considered the most important Śaiva poets. This chapter includes an overview of the Śaiva Siddhānta tradition. The end of the chapter provides a brief introduction to the structure of Tamil poetry.

Chapter 2 analyzes Kāraikkāl Ammaiyār's poetry in detail in an attempt to understand it in its own context and to reveal the contours of a new devotional community emerging from an ancient Tamil landscape. Kāraikkāl Ammaiyār's poetry reveals the process of localizing the Sanskritic god Śiva in the Tamil landscape, importing his myths and shaping a devotional path among competing religious traditions. Ammaiyār locates herself as Śiva's *pēy* or demon, part of his troupe of ghouls accompanying him as the dancer in the cremation ground. In addition to this theme, Kāraikkkāl Ammaiyār's poetry conveys a detailed iconographic portrait of Śiva as the heroic god who bestows his grace on those devotees who love and serve him.

Chapter 3 discusses the narratives about Kāraikkāl Ammaiyār's life, beginning with Cēkkiḻār's foundational hagiography in his twelfth-century *Periya Purāṇam,* which provides biographical details absent in the poetry; this narrative supersedes the poetry in terms of popularity, and highlights cultural tensions surrounding the roles of women and their participation in the devotional path. This chapter also investigates some contemporary film and literary narratives.

Chapter 4 explores the two towns and temples associated with Kāraikkāl Ammaiyār. The town of Kāraikkāl (Karikal) on the coast south of Pondicherry, as her name suggests, is considered Ammaiyār's birthplace. Cēkkiḻār's story makes this area the setting for her life as a wealthy merchant's devoted wife. There is a temple dedicated to Kāraikkāl Ammaiyār, which hosts a very popular annual mango festival. The other place closely connected to Ammaiyār, and probably more important in the Śaiva tradition, is Tiruvālaṅkāṭu, which means "sacred banyan tree forest," and is a small village approximately 50 kilometers west of Chennai. Ammaiyār wrote two poems of eleven verses each dedicated to this place. In Cēkkiḻār's story Śiva tells Ammaiyār to go to Tiruvālaṅkāṭu to be the perpetual witness to his dance. The temple *mahātmya* or myth of how the deities took up residence here, tells the story about the dance contest between Śiva and Kālī, a narrative that seems to have originated in Tamilnadu and which is most closely associated with the famous Chidambaram temple. Ammaiyār's poetry, and the temple myth, suggest that Tiruvālaṅkāṭu may be an even earlier site for this dance. The Tiruvālaṅkāṭu temple to Śiva as Vaṭāraṇyēśvarar fairly recently began to celebrate an annual festival to Kāraikkāl Ammaiyār on her star day, which includes a ritual in which Ammaiyār achieves liberation through Śiva's grace. The shrine commemorating Ammaiyār's liberation is behind the Ratna Sabhai, or jeweled hall, in which Śiva performs his *ūrdhva tāṇḍava* dance while Ammaiyār sings at his feet. This chapter also explores the ancient associations between Tiruvālaṅkāṭu and the contiguous town of Paḻaiyaṉūr.

The final Chapter 5 provides a full translation of Kāraikkāl Ammaiyār's poetry, which I made in partnership with Dr. R. Vijayalakshmy, Professor Emeritus at the International Institute of Tamil Studies.[5] The poems are annotated and can be read without benefit of the preceding chapters.

1

The Place of Kāraikkāl Ammaiyār in South Indian History

Kāraikkāl Ammaiyār's poetry bridges the classical Tamil world and the devotional milieu in which Sanskritic myths are localized in a Tamil landscape and infused with Tamil modes of relating to the divine. Although Ammaiyār does not directly praise the Tamil land or Tamil language as the later Śaiva poets do, her poetry is animated by literary and cultural elements that are defining features of the classical Tamil world. Ammaiyār makes reference to many of Śiva's heroic deeds as related in Sanskrit myths and epics, but she is especially devoted to Śiva dancing in the cremation ground, a scenario that resonates profoundly with Tamil ideas of death and dessicated wastelands. In order to understand how Ammaiyār's poetry situates Śiva in the Tamil landscape, in this chapter I present a brief historical overview of the milieu in which Kāraikkāl Ammaiyār composed her poetry, including the literary traditions that inform her work.

A vivid portrait of life in Tamilnadu in the early centuries of the Common Era emerges from the earliest surviving Tamil literature, which was likely composed or compiled between the first century BCE and the fifth century CE. Literature can convey certain social and cultural facts, but since it "refracts as much as it reflects," it is necessary to "enter the realm of the symbolic values that writers express through the 'facts' and 'objective entities'" (Ramanujan 1999a, 52). In classical Tamil literature human behavior and natural landscape are key components of a poetic system that reflects and structures the values and aesthetics of the Tamil world during the centuries leading up to the beginnings of devotional Hinduism. By outlining a chronological development of cultural and literary ideas and practices in Tamilnadu, I aim to convey the complex environment that Richard Davis describes as the "shared religious culture where divine figures, literary tropes, and ritual forms could all be reincorporated, reformulated, and resituated for polemical purposes" (Davis 1999, 218).

This early literature consists of the first Tamil work on grammar and poetics, the *Tolkāppiyam*; ten long poems by ten different poets called the *Pattuppāṭṭu*; and eight anthologies (*Eṭṭutokai*) of poetry that is divided into two types: *akam*, "inner" or love poems; and *puṟam*, "outer" or public poems about kings, war, heroism, death, codes of conduct, and so on. These poems were composed by Pulavaṉs, "wise men." Although the poems are clearly rooted in an oral culture, they are syntactically too complex to have been simply extemporized, and may have been composed in writing; A. K. Ramanujan calls the poems "witnesses to a transition" (1985, 273). The Brāhmī script, which was probably the first script used for Tamil, was introduced into Tamilnadu in approximately the second or third century BCE. From ancient times two forms of Tamil seem to have been in use: a spoken form with many dialects, and a written, standardized language. Several centuries after the texts' composition, this classical literature was labeled "Caṅkam" literature, referring to three *caṅkams* or academies of poets that, according to legend, each met for thousands of years in ancient kingdoms in or near the city of Maturai that were subsequently washed away by floods. In addition is the *Tirukkuṟaḷ*, traditionally attributed to Tiruvaḷḷuvar and probably composed 450–550 CE, a compendium of aphoristic verses about ethics, virtue, love, politics, and economic issues that continues to be esteemed in Tamil culture.[1] The *Tirukkuṟaḷ* delineates the social and moral milieu in which Ammaiyār composes her poetry, but it is the *akam* and *puṟam* poetry that Ammaiyār draws on to give voice to her uncompromising love of Śiva and her conviction that he is the divine hero who conquers evil and through whom the devotee can conquer death. The varied scenes of love and heroism in the classical poetry become the stages of devotion to Śiva and the arenas of his heroic activities.

In the *Tolkāppiyam* the *akam* and *puṟam* poems are characterized by *tiṇai*, which is most often translated as "landscape" or "poetic situation." But Martha Ann Selby suggests these words are inadequate to convey the scope and boundary of this concept. She says, "*Tiṇai* is, in a very real sense, the artistic space circumscribed by the poets, along with everything contained therein. I tentatively choose the word 'context' to translated *tiṇai*, but what must be understood is that this context includes geographical space, time, and everything that grows, develops, and lives within that space and time, including emotion" (2000, 33). There are seven *tiṇai* or contexts for *akam* and for *puṟam* poems; each of the five major or "middle" contexts is assigned to a geographical landscape that contains characteristic flowers, birds, animals, people, drums, and gods; each landscape is connected to a particular season, time of day, and subcategory or theme (*tuṟai*); and finally, each context has a fixed behavior, mood, or emotion that on one level defines the context. The behavior or mood of each *akam* poem is a phase in the love relationship between a man and a woman. The five main *akam* contexts, named after a flower or plant found in each landscape, are: mountain (*kuṟiñci*), first union; pasture (*mullai*), waiting for a lover to return; countryside (*marutam*), infidelity and resentment; seashore (*neytal*), lamenting the lover's absence; and wasteland (*pālai*), separation. Many of Kāraikkāl Ammaiyār's poems take place in a *pālai* landscape. The last two situations in *akam* poetry are not related to a particular landscape and are not the subject of true love poetry, which is well-matched or proper love. These situations are mismatched love (*peruntiṇai*), and unrequited love (*kaikkiḷai*). The characters in *akam* poetry are not named, but are restricted to a few anonymous, conventional types: the hero and heroine, the heroine's foster-mother, friends and messengers, the concubine. The poet does not speak directly to the reader or use the poet's own voice, but rather allows the reader to overhear the characters' dialogue or monologue: The heading for a poem might be "What Her Girl Friend Said."

According to the *Tolkāppiyam* the seven *tiṇai* for *puṟam* poems are parallel to the landscapes for *akam* poems; six of the seven are given a plant name. The seven *puṟam* contexts are: cattle raid (*veṭci*), invasion (*vañci*), siege (*uḻiñai*), battle (*tumpai*), victory (*vākai*), struggle, endurance (*kāñci*), and praise of heroes (*pāṭāṇ*). Although the correspondences between the *akam* and *puṟam* contexts may not be immediately clear, the *Tolkāppiyam* commentators explain that the first union of lovers, for instance, corresponds to a cattle raid because both are first encounters, and take place in the middle of the night, in the mountains, and in secret. In contrast to the overheard dialogues of conventional character types in *akam* poetry, the *puṟam* poets speak in their own voices, or as a bard or drummer, specify individuals by name, and portray particular circumstances and "real" people in history. The contexts of the poetry provide a provocative outline of some of the important social, cultural, and religious themes in Tamilnadu during this period, as well as the imagery that will inform the work of Kāraikkāl Ammaiyār. Ammaiyār speaks in her own voice as Śiva's *pēy* and ardent devotee. She builds a vivid and adoring image of Śiva as the Lord of the Universe by evoking his many heroic deeds and describing his attributes in detail.[2]

Although *akam* and *puṟam* poems are categorized separately, in practice they overlap and intersect: The two genres of poems differ in theme and emotion, but share a repertoire of imagery, "a live vocabulary of symbols; the actual objective landscapes of Tamil country become the interior landscape of Tamil poetry" (Ramanujan 1994, 108). In this poetry nature and culture are not opposed, but work together to embody meaning concretely, not through metaphysical abstraction but through physical detail (Ramanujan 1985, 286–287). The geographical landscape becomes a kind of map of the human self. Selby cites a vivid example of one *akam* poem in which a woman talking to her mother laments her absent lover; in the last few lines of the poem elements of the seashore (*neytal*) context are literally mapped onto her body:

> The place between my breasts
> has filled up with tears,
> has become a deep pond
> where a black-legged
> white heron feeds.

Here the woman's salty tears correspond to the pond on the seashore; the heron is her lover, feeding on her. In this poem the environmental imagery remakes the woman's body. Although every poem in the anthologies does not unify the geographical landscape with the speaker's body this literally, the geographical imagery of the poetic system stimulates and articulates the transformation of human emotions, thoughts, and desires (Selby 2000, 52–54).

Whereas *akam* poetry is concerned with the many phases of human erotic love, *puṟam* poems focus largely on kings and heroes. Many (if not most) of the *akam* poems are in the voices of women, as opposed to the overwhelmingly masculine voices of the *puṟam* poems. During the Caṅkam age there were many small kingdoms, or *nāṭus*; the most powerful kings of the time were the Cōḻas, Cēras, and Pāṇṭiyas. The king was expected to rule justly, ensure a rich harvest, be a generous patron, and achieve victory on the battlefield. War seems to have been virtually constant, and many of the *puṟam* poems describe in vivid detail the extraordinary heroism and strength of the king and his warriors and the bloody carnage on the battlefield. Victory and a hero's death on the battlefield both bring honor; having a good name in public is a central concern. Women in the *akam* poems fear that their lovers will betray or desert them, thereby robbing them of their chastity (*kaṟpu*), and their good public name. Wives and mothers in the *puṟam* poems dread hearing gossip that their husbands or sons were killed running from the enemy, and rush onto the battlefield to see their men's wounds:[3]

When she heard the many voices saying . . . "her son was afraid of the enemy army
and he showed them his back and ran!" then rage overcame her . . .
And when she found her son who was scattered
in pieces, she felt happier than she had been the day she bore him.[4]

Widows were expected to maintain their chastity after their husband's death by living restrained, ascetic lives, giving up their ornaments and shaving their heads. Some widows chose instead to accompany their husbands in death, sometimes by immolating themselves on their husbands' funeral pyres, or taking their own lives and being buried in the same urn with their husband. A memorial stone (*naṭukal*) was erected to house the powerful spirits of heroic warriors and chaste wives, which would be worshiped with offerings. Heroic warriors earned war anklets (*kaḻal*), made of gold, which symbolized their victory over their enemies and which were distinct from the anklets worn by women (*cilampu*). The war anklet is one of the elements signifying heroism that Kāraikkāl Ammaiyār uses to convey the victorious stature of the god Śiva.[5]

Although Caṅkam poetry is concerned mostly with the elite members of Tamil society, the *cāṉṟōr* or "noble ones," and reflects their aristocratic values, the poems are also populated by many groups or castes (*kuṭi*) of people that are identified by their occupation and which form a Tamil social hierarchy or caste system that existed before the North Indian *varṇa* system spread into South India and the two systems fused together. Several important castes are considered to be of lower birth, or Pulaiyaṉs, people whose occupations brought them into contact with polluting or threatening forces, such as death, and who were restricted in their interactions with higher castes. Many of these low castes were bards and musicians that performed a variety of functions in society; they were clearly distinct from the Pulavaṉs or poets who composed the poems. Bards sang the praises of kings, and played drums in battle. Drumming is particularly important in the Caṅkam world; many groups of drummers are frequently mentioned.[6] Dancing is also an important activity; the poetry describes many festivals at which crowds of people, especially girls, come together in joyful dances, such as the *tuṇaṅkai*. Music and dancing are integral to the ritual worship of Murukaṉ, whose name means "one who is youthful, beautiful." He is one of the few named deities in the Caṅkam poems, and appears to be an indigenous Tamil god.[7]

Drums were integral to the king's activities, especially warfare; they contained a kind of power that infused the king and his army. Each ruler possessed symbols of authority such as a tutelary or protected tree and a royal drum, or *muracu*; a victorious king would cut down his enemy's tree and take his drum. The *muracu* or royal drum was bathed and offered sacrifices of blood and liquor. Before the battle began, a drummer beat a huge drum to call the soldiers to the battlefield; drums were said to cause enemies to be defeated. When a warrior did not achieve victory and was wounded, drummers and bards played for him, providing a kind of protection from the forces unleashed around him. In many poems the carnage of the battlefield is described in gruesome detail: rivers of blood flow, dead bodies pile up, and severed body parts are scattered everywhere:

> How can the war flare up now and soldiers brace against
> advancing troops?
> Demonesses, garishly glowing, plunge their hands into the
> wounds of warriors
> who have died there in battle and smearing their hair red
> with the blood,
> they dance then to the sad throb of the paṟai drums beaten
> in slowed pain.
> Vultures are feasting on the army . . .[8]

The battlefield draws spirits and other creatures that feast on dead bodies and inhabit places of death. The Tamil word for demon or ghoul is *pēy*, the word Kāraikkāl Ammaiyār uses to describe herself in her poetry. Male and female demons are common beings in particular Caṅkam landscapes, along with spirits that are generally malevolent and cause suffering. The battlefield is another arena where particular kinds of dances take place. Here the *tuṇaṅkai* is performed by female demons and corpses that rise up in response to the dance's rhythm; Koṟṟavai, the goddess of war and victory who lives in the forest, is also said to dance the *tuṇaṅkai*. Demons dancing the *tuṇaṅkai* appear in Kāraikkāl Ammaiyār's poetry.[9]

The battlefield is a place of brutal death, but it is also a realm of transition; the death or defeat of one king brings increased honor and power to the conqueror. The heroic king brings in "an unfailing harvest of victorious wars" (Ramanujan 1985, 115), and the battlefield is often homologized to the process of the harvest:

> . . . I have come here, to the field where the gurgling
> blood rises

and spreads across the earth, since a cloud of glowing weapons
has rained down the ripe, wished-for fruit and when the rich
curving grain is cut, the stems heap up and elephants circle
like buffaloes to thresh and reduce the many piles of fallen corpses. . . .[10]

In addition to the battlefield, fearsome beings inhabit the cremation ground, another place of death and transition that is described in many *puṟam* poems. The burning ground is salty, dessicated, a wasteland where only plants that can survive extreme heat and aridity can live. Owls shriek; scavenging animals, ghouls, and demonesses feast on the rotting flesh of corpses left among the ash and bones. Low-caste men perform the funeral rituals. On the battlefield the victorious warrior fights his way to honor and fame; but the cremation ground is everyone's ultimate destination:

. . . This ground,
it is the end
of everyone in the world,
looks upon the backs of all men,
and hasn't seen anyone yet
who will look upon its back.[11]

The word most often used in the poetry for cremation ground or burial ground is *kāṭu*, which also means "forest," "jungle," "desert," "dry land," "place," and "border, limit." In Tamil Caṅkam culture the *kāṭu* is conceived of as a dangerous, uninhabitable wilderness area outside of human control, and has traditionally been contrasted with the *nāṭu*, the agricultural and inhabited land, and the *ūr* or village, a distinction that continues to be a vital part of Tamil culture today.[12]

The *kāṭu* is connected to the *pālai* landscape of *akam* poetry, the wilderness or desert wasteland that signifies separation. The *pālai* is a kind of drought-resistant tree; this landscape has no specific geographical location, but is any area that the midday summer heat has burned into a wasteland. *Pālai* poems may describe the lovers' elopement and the hardships they endure, including the pain of separation from their families. But the most common *pālai* poems describe the hero's solo journey through a harsh and dangerous wasteland in search of wealth or education so that he can marry his lover. The wasteland is a chaotic territory of transition between settled, inhabited landscapes.

The extreme heat, dessicated plants, and wild animals and birds mark the landscape as an alien world that the hero endures by thinking of his beloved. Many of the poems move from outside to inside, from the desolate landscape outside to the hero's heart and the image of the lover he had to leave. The *puṟam* situation of *vākai* or victory in war also takes place in a wasteland; the poems praise the achievement of the hero, who has survived the dangers of the battlefield and endured the long separation from his wife.[13]

In the post-Caṅkam period this poetic system will be used to portray outer and inner devotional landscapes. The longing for a lover and the pain of separation in *akam* poems will be redirected toward god in devotional poetry. Likewise, the praise of a king or hero that is central to *puṟam* poetry will provide a language and set of images through which devotees envision and connect to the divine. Fear of public shame will become the sense of separateness from others as an emerging devotional community. The cremation ground with its fearsome creatures will carry over into Kāraikkāl Ammaiyār's poetry, but will convey a devotional vision of the world.

Caṅkam literature reveals a social, cultural, and religious milieu characterized by North Indian as well as indigenous Tamil elements. Scholars have long debated how much of the culture depicted in the poems comes from North India, and how much is "pure" Tamil. The elements of the poetry and the Caṅkam world discussed so far seem to predate the introduction of North Indian culture, but cultural elements from regions north of the Tamil country were clearly impacting the South Indian world from early on; the way that Sanskrit language and North Indian ideas and practices were selectively woven into Tamil culture is hugely important in the later development of devotional Hinduism, as well as in Kāraikkāl Ammaiyār's poetry.[14]

Some features in Caṅkam literature obviously spread into the Tamil land from the north. Vedic sacrifice, Brahman priests, and Vedic literature had spread throughout the subcontinent by the turning of the Common Era. There are many descriptions of Brahmans reciting the Vedas and performing sacrifices in Caṅkam literature. Brahmans apparently lived apart from other groups and kept away from polluting animals like dogs. At least some Brahmans were vegetarian; some of the poets were Brahmans. Some poems make references to the epics *Mahābhārata* and *Rāmāyaṇa*. The *Tirukkuṟaḷ* is organized according to the Sanskritic three aims of life, which also appear in the poems: *dharma* (*aṟam*) or morality; *artha* (*poruḷ*) or wealth, public life; and *kāma* (*iṉpam*) or sexual pleasure. There are several descriptions of ascetics who have renounced the world and practice *tapas*, or austerities in order to achieve liberation, *mukti*, the fourth aim of human life. Many poems include the doctrine of karma and reincarnation.[15]

Brahmanical deities from the North were well known in the Tamil country by the Caṅkam period. Indra, Kubera, Varuna, Paraśurāma, Balarāma, and the devoted wife Arundhatī are mentioned in the poetry. There are several references to Māyōṉ, the Tamil name for Viṣṇu/Kṛṣṇa.[16] Although the name "Śiva" does not appear, there are a few references to the god Śiva in Caṅkam poetry: He is described variously as blue-throated, having an eye in his forehead, wearing a crescent moon, bearing Gaṅgā in his matted hair, and possessing a banner marked with a bull. He gave the gods victory when he conquered the three-walled city with an arrow; he prevented the demon from raising the mountain he is sitting on. He is associated with Death. He is called the Primal Being, and is associated with the four Vedas. He is also described as the god worshipped by sages or Brahmans in a temple.[17]

The *Cilappatikāram*

According to Zvelebil (1973, 172), "the first literary expression and the first ripe fruit of the Aryan-Dravidian synthesis in Tamilnad" is the epic *Cilappatikāram*, "The Story of the Anklet," written in approximately the fifth century and traditionally ascribed to the Jain prince-ascetic, Ilāṅkō Atikaḷ.[18] The epic tells the story of the hero and heroine, Kōvalaṉ and his chaste wife Kaṇṇaki. The action takes place in all three of the Tamil kingdoms: the Cōḻa, in the northeast part of the Tamil country; Pāṇṭiya, in the south and southeast; and the Cēral, on the west coast (what is now the state of Kerala). The epic is divided into three books, each of them named after the three capitals. Each book embodies a different dimension: the Caṅkam poetic categories of *akam* and *puṟam*, to which is added the mythic (*purāṇam*) realm. "The Book of Pukār" explores and celebrates the many facets of love through *akam* conventions; "The Book of Maturai" describes the heroine Kaṇṇaki's destruction of the city of Maturai and her transformation into the goddess Pattiṉi; "The Book of Vañci" uses *puṟam* conventions to praise the king and celebrate his victory in war. *Cilappatikāram* encapsulates many facets of the complex cultural and religious milieu of the Tamil country in which Kāraikkāl Ammaiyār composed her poetry. Part of the "Aryan-Dravidian synthesis," the epic expresses a broader portrait of Śiva than is seen in Caṅkam literature, including his connections to both Sanskritic and Tamil goddesses. In the epic Śiva performs his dance of destruction in the cremation ground, an image that is central to Ammaiyār's devotional world. The doctrine of karma and rebirth is integral to the Jain epic, as well as to Ammaiyār's poetry, although the paths to liberation from rebirth are different for each poet. In addition to the epic's rich evocation of the Tamil world that informs Ammaiyār's poetry, the figure of Nīli, who plays a part in Kōvalaṉ's fate, bears important associations with the story of Kāraikkāl Ammaiyār and the temple town of Tiruvālaṅkāṭu.[19]

The story of the epic *Cilappatikāram* begins in the Cōḻa capital of Pukār (Pūmpukār) on the east coast, where the hero and heroine, Kōvalaṉ and Kaṇṇaki, belong to prominent merchant families. They marry and enjoy many years of wedded bliss. Then Kōvalaṉ abandons his wife for the courtesan Mātavi; Kaṇṇaki is heartbroken but faithfully waits for his return. Kōvalaṉ squanders all of his wealth on Mātavi, but sours on their affair and returns, remorseful, to Kaṇṇaki, who as a devoted wife not only accepts him back but also gives him one of her jeweled anklets to sell in order to begin a new life. They travel through the forbidding, desolate forests to the city of Maturai, the capital of the Pāṇṭiyaṉ kingdom, along the way meeting the Jain ascetic Kavunti, who becomes their guide and companion. In the forest a Brahman on pilgrimage from the Cōḻa country tells Kōvalaṉ that Mātavi has given birth to their daughter Maṇimēkalai, who is the heroine of the great Tamil Buddhist epic *Maṇimēkalai*. But Kōvalaṉ had a dream about his own death and fears returning to Pukār, so he and Kaṇṇaki continue on toward the capital.

Kōvalaṉ leaves Kaṇṇaki in the care of a herdswoman outside the city and reaches Maturai alone. He fatefully sells the anklet to the king's goldsmith, who has stolen the queen's anklet but falsely accuses Kōvalaṉ of the theft. The Pāṇṭiyaṉ king responds hastily to his goldsmith's accusation and without a trial orders Kōvalaṉ to be executed. When Kaṇṇaki hears about her husband's tragic death, she rushes into the city and finds him in a pool of blood. She has a vision that he ascends to heaven. Kaṇṇaki then goes to the palace to confront the king; she breaks open her anklet to prove Kōvalaṉ's innocence: her anklets contain rubies; the queen's contain pearls. The king realizes his guilt and his failure to rule righteously and dies; the grief-stricken queen dies after him. Kaṇṇaki then tears off her left breast, curses the unrighteous city, and throws it at Maturai, her chaste power burning the city down, sparing only "Brahmans, good men, cows, chaste women/The old, and children."[20] The goddess of Maturai comes to Kaṇṇaki and tells her that events in Kōvalaṉ's past life resulted in his death in this life. He was a man named Bharata and worked for a king; he mistakenly thought a merchant called Caṅkamaṉ was a spy and beheaded him. Before Caṅkamaṉ's wife Nīli took her own life, she cursed Bharata. The goddess then tells Kaṇṇaki that she will soon join her husband in heaven.

Kaṇṇaki journeys west to Neṭuvēl (Murukaṉ) Hill in the Cēral country. There the local hill dwellers witness the gods taking her up to heaven. The hill people take their story to the Cēral king, Ceṅkuṭṭuvaṉ; a poet tells the king about the tragic events in Maturai. The queen wants Kaṇṇaki to be worshiped as a goddess. Ceṅkuṭṭuvaṉ declares that he will install a memorial stone (*naṭukal*) for Kaṇṇaki brought down from the Himalayas. During his march north he conquers several North Indian rulers, who then carry the stone south to the capital city Vañci, where the king installs the stone image of Kaṇṇaki, now the goddess Pattiṉi ("chaste woman"), in a temple. In response to the Brahman Māṭalaṉ's counsel, the king performs the royal sacrifice (*rājasūya*) to establish himself as the ruler of the entire Tamil country, and along with the invited kings, worships Pattiṉi.[21]

Cilappatikāram contains many elements that are familiar from Caṅkam poetry. The epic is filled with detailed descriptions of music and dance, including the frenzied dancing of a possessed temple oracle (Canto 12). The god Murukaṉ is prominent, and in a few songs the mother of a love-sick girl thinks she is possessed by him (Canto 24). After burning the city of Maturai, Kaṇṇaki, now a widow, goes to the temple of the goddess Koṟṟavai and breaks off her bangles (23.181). Kings are praised for their righteous rule, their generosity, and their prowess in battle. Demons and demonesses (*pēymakaḷ*) dance on the battlefield and feast on corpses; the battlefield is compared to a cremation ground (Canto 26). When Kaṇṇaki and Kōvalaṉ leave their families in Pukār and go to Maturai, they travel through a threatening, desolate *pālai* landscape (Canto 11). When the Cēral king hears the story of Kaṇṇaki's ascension to heaven, he installs a memorial stone (*naṭukal*) to the woman who was deified through her power of chastity (The Book of Vañci). This is the first Indian record of the deification of a woman of the Vaiśya caste.[22]

In addition to familiar Caṅkam characteristics, the epic encompasses many elements of northern provenance that have clearly pervaded the Tamil country by the fifth century and become integral to the culture. The doctrine of karma and reincarnation is central to the epic; Kōvalaṉ's untimely death is precipitated by his actions in a previous life (23.145–176), and Kaṇṇaki's tragic situation results from her failure to observe a vow for her husband in an earlier life (9.54–56). One of the main characters, Kavunti, is a Jain ascetic; she serves as a guide and protector for the hero and heroine, and when she hears about the terrible events in Maturai, she starves herself to death (*uṇṇāṉōṉpu/sallekhana*) in penance (27.82–83).[23] In addition to Jains, there are references to Buddhists, yogis, ascetics, Ajivikas. Girls perform the dance of Kṛṣṇa (Māyavaṉ) and his consort Piṉṉai;[24] several other avatars of Viṣṇu are praised (Canto 17). The Caṅkam goddesses Aṇaṅku and Koṟṟavai are identified in the epic with several Sanskritic goddesses, including Durgā, who rides a lion and killed the buffalo demon, and Umā/Pārvatī, the consort of Śiva (Canto 12; 20.34–36). Kālī is said to live in the forest, like Koṟṟavai (20.39). When Kaṇṇaki arrives at the palace gates to confront the king about her husband's death, the gatekeeper describes the enraged and vengeful woman to the king as "not Koṟṟavai . . . not Aṇaṅku . . . not Kālī . . . not Durgā" (20.35–44), foreshadowing the divine power she utilizes in destroying the wicked city.[25]

In contrast to his marginal presence in Caṅkam poetry, Śiva plays a larger, though not major, role in *Cilappatikāram*. There are references to Śiva throughout the epic, and some of his attributes are familiar from Caṅkam poetry. Drums sound from his temples (13.137–138; 14.7–14). In the epic Śiva is described as residing in the Himalaya mountains (28.225–229); as manifesting in himself the entire universe (26.55–59); and as causing events through his grace (30.140–141). Śiva is also explicitly connected to the goddesses Umā and Kālī; one passage refers to the marriage rituals for Umā and Śiva (25.132–134). There are also two descriptions of Śiva dancing his dance of destruction, which will be discussed in the next chapter.[26]

Early Devotional Poetry

In general, Caṅkam poems did not convey overtly religious themes; although some poems allude to various deities and practices related to them, these are secondary to the focus on the natural and social worlds. There are, however, two exceptions from the later Caṅkam period (ca. fifth–sixth century CE) that mark the beginning of devotional poetry in the Tamil land. One of the ten long poems, the *Tirumurukāṟṟuppaṭai*, praises the Tamil god Murukaṉ, who by this period had become fused with the Sanskrit god Skanda, the son of Śiva and Pārvatī who was born to battle the demons. In the Caṅkam literature he is associated with the hills, and is said to live in trees, especially the *kaṭampu* tree; he rides a peacock; and he is called Cēyōṉ, the Red One. He is also called *kaṭavuḷ*, a term for the divine that in a later period designates a transcendent divinity, but which in the Caṅkam context appears to mean a deity one should sacrifice to or worship. Murukaṉ is also associated with another important word for divine power in Caṅkam literature, *aṇaṅku*, which means "affliction," "suffering," "fear," and "killing," as well as "deity," "celestial woman," "demoness," and "demon." *Aṇaṅku* can possess a person or dwell in a particular object; Murukaṉ is said to cause and dispel *aṇaṅku*, especially in young women. In several *akam* poems, the mother brings a love-sick girl to the vēlaṉ, Murukaṉ's priest, not knowing the girl is in love and thinking she is possessed. The vēlaṉ, "he who has a spear," dances his frenzied possession dance, the *veṟiyāṭu*, to diagnose the girl's affliction. Sometimes a priestess or woman diviner (*kaṭṭuvicci*) was called on. In other worship contexts, crowds of girls perform the *veṟiyāṭu*; lutes, pipes, and drums are played. This kind of ecstatic connection to an immanent divine will carry over into devotional worship.[27]

The *Tirumurukāṟṟuppaṭai* is a "guide poem" (*āṟṟuppaṭai*), a *puṟam* form in which two bards meet on a road and converse; one bard praises his patron's generosity and prosperous realm, and urges the other bard to visit this ruler's court to seek his patronage. In the *Tirumurukāṟṟuppaṭai* a Murukaṉ devotee tells a neophyte about the beautiful god and the six hills that are his sacred dwelling places in Tamilnadu. The six sacred places are identified with Murukaṉ's six faces, so that the Tamil land is made into the body of the god. Instead of the wealth given by a king, Murukaṉ bestows personal salvation on his worshipers. Here the Sanskrit gods Viṣṇu, Śiva, Indra, and Brahmā are subordinated to Murukaṉ. He has a Sanskrit wife from the heavens, Teyvayāṉai, the daughter of Indra; and an earthly Tamil wife, Vaḷḷi, daughter of a hunting tribe.

In this poem, the poet describes one of the places where Murukaṉ dwells, accessible to his devotees:

> Where goats are slaughtered,
> where grains of fine rice are offered
>   in several pots with flowers,
> and His cock-banner is raised . . .
>
> wherever devotees praise
> and move His heart;
>
> where His spear-bearing shamans
> set up yards
> for their frenzy dance . . .

and in the awesome vast temple
where the daughter of the hill tribe
worships . . .
    singing *kuriñci* songs . . .
where the daughter of the hill tribe
sounds Murukaṉ's favorite instruments
and offers worship to Murukaṉ
till He arrives
and comes into her
to terrify enemies and deniers . . .

He dwells in all such places
and I speak what I truly know. (Ramanujan 1985, 215–217)

In this poem the description of the worship of the god evokes the Caṅkam descriptions of the frenzied dancing and music that were integral to the worship of Murukaṉ, the participation of women in his worship, and the shaman-priest's and the woman's possession by the god. Murukaṉ dwells in the hills; the "daughter of the hill tribe" sings *kuriñci* songs. In the *akam* landscape the heroine meets her lover in the hills; here, the woman is possessed by the god. In the Caṅkam poetry the worship of Murukaṉ was a subsidiary element, serving to highlight the love-sickness of the heroine; here the *akam* landscape localizes the god, who is praised in the *puṟam* mode as a powerful god whose heart is tender, but who terrifies his enemies, and lives in a vast temple in a beautiful realm. In the eleventh century the *Tirumurukāṟṟuppaṭai* was included in the Tamil Śaivite canon; it is the only Caṅkam poem that is also part of a devotional corpus.[28]

The Caṅkam anthology *Paripāṭal* originally contained seventy poems to the gods Cevvēḷ (Cēyōṉ/Murukaṉ), Tirumāl (Viṣṇu), the river Vaiyai (Vaikai), and the Pāṇṭiya capital Maturai located on this river. Only twenty-four poems have survived, seven of them to Tirumāl, and they are the only Caṅkam poems dedicated to Viṣṇu. These are likely the earliest devotional poems in Tamilnadu, as well as in India.[29] One *Paripāṭal* poem celebrates one of Tirumāl's sacred places, Māliruṅkuṉṟam, "Tirumāl's Dark Hill," near the city of Maturai and still the location of a popular Viṣṇu temple, called Aḻakar Kōyil. The praise of the god's sacred place parallels the *puṟam* praise of the king's prosperous, well-protected realm, as well as the close attention to the natural landscape in *akam* poetry.

. . .
fragrant blue lilies

blossom in all its ponds,
the branches of *aśoka* trees
growing at their edge
are covered with blossoms . . .
the beauty of this place
is like the Black God himself . . .
the name Iruṅkuṉṟam

has spread far and wide,
on this great, bustling earth
it boasts fame in ages past
for it is the home of the dear lord
who eradicates delusions
for people who fill their eyes
with his image. (Ramanujan 1999d, 241)

The *Paripāṭal* poems incorporate elements of the *puṟam* mode of praise for a heroic king, but instead celebrate the heroic feats and generosity of the god. In Ramanujan's translation of *Paripāṭal* 2 we read:

. . .
O lord fierce in war,
the discus in your hand
cuts off the sweet lives
of enemies:
heads fall and roll
wreaths and all . . .
and lie dead at last
in a mire of blood.

That discus
consumes enemies at one stroke:
Death is its body,
its color the leaping flame
of bright fire
when gold burns in it.

The battle scene, with the heads rolling in blood, echoes the macabre battlefield scenes depicted in *puṟam* poetry; but here we know the hero is not a human king, but the god Tirumāl/Viṣṇu because of the discus in his hand, a reference from Sanskritic myth and iconography.

In another verse of the poem Tirumāl's grace is said to be "a sky of rain-cloud/fulfilling everyone." Rain signifies generosity in the Tamil land where rains are often scarce; in *puṟam* poetry a ruler's generous patronage is often likened to the rain. In addition, here the darkness of a storm cloud evokes Tirumāl's blue-black color. In contrast to the shaman-priest (Vēlaṉ) who performs rituals to Murukaṉ, in later verses of this poem Tirumāl is identified with a carefully delineated Vedic sacrifice performed by Brahmans. *Paripāṭal* 3 celebrates Tirumāl by saying "In the Vedas, you are the secret./Of the elements, you are the first." In other verses of the *Paripāṭal* poems Tirumāl is the One, beyond understanding, transcending time, the essence of the universe. The Tamil sense of the sacred as immanent in special places, people, and things localizes Tirumāl in the Tamil land, but he is at the same time conceived of as the transcendent Absolute. These early poems represent the first time in India that philosophical and religious concepts are conveyed in a vernacular language instead of Sanskrit. They extend the classical landscapes and motifs into the devotional realm, but it is with the hymns of the poet-saints that devotional poetry truly flowers.[30]

Bhakti

Historical changes during the late Caṅkam era would help usher in the period in which devotional poetry flourished. In North India the Guptas (320–540 CE) identified themselves as *bhāgavatas*, devotees of god; they officially sponsored Viṣṇu, whose mythology became part of their politics, and they built temples. The earliest *purāṇas* or mythological texts were recorded during this period. In South India the Kalabhras (Tamil Kaḻappāḷar) ruled from the third to the sixth century; the historical record for this period remains thin, but it is clear that the Kalabhras supported Buddhism and Jainism, both of which prospered during this period—Jainism, in particular, flourished. From approximately 550 to 900 CE, the Pallavas ruled from their capital in Kāñcipuram, and the Pāṇṭiyas reigned in Maturai. Both of these kingdoms were powerful supporters of the devotional traditions, patronizing Brahman priests and constructing temples. People and influences from the north moved southward more rapidly during this period. Devotees composed devotional poems to Śiva and Viṣṇu, becoming the poet-saints of the traditions, and initiating the vernacular bhakti movements that would spread throughout the subcontinent.[31]

Bhakti is usually translated as "devotion," but the English word does not adequately convey the multivalent meanings of the Sanskrit term, which is derived from the verb *bhaj*, which means "to share with," "bestow," "serve." *Bhakti* encompasses the sense of participation and love between god and devotee that characterizes the hymns of the devotional poets.[32] Bhakti developed from Vedic roots, revisioning both the Vedic notion of action in the world in pursuit of religious goals and the Upaniṣads' solitary pursuit of liberation. In the dominant Upaniṣadic path, the renouncer engages in reverent meditation on the Ātman-Brahman in order to realize the identification of his true Self with the Absolute. Theistic conceptions of the impersonal Absolute emerge in two late *Upaniṣads*: Viṣṇu in the *Kaṭha* and Rudra-Śiva in the *Śvetāśvatara*. In these texts the Lord is the transcendent creator who is also immanent in the human self. It is also in these two texts that the concept of divine grace appears. The *Śvetāśvatara* emphatically proclaims that the creator of the universe and the cause of liberation are one God. Through the power of his austerities, his deep love (*bhakti*), and God's grace, the devotee knows the Lord and achieves salvation.[33]

Bhakti as the path to salvation through the love of God is fully explicated for the first time in the *Bhagavad Gītā* (ca. 300 CE), in the context of the *Mahābhārata*. This text introduces concepts that will remain central to later bhakti texts and practices, including the poetry of Kāraikkāl Ammaiyār. In this text Kṛṣṇa explains the path of bhakti-yoga to the hero Arjuna: one should act in the world but relinquish the fruits of action and dedicate them to the Lord. Like the renouncer the bhakta should sever his passionate attachment to worldly goals, yet unlike the renouncer he should not pursue salvation physically removed from the social world. In contrast to the Vedic structure of performing rituals in prescribed spaces and at prescribed times, the bhakta should at all times be focused on the Lord, performing all action as a sacrifice to him, pursuing liberation in the world. This interaction between the perspectives of renunciation and commitment to action in the social world is inherent in the bhakti path.[34]

The bhakti path that Kṛṣṇa lays out in the *Gītā* is not simply one of faith or reverence (*śraddhā*). In a vivid illustration of the breadth of the bhakti path, Kṛṣṇa delineates four kinds of bhaktas: the afflicted (*ārta*), the seeker of wealth (*arthārthī*), the seeker of knowledge (*jijñāsur*), and the sage who has the true knowledge of the Self (*jñānī*). Kṛṣṇa says the *jñānī* is the highest of the bhaktas:

> They are all noble, but I regard
> the man of knowledge to be my very self;
> self-disciplined, he holds me
> to be the highest way.

At the end of many births,
the man of knowledge finds refuge in me;
he is the rare great spirit who sees
"Krishna is all that is."[35]

Kṛṣṇa makes it clear that knowledge is necessary for liberation from the cycle of rebirth. The bhakta's direct emotional connection to the Lord is grounded in the understanding that Kṛṣṇa is the Absolute, the All. This tension between knowing the Lord as the Supreme Principle of the universe (*nirguṇa*), and as the loving individuated God with particular attributes (*saguṇa*) is integral to the hymns of the devotional poets, including Ammaiyār.[36]

The Tamil poems of the *Paripāṭal* and the *Tirumurukāṟṟuppaṭai* are considered the first devotional poems written in a vernacular language in India.[37] Between the fifth and tenth centuries the Tamil poet-saints, the āḻvārs and the nāyaṉmārs, wrote devotional poetry to Viṣṇu and Śiva, wandering from place to place singing about god, spreading temple worship, creating a sacred geography and firmly establishing the bhakti traditions in Tamilnadu. Their poems became part of the sectarian traditions and are still sung in temples today.

The twelve āḻvārs, "those who are immersed," wrote poetry to Viṣṇu. The tenth-century devotee Nātamuṉi collected and arranged their poetry in the *nālāyira-tiviya-pirapantam*, "The Four Thousand Sacred Hymns." The *mutal mūvar* or "first three" poets were Poykai, Pūtam, and Pēy, and probably lived in the sixth or early seventh century, possibly during the same time as Kāraikkāl Ammaiyār. These three poets each composed an *antāti* of one hundred verses in *veṇpā* meter, all similar in content. This is the same form as two of Ammaiyār's poems. The lives of the āḻvārs were collected in the Sanskrit text *Divya-suri-caritam*, "Characters of the Sacred Ones." According to legend, the three poets met each other at the temple in Tirukkōvalūr, where, as they huddled together in the darkness during a severe thunderstorm, they felt the presence of a fourth person and realized that Viṣṇu had joined them. The legend says that their close encounter with the Lord inspired each poet to write the first verse of his *antāti*. Pēy ("Demon") and Pūtam ("Ghost") probably received their names because they were "god-possessed." The poetry of these first three Vaiṣṇava saints is more personal than the classical poetry or the early devotional poems; the personal voice of the poet characterizes bhakti poetry. Viṣṇu temples usually contain shrines with figures of the twelve āḻvārs.[38]

The Tamil Śaiva Tradition

The sixty-three nāyanmārs, "leaders," are the saintly devotees of Śiva canonized in the Śaiva tradition. Only six of these saints wrote poetry, including the *mūvar mutalikaḷ*, the "First Three Saints," commonly known as Appar (Tirunāvukkaracar), Campantar (Tiruñāṉacampantar), and Cuntarar (Nampi Ārūrār). The corpus of their hymns would later become known as the *Tēvāram*, part of the central Tamil Śaiva scripture. Cuntarar, who lived two centuries after Appar and Campantar and whom scholars date between the late seventh century and the first half of the ninth century, is responsible for compiling the list of saints in an eleven-stanza poem called *Tiruttoṇṭattokai*, "The List of the Holy Devotees," in which he names sixty-two saints.[39] A fourteenth-century work, the *Tirumuṟaikanta purāṇam*, "The Story of the Discovery of the Sacred Text," describes how the eleventh-century Cōḻa king Apayakulacēraṉ, after hearing some of the poems sung to Lord Śiva in a temple, asked the poet Nampi Āṇṭār Nampi to find and organize the hymns of the Tamil saints. Helped by the god Gaṇeśa, Nampi found the ant-eaten manuscripts of the saints' hymns in a sealed room behind the dancing Śiva in the great Chidambaram temple. Nampi organized the hymns into the Tamil Śiva-bhakti canon, the *Tirumuṟai*: The mūvars' hymns, the *Tēvāram*, form books one through seven; the *Tiruvācakam* and *Tirukkōvaiyār* of Māṇikkavācakar became the eighth book. The ninth-century Māṇikkavācakar was never added to the official list of sixty-three saints, but he and the First Three are considered the *nālvar*, the "Four Revered Saints" in the Śaiva tradition. The ninth book of the *Tirumuṟai* contains musical compositions probably sung in Cōḻa temples. Book ten is Tirumūlar's sixth- to seventh-century work *Tirumantiram*, considered the earliest work of Śaiva Siddhānta philosophical speculation. The eleventh book is a compilation of many texts spanning several centuries, including the poems of Aiyaṭikaḷkāṭavarkōṉ, a Pallava ruler and early Śiva devotee, and Kāraikkāl Ammaiyār, who is considered by many scholars to be the earliest poet to write poems to Śiva in Tamil. Nampi Āṇṭār Nampi's work, including his hagiography of the Śaiva saints, concludes the eleventh book. The twelfth and final book of the canon is the twelfth century *Periya Purāṇam*, "Great Story" of Cēkkiḻār, the definitive narrative of the sixty-three saints.[40]

One of the major issues in scholarship on bhakti is whether, and to what degree, bhakti is a movement of social protest against caste hierarchy, status, and orthodoxy. Overall, bhakti poetry extols the meaninglessness of caste in the eyes of the Lord, in contrast to the overtly aristocratic poetry of the classical age. However, approximately one-third of the Tamil poets are of Brahman origin, including the four major Śaiva poets and eight of the twelve āḻvārs. Āṇṭāḷ is the only female āḻvār; Kāraikkāl Ammaiyār is the only female nāyaṉmār poet. A large segment of the sixty-three Śaiva saints comes from the high-ranking Vēḷāḷar peasant caste and the chieftains associated with them.[41] Both the Vēḷāḷar landowners and the Brahmans supported the worship of Śiva and Viṣṇu. At the same time that the Śaiva poets sang about the temples emerging in the Tamil land, temple rituals were being created and compiled in Sanskrit liturgical texts called Āgamas, the earliest of which appeared by about 700 CE. The Āgamas are considered revealed texts, originally coming from Śiva himself; they detail all aspects of temple worship, including the transformative rituals that lead the priests (*ācāryas*) and adepts (*sādhakas*) toward liberation. The Pallava kings instituted the singing of the nāyāṉmārs' hymns during worship in the temples, a practice the Cōḻas continued.[42]

Śaiva Siddhānta, "perfected Śaivism," was the system of philosophy and ritual practice that emerged from the Āgamas, and was the dominant Āgamic school by the ninth and tenth centuries. The origins of Śaiva Siddhānta are not entirely clear, but it apparently developed in central and northern India, then spread to the south through Brahman preceptors connected to temples or to monastic lineages. Śaiva Siddhānta seems to have emerged as a distinctly named order in approximately the ninth century, after the rise of Śaṅkara's non-dualist Advaita Vedānta philosophy, when observers divided the greater Śaiva community into four orders: the Pāśupatas, Kālāmukhas, Kāpālikas, and Śaivas. From the tenth through twelfth centuries, Śaiva Siddhānta spread to many regions of India. Due to political changes in North India in the thirteenth century, Śaiva Siddhānta lost its royal patronage and rapidly died out in northern areas.

In the Tamil land, inscriptions state that the Pallava king Siṃhaviṣṇu (ca. 550–610) studied the Āgamas, and the Pallava king Narasiṃhavarman II (ca. 690–728) was well informed about the Śaiva Siddhānta path. In the sixth- to seventh-century work the *Tirumantiram*, the tenth book of the Śaiva canon, Tirumūlar refers to nine Āgamas, as well as specific Āgamic rites and temple worship. All three *Tēvāram* poets Appar, Campantar, and Cuntarar mention the Āgamas; these bhakti poets delineated movements that self-consciously created Tamil Hindu solidarity centered on temple worship. As Śaiva Siddhānta became established in the Tamil land, several endogamous clans of the Ādiśaiva or Gurukkaḷ (Kurukkaḷ) Brahman subcaste transmitted the Āgamas to their initiates, gaining control of the Śaiva temples in the Tamil region. As the Śaiva Siddhānta temple ritual developed, it included Tamil devotional elements as well as Vedic practices. After Cēkkiḻār's twelfth-century *Periya Purāṇam*, from the thirteenth century on, a distinct Tamil Śaiva Siddhānta develops. The central Śaiva Siddhānta works in Tamil, rather than Sanskrit, commence with the Vēḷāḷar saint Meykaṇṭār's work *Civañāṉapōtam* (ca. 1223), the first systematic treatise on Tamil Śaiva Siddhānta. Meykaṇṭār is one of eight philosophers who wrote fourteen canonical texts called the *Meykaṇṭa cāttirams*; eight of these works are attributed to Umāpati Civācāriyar, the fourteenth-century philosopher who systematized Śaiva Siddhānta. These works recognize not only the Āgamas as authoritative texts, but also the Vedas and the *Tirumuṟai* of the Tamil Śaiva saints. In contrast to the Āgamic focus on ritual, the Tamil texts foreground devotion and spiritual knowledge. The Śaiva Siddhānta tradition recognizes four components of the canon: the Vedas, the twenty-eight Śaiva Āgamas, the *Tirumuṟai*, and the fourteen *Meykaṇṭa* texts. Since the sixteenth century, Tamil Śaiva Siddhānta has been transmitted through lineages of Vēḷāḷar ascetics in *maṭams* or monasteries. Śaiva Siddhānta exists today only in Tamilnadu and in Tamil diasporic communities.[43]

According to Śaiva Siddhānta dualistic philosophy, the universe is made up of three fundamental but separate, distinct realities: the Lord Śiva (*pati*), individual souls (Sanskrit *paśu*, Tamil *pacu*); and fetters or karmic bonds (Sanskrit *pāśa*, Tamil *pācam*). These three realities interact in complex ways, engendering phenomenal existence (*samsāra*). The Lord Śiva is omniscient and omnipotent, the master of the universe and cause of all beings who is beyond form. Śiva directs the emitting and reabsorbing of the material worlds, performing his five cosmic activities (*pañcakṛtya*) of creation, preservation, veiling or concealment, destruction, and grace. Like Śiva, souls by nature possess consciousness (*cit*), which animates them, distinguishes them from the inanimate elements of the universe (*jaḍa*), and endows them with latent powers of omniscience and omnipotence. However, souls are in a state of spiritual bondage. Three fetters—*mala* or primordial stain, *karman*, the consequences of past actions, and *māyā*, the elements of the material universe—all constrain the souls and keep them in a state of bondage. Souls can escape these fetters and realize their innate powers and freedom only through Śiva's grace (*aruḷ*). However, human effort is also necessary to remove the fetters and allow the soul's powers to manifest. The devotee must be initiated into the Śaiva path by a guru; the ritual burns up the fetters in the sacrificial fire to free the initiate from the cycle of rebirth. In addition, the initiate must follow a fourfold path, each stage activated by Śiva's grace: proper conduct or service (*caryā*), ritual action (*kriyā*), disciplined concentration and meditation on Śiva (*yoga*), and finally, supreme knowledge (*jñāna*) of Śiva, which is liberation (*mukti*). The devotee is purified of all impurities and attains a state like Śiva (but not identity), enjoying supreme bliss. Kāraikkāl Ammaiyār's poetry is very early in the history of the Tamil Śaiva tradition, yet some verses of her poetry foreshadow more fully developed Śaiva Siddhānta philosophy.[44]

As the Tamil Śaiva community carved out a self-conscious identity, the Śaiva poets' most vehement opposition was to Jainism and Buddhism, which were seen as alien religions. The Tamil Śaiva community was forged partly by the harsh rhetoric of the Tamil Śaiva saints against the Buddhists and Jains. The Jains, in particular, were denounced as heretics who do not uphold the Vedas and whose false doctrines do not lead to Śiva; they are also ridiculed for their ascetic practices. Peterson argues that "the negative representation of Jains was an important part of a process of self-definition and consolidation of power for the Tamil Śaiva sect . . . Jains were not only a threatening rival group, but a very useful foil against which to establish the superiority of the Śaiva religion . . . the attack on Jains was part of a larger Tamil Śaiva project, of fashioning a communal identity for Tamils, based on the celebration of Śaiva sectarian ideals and the exclusion of non-Śaiva ones." This Tamil identity constructed by the bhakti poets would eventually displace the regional identity conveyed by the Jain epic *Cilappatikāram*.[45]

The *Tēvāram* poets Appar and Campantar regularly denounce Buddhists, and Jains in particular. The most dramatic episodes of Śaiva-Jain antagonism may take place in Cēkkiḻār's life story of Appar, who though born in a Śaiva family, became a Jain monk and was given the name Tarumacēṉar (Sanskrit Dharmasena). His sister, a devout Śaiva, was in despair over his conversion and prayed to Śiva for help; Śiva responded by afflicting Tarumacēṉar with an acutely painful abdominal disease. His sister convinced him to appeal to Śiva; he was completely cured and converted back to his family's Śaiva path. The Jain monks were outraged at his conversion and persecuted Tarumacēṉar; however, he survived his tortures unscathed, and he converted the Jain Pallava ruler to Śaivism. Appar's poetry is infused with guilt over his sin of converting to Jainism.[46]

Although some narratives within the Śaiva tradition and in scholarship on bhakti proclaim the dramatic triumph of devotional Hinduism over Buddhism and Jainism, causing their rapid demise, several scholars have recently dissected this narrative to provide a more nuanced understanding of the historical, religious, and social changes of this period. Beginning in the Pallava era, rulers did patronize Hindu cults and built temples to Hindu deities, which helped institute major cultural and religious changes in the Tamil land. However, it is clear from the inscriptional record that Jainism in particular continued to be a significant part of Tamil society until the thirteenth century; Jain Tamil scholarship continued into the sixteenth century. Encounters and interchanges between the developing devotional sects and Jainism in particular took place over many centuries. As the Tamil nāyaṉmārs pioneered "emotional bhakti," the Brahmans who transmitted the Āgamas were formulating a Śaivism that was more ritualistic and ascetic, like Jainism. It is important not to reify the boundaries of religious communities, especially during the more fluid period when Kāraikkāl Ammaiyār composed her poetry. The epic *Cilappatikāram* portrays the Tamil land as a region of mutual tolerance among religious groups. Ammaiyār's poetry illuminates a period during which religious communities were just beginning to define themselves in a more self-conscious way, which we will explore in chapter two.[47]

Praising Śiva

As we have seen, Śiva did not have an indigenous form in the Tamil land, as did Māyōṉ/Viṣṇu, the Caṅkam god who absorbed Sanskritic elements. Śiva has Vedic roots; he encompasses aspects of the god Indra, and the fire god Agni, but many of his characteristics can be traced back to Rudra, the "howler" or "ruddy one," the god of death and destruction. The hymn the *Śatarudrīya Stotram,* "The Hymn to the Hundred Rudras" (ca. 1000 BCE), in the *Yajur Veda,* is an early *stotra* or praise poem and the most complete ancient description of Śiva's deeds and attributes. Popularly known as the *Rudram,* it consists of sixty-six mantras that vividly portray the paradoxical Rudra and list his one hundred names and epithets. In the Vedic context the hymn was recited to accompany the oblations to the one hundred Rudras (or Rudra's one hundred aspects) during the construction of the fire-altar (*agnicayana*). Śiva's five-syllable mantra, the *namaḥ śivāya,* which is central to Tamil Śaiva doctrine, first appears in this text. The hymn praises Rudra as the blue-throated, red-bodied embodiment of wrathful, destructive forces as well as of benevolence and grace; he has a dreadful body (*ghora*) and an auspicious body (*śiva*). He is a powerful archer with a fierce weapon; he has braided hair and one thousand eyes; he inflicts disease and is the divine healer; he is the cause of prosperity and happiness; he frequents isolated wilderness areas, forests, and mountains, attended by his troops of ghosts, goblins, and spirits.[48] The hymn invokes his grace:

> Reverence be to the bestower of welfare, to the master of animals, to the dreadful and to the terrible, to him who slays before and to him who slays from afar, to the slayer and to the extremely destructive, to the trees with green-locks and to the deliverer . . .
>
> Most bountiful one, most benevolent, be kind and gracious to us. . . .[49]

According to Peterson (1989, 26), the *Rudram* is the most influential Sanskrit model for the poetry of the *Tēvāram*. Some of the Tamil devotional poems are closely linked to the Sanskrit *stotra* hymns, particularly in terms of content; descriptions of Śiva's attributes and deeds are central to *bhakti* poetry. The form of the Tamil hymns also contains some affinities to the Sanskrit hymns: For instance, the short, vividly descriptive phrases for Śiva in the Tamil hymns echo the compound epithets in the *stotras*. The *Rudram* is the main Vedic text used in Āgamic temple rituals, and today is still the most important Sanskrit text used in daily temple rituals, as well as festivals and processions. Some of the imagery of Śiva's attributes and nature in Kāraikkāl Ammaiyār's poetry is the same as in the *Rudram*.

Stotras praising the Purāṇic gods and goddesses are included in larger sacred texts such as the *Mahābhārata* (ca. 300 BCE–300 CE). Several stories about Śiva ("The Auspicious One") are told in the *Mahābhārata*, including Śiva drinking the poison that arose from the churning of the ocean, and his destruction of the three cities of the demons. Śiva's paradoxical nature is vividly apparent in this epic: He is the terrifying god who destroys the world with purifying fire at the end of each age so that it can be renewed; he is the ascetic yogi who wears a snake and lives in cremation grounds; yet he is also the compassionate, gracious god who is united with the goddess Umā and carries Gaṅgā on his head.[50]

The Tamil *bhakti* poets drew many elements from Caṅkam poetics that they molded into devotional poetry. The Tamil poets drew also from classical Sanskrit literature. The poetry by Kāraikkāl Ammaiyār and the *Tēvāram* poets often contains stanzas of four short lines; even when part of a longer poem, each stanza can be understood and savored alone, as in Sanskrit court poetry. The myths and iconographic descriptions of the gods and goddesses were popular and important elements in Sanskrit court poetry. The great fourth-century Sanskrit poet Kālidāsa composed the earliest descriptions of Śiva in court poetry; the conception of Śiva as *aṣṭamūrti* (Tamil *aṭṭamūrtti*), as sustaining the universe in his eight forms, is central to Kālidāsa's work. As in the *stotras* and Kālidāsa's work, Ammaiyār's poetry praises Śiva by stating his epithets, attributes, deeds, nature, and identity, in order to create a concrete and vivid image of Śiva for the devotee. But Ammaiyār and the other Śaiva saints molded these many poetic elements into something new: By focusing on their personal relationship with the Lord, by describing their personal feelings and experiences of God, they presented a direct understanding of God achieved through perpetual, loving devotion.[51]

The Poetry and Its Structure

Kāraikkāl Ammaiyār composed four works that are included in the eleventh book of the *Tirumuṟai*, the Śaiva canon. The longest is the *Aṟputat Tiruvantāti* ("Sacred Linked Verses of Wonder") with 101 *veṇpā* verses; in the final verse she identifies herself as "Kāraikkāḷ Pēy." In the *antāti* form the last word in one verse is the first word of the next verse, thus linking the verses together. The second work is the *Tiruviraṭṭai Maṇimālai* ("The Sacred Garland of Double Gems") with twenty stanzas alternating in *veṇpā* and *kaṭṭalaik kalitturai*, also in the *antāti* form; Kāraikkāl Ammaiyār likely introduced the *kaṭṭalaik kalittuṟ ai* meter, perhaps the first post-classical meter in Tamil poetry. These two works do not seem to have been set to music. The last works are the two *patikams* called *Tiruvālaṅkāṭṭu Mūtta Tiruppatikaṅkaḷ* ("First Sacred Verses on Tiruvālaṅkāṭu") which are ten-verse poems with an eleventh "signature" verse each. These poems are set to music: The *paṇ* or musical mode for the first *patikam* is *naṭṭapāṭai*, and *intaḷam* for the second. Ammaiyār identifies herself as Kāraikkāḷ Pēy in the eleventh verse of each of these poems. Kāraikkāl Ammaiyār's poems are probably the first examples of *prabandha* literature in Tamil (*pirapantam*), genres established according to their content or form, or both. Accounts of Ammaiyār's life suggest she wrote the first two works before going to Mt. Kailāsa, then wrote the Tiruvālaṅkāṭu poems when she arrived there.[52]

Tamil poetic meter "can be described, in a qualified sense, as a time-oriented, rather than a stress-based or syllabic prosody" such as governs English verse (Peterson 1989, 77). The basic metrical component is called *acai*, which contains two types: *nēr* or one long or short syllable (¯), and *nirai* or two short syllables (˘˘). The foot or *cīr* is made up of combinations of these *acais* from the smallest foot of one *acai* to feet made up of several *acais*, such as *akavaṟcīr* which contains two *acais* (*nēr nēr*, *nirai nēr*, *nēr nirai*, or *nirai nirai*), and *veṇcīr* which consists of an *akavaṟcīr* plus a *nēr*. Ammaiyār's long poem *Aṟputat Tiruvantāti* is composed in the classical meter *veṇpā*; each verse contains four lines, and each of the lines contains four *cīr* except the last line which contains three. In addition to the meter the poems contain several kinds of rhyme, between and within the lines. The third verse of *Aṟputat Tiruvantāti* is schematized below; the bold type at the beginning of each line shows the *etukai* rhyme in which the second syllable or a cluster of syllables is repeated; the italicized letters show alliteration between feet within a line.[53]

Below the schematized poem is a literal translation of the Tamil phrases, which shows that "the 'left-branching' syntax of Tamil is most often a reverse mirror image of the possible English."[54] This verse also exemplifies the pattern of a sequence of nouns, epithets, or descriptive words leading up to a verb that is commonly used by Ammaiyār and later poets. Another common pattern seen in this verse is a new image or idea begun in one line but continued in the next line. This verse contains three lines describing that the devotees are servants only of Śiva, with one line describing Śiva himself. The first word in the first two lines ends in "ē" which is an emphatic marker that stresses the devotees' service "to *Him* [Śiva] only." Where possible, as in this verse, I have tried to keep the same order of the lines in the English translation.

˘ ˘ ¯ / ¯ ˘ ˘ ˘ ˘ / ¯ ¯ ¯ / ¯ ¯
avarkkē / eḻupiṟappum / āḷāvōm / *e*ṉṟum

˘ ˘ ¯ / ¯ ˘ ˘ ˘ ˘ / ¯ ˘ ˘ ˘ / ˘ ¯
avarkkē / nām aṉpāva tal / lāṟ—pavarc / caṭaimēṟ

¯ ¯ ¯ / ¯ ˘ ˘ ˘ ˘ / ¯ ¯ / ¯ ˘ ˘
pākāppōḻ / cūṭu *ma*varkkal / lāl *maṟ* / ṟoruvark

¯ ¯ ¯ / ¯ ¯ / ¯ ¯
kākāppōm / eññāṉ / ṟum āḷ

To Him / for seven births / we will be servants // Always
For Him / we—love—only // dense matted hair—on
Indivisible piece—wearing / for Him—except—for others
We will not be / always / slaves

For all seven births we will be only His servants.
We will always love only Him—
the One who wears the crescent moon in His thick, matted hair.
We will never be slaves for anyone except Him.

Like the other nāyaṉmār poets, Kāraikkāl Ammaiyār presented vivid, detailed iconographic portraits of Śiva to instill a concrete devotional image in the devotee's mind. Such detailed poetic iconography is a central component of Tamil bhakti poetry. It is possible that Ammaiyār was seeing physical images of the Lord.[55] Physical representations of Śiva appear as early as the third or second century BCE; many of the early images are *liṅgas*. During the Kuṣāṇa period (ca. first–third century CE) the images proliferate, on coins and seals as well as in stone. Among these images are Śiva as Ardhanārīśvara, or the Lord as half male and half female; Harihara—half Śiva, half Viṣṇu; as the beggar; and as the lord of the *gaṇas*, the ghoulish beings that form Śiva's fearsome retinue as he plays and dances in the cremation ground.[56] In her poetry Kāraikkāl Ammaiyār calls herself one of Śiva's *gaṇas*, one of the beings that perpetually witness the Lord's dance in the cremation ground. Śiva dancing in the cremation ground is a central image in Ammaiyār's poetry, which we turn to now.

2

Kāraikkāl Ammaiyār Through Her Poetry

Śiva's *Pēy*

The standard stories about Kāraikkāl Ammaiyār stress that she is a beautiful and devoted wife before her husband renounces her and she is free to devote her life to Śiva. But in her poetry, Ammaiyār gives no personal history, other than to say to Śiva that she has worshiped him as soon as she could speak, in the first verse of her long poem *Arputat Tiruvantāti*:

> Ever since I was born in this world, and learned to speak,
> with overwhelming love I have always remained at
> Your beautiful feet.
> O God of the gods, whose blue-suffused throat
> shines incandescently,
> when will You take away my sorrows?

In the earlier Caṅkam *puram* poetry the poet speaks in his own voice but focuses on praising kings and heroic warriors and describing events around him. In devotional poetry the poet speaks in his or her own voice and praises the god, but in contrast to Caṅkam poetry, the interior state of the poet, the "I" is foregrounded, as in this poem. Ammaiyār reveals the consuming love she has always felt for Śiva, in addition to praising him as the greatest of the gods and appealing to him to show her his grace by removing the miseries of earthly life. This poem follows a pattern that many *bhakti* poems will follow. The first two lines of the poem focus on the subject or author, Ammaiyār, conveying her interior state and the actions she performs to Śiva. The second two lines convey the qualities of the god Śiva, the object of Ammaiyār's devotion, and the reaction to her worship that she desires him to have.[1] In many of her poems, such as this one, Ammaiyār addresses Śiva directly; in several other poems she speaks to her own heart, either chiding herself for her shortcomings in worshiping, or rejoicing in her intimate relationship with Śiva. In some poems she speaks directly to other devotees or potential devotees, or to those ignorant people who do not worship Śiva, but whether or not the devotees are addressed directly, it is clear that the poems are meant to be heard and that Ammaiyār is explicating the path that defines and unites the emerging community of devotees.[2] Each "bhakti poem functions as both a description of and a medium for" the emotional, intimate communion the poet experiences with god (Cutler 1987, 11). As the Caṅkam poets praised the king by narrating his victorious actions on the battlefield, Ammaiyār praises Śiva by referring to his heroic deeds narrated in Sanskrit myths. As in this poem, Ammaiyār often refers to Śiva as blue-throated, which occurred when Śiva swallowed poison:

> In order to obtain *amṛta* (ambrosia), the elixir of immortality, the gods and demons churned the ocean of milk. Mount Mandara was the churning stick, supported by Viṣṇu; the snake king Ādiśeṣa (or Vāsuki) was the rope. The gods held one side of the rope, the demons the other. As they churned the ocean a burning black mass of poison, the terrifying Kālakūṭa, emerged. In order to save the world Śiva immediately swallowed the poison, holding it in his throat, which turned his throat blue-black.[3]

Throughout her poetry Ammaiyār combines several Sanskritic myths with Caṅkam elements to build a vivid portrait of this heroic god who she has devoted herself to with all her heart.[4] As we saw in Chapter 1, male and female demons or *pēys* were common characters in Caṅkam poetic scenes, often dancing among the corpses lying on battlefields or in the desolate landscape of the cremation ground. The Caṅkam *pēy* or demons are not necessarily evil; they are ghoulish, frightening, and haunt forbidding places, transgressing ordinary human boundaries.

> Those who say the words of this garland of *antāti veṇpā* verses
> uttered by Kāraikkāl Pēy, melting with love,
> and worship with everlasting devotion

will reach the Lord and praise Him with unceasing love.
(*Aṟputat Tiruvantāti* 101)

Ammaiyār characterizes herself as the demon or *pēy* from Kāraikkāl in the last verse of three of her four verses, as in this final, signature verse of her long poem.[5] This is all Ammaiyār says about the town of Kāraikkāl, currently called Karikal, which is located about 150 kilometers south of Pondicherry, but the place name localizes the mythic actions of Śiva and his interactions with his devotees in the Tamil country.

Ammaiyār focuses two of her poems on the place called Tiruvālaṅkāṭu (Tiruvalangadu), which is approximately 50 kilometers west of Chennai and far to the north and west of Karikal, at the northern edge of the Tamil land made sacred by the later *Tēvāram* poets.[6] Cēkkiḻār's story of Ammaiyār describes how Śiva told her to go to Tiruvālaṅkāṭu to witness his dance after she walked to Mt. Kailāsa on her hands, but such autobiographical details are not included in the poetry; Tiruvālaṅkāṭu is simply the place where Śiva dances in the cremation ground. In the last verse of each of the two Tiruvālaṅkāṭu poems, Ammaiyār again signs the poems as Kāraikkāl Pēy, describing herself in the first poem as having "uncombed hair" and in the second as having "teeth and a fiery mouth," descriptions that resonate with the demonic figures in Caṅkam poetry.[7] (See Figure 2.1.)

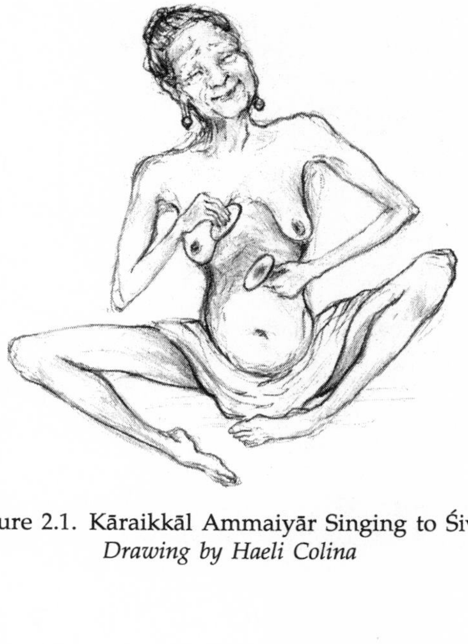

Figure 2.1. Kāraikkāl Ammaiyār Singing to Śiva.
Drawing by Haeli Colina

The first verse of the Tiruvālaṅkāṭu poems describing a female *pēy* is commonly understood to be Ammaiyār's self-description:[8]

> A female ghoul with withered breasts, bulging veins,
> hollow eyes, white teeth, shriveled stomach,
> red hair, two fangs,
> bony ankles, and elongated shins,
> stays in this cemetery, howling angrily.
> This place where my Lord dances in the fire with a cool body,
> His streaming hair flying in the eight directions,
> is Tiruvālaṅkāṭu. (*Tiruvālaṅkāṭṭu Mūtta Tiruppatikam* 1.1)

Śiva's dancing has Vedic roots, and there are sculptural forms of Śiva dancing from at least the Gupta period. The iconographic image of him as the great dancer attired in elephant skins and ornamented by snakes, accompanied by his *gaṇas* or troupe of ghouls, dancing while Pārvatī watches (and sometimes takes part) is clearly conveyed in the *Mahābhārata*.[9] Śiva's *gaṇas* or *bhūtagaṇas* are squat, impish, grotesque creatures who play a variety of musical instruments to accompany Śiva's dance. Śiva's *gaṇas* accompany him in Caṅkam poetry, localizing his troupe in a landscape already filled with *pēys* and other ghoulish beings. In the fifth-century Tamil epic *Cilappatikāram*, there are several scenes in which Śiva dances, including in the cremation ground while Pārvatī watches.[10]

In many of Ammaiyār's poems Śiva is accompanied by his *gaṇa* ensemble while he dances and Pārvatī watches, including this one:

> You who possess a five-headed cobra spitting fiery
> poison from its gaping mouths,
> the dance that You perform,
> is it for the One with young, tender breasts shaped like a
> round pot to see?
> Or is it for the troupe of ghouls in the burning cremation
> ground to see?
> You tell me once. (*Aṟputat Tiruvantāti* 99)

The cremation ground as the stage of Śiva's dance is a central motif in Ammaiyār's poetry. In the *Mahābhārata* Umā asks Śiva why he dwells in cremation grounds:

> Maheśvara, the Great Lord, replied to the Goddess that in the past he had been looking a long time for a pure place to

dwell in. He could not find one, was frustrated, and out of anger against procreation he created the *piśācas*, flesh-eating ghouls and goblins, and the *rākṣasas*, intent on killing people. Out of compassion and to protect people and alleviate their fear, however, he kept these ghosts and fiends in cremation grounds. Since he did not want to live without the *bhūtas* and *gaṇas*, he chose to live in a cemetery. The brahmins worshiped him in daily sacrifices, whereas those who desired liberation took the terrible Rudra vow. Only heroes (*vīra*) could stay in such a place. It was not fit for seekers of long life or for the impure. None but Rudra could free people from fear. When the ghosts stayed with him, they caused no harm. It was for the well-being of the world that Rudra lived in cemeteries. (Kramrisch 1988, 395–396)

In Ammaiyār's poetry, the burning ground is the site of Śiva's universal dance of creation and destruction, the gruesome place where "[r]evulsion in its last degree of sublimation reaches up to holiness" (Ibid. 299) where the devotee transcends ordinary awareness to realize Śiva's divine play and the ultimate salvation he brings. The dancing demons in the cremation ground are enraptured by Śiva's dance, embodying pure devotion to Śiva, pure awareness only of him.[11] As his fervent *pēy* devotee Ammaiyār describes herself as a member of Śiva's troupe of ghouls, explicitly linking the Tamil *pēys* with Śiva's *gaṇas*:

> The One who has kept another eye on His forehead,
> has made me understand a little of Him.
> I am one of the *pēys* among his good *gaṇas*.
> Whether or not this grace lasts,
> I don't want anything else. (*Aṟputat Tiruvantāti* 86)

Śiva as the Heroic Lord

In one poem Ammaiyār describes Śiva himself as having a ghoul form:

> All those other people who do not understand that
> He is the real truth,
> have seen only His *pēy* form:
> His lotus-like body smeared with ash and garlanded
> with bones.
> You see that they ridicule Him! (*Aṟputat Tiruvantāti* 29)[12]

Through her powerful poetry, Kāraikkāl Ammaiyār reveals that seeing the terrifying form of Śiva performing his dance of destruction in the cremation ground is really the most sublime and blissful experience of the Lord. She makes the terrible beautiful, and leads the devotee beyond the limits of ordinary awareness into a transcendent knowledge of Śiva as Truth, as the cosmic dancer who also lives in the heart of his adoring devotee.[13] Ammaiyār conveys a vivid iconographic portrait of Śiva by describing his form and attributes in loving detail, and by praising the heroic deeds he performs. Śiva's form and deeds are drawn from Sanskritic myths, but in her poetry Ammaiyār makes Śiva a local hero, praising him as the Caṅkam poets praised victorious warriors. In the first sectarian poetry in the Tamil region Ammaiyār illuminates Śiva's cosmic identity yet declares that those who truly love him will see him.[14]

> He is the One who knows.
> He is the One who makes us know.
> He is the knowledge that knows.
> He is the truth that is to be known.
> He is the moon, sun, earth, sky, and all the other elements.
> (*Aṟputat Tiruvantāti* 20)

> He is the sun, moon, fire, and space;
> He has become earth, water, air.
> He is the One who is the soul,
> and who has taken eight forms.
> He has come and revealed Himself as knowledge. (*Aṟputat Tiruvantāti* 21)

These two poems elucidate Śiva's nature as encompassing eight forms, or Aṣṭamūrti (Tamil *aṭṭamūrtti*): He is the five elements of earth, water, air, fire, and space; the sun and the moon; and the sacrificer.[15] Śiva has created the elements of the cosmos and has become them himself; he is both manifest in forms (*cakaḷam*) and is beyond form (*niṭkaḷam*).[16] In these two poems Śiva is not only manifest in all forms in the cosmos and the cause of all life forms, he is also the ultimate knowledge that liberates the souls bound to the cycle of reincarnation. In the Vedic system the sacrificer is the central agent in the performance of the sacrificial ritual that maintains cosmic order. The Tamil word for sacrificer, *iyamāṉaṉ* (Sanskrit *yajamāna*) also means life or soul.

As we saw in Chapter 1, in Śaiva Siddhānta philosophy the soul is the central agent in its own release from bondage. The soul achieves liberation only through Śiva's grace, but it must make an effort to remove the fetters and activate its powers. In the Śaiva Siddhānta path the devotee must be initiated by a guru and then must follow a fourfold path: proper conduct or service (*caryā*), ritual action (*kriyā*), disciplined concentration and meditation on Śiva (*yoga*), and finally, supreme knowledge (*jñāna*) of Śiva, which brings liberation (*mukti*). Śaiva Siddhānta is not fully systematized for several centuries after Kāraikkāl Ammaiyār lived; the intricate philosophy, technical details, and hierarchical divisions that are central to the Śaiva Siddhānta path are not evident in her poetry. But Ammaiyār's poetry does contain the seeds of the devotional principles that infuse the hymns of the later *Tēvāram* poets and that will be fully developed in the ensuing centuries.[17] In Caṅkam poetry the poet praises his king and patron; in Ammaiyār's poetry and later *bhakti* works this hierarchical relationship is transposed into one in which devotees perform humble service for Śiva out of consuming love for him. Ammaiyār makes it clear in her poems that the devotee should meditate on Śiva, love, serve, and worship him, and understand that he is the ultimate truth of the universe who through his grace grants souls liberation from rebirth.[18]

Those who speak about bookish knowledge,
who do not have real knowledge of the truth,
let them wander.
The nature of the One whose throat is like a blue jewel
is beyond limits.
To those who practice any kind of austerities,
who imagine Him in any form,
He will appear in that form. (*Aṟputat Tiruvantāti* 33)

O ignorant heart, you have attained a great refuge—
rejoice!
Shine among humans!
Nurture still more the great love that comes from being
the slave to the One who wanders,
wearing the bones of all, without contempt. (*Aṟputat Tiruvantāti* 31)

To those who follow the great path of focusing on Him,
the Lord,
desiring the Lord's great grace,
and who ask, "Where has He, the Lord, gone?"
He is very easy to see:
He is even here, in the mind of
people like me. (*Aṟputat Tiruvantāti* 45)

On that day I became Your servant without seeing
Your divine form.
Even today I have not seen Your sacred form.
To those who ask,
"What is your Lord's permanent form? "
What can I tell them?
What is Your form? (*Aṟputat Tiruvantāti* 61)

In these poems Ammaiyār declares that if devotees truly love Śiva, perpetually serving him and meditating on him, through his grace they will see him and understand him as the ultimate reality. The first poem emphasizes the inadequacy of texts in realizing Śiva as the truth. In the second poem Śiva is garlanded with the bones of everyone, signifying that birth status does not matter to the Lord, he accepts all devotees who serve him. In the third poem, as in many of her poems, Ammaiyār celebrates her select status as one of Śiva's true devotees, the recipient of his grace. But in the last poem Ammaiyār expresses the despair and longing of the devotee who serves Śiva but has not yet been granted a divine vision. The mysterious Śiva does not reveal himself as part of his grace and divine play, arousing the devotee's intense love and service.[19] Śiva's nature is "beyond limits" yet Ammaiyār craves a form on which to focus her meditation, her service, and her praise.

In many of her poems Ammaiyār paints a vivid iconographic image by describing Śiva's beautiful form in loving detail, paying particular attention to his matted hair and to the snakes that adorn his body:

The curls of His matted locks hang down,
shining like a golden mountain.
On the golden chest of the One with the throat like
darkness,
a snake hangs closely around Him,
glittering near His garland of bones. (*Aṟputat Tiruvantāti* 26)

For those who look,
the golden matted hair of our Lord
who has tied a snake around His head,
with its crown of beautiful, flourishing *koṉṟai* flowers
and the Gaṅgā river, flowing abundantly from heaven,
looks like the rainy season. (*Aṟputat Tiruvantāti* 53)

These poems describe Śiva as the ascetic yogi: His head is covered with matted hair, snakes coil around his chest and head, he wears a garland of bones, a crown of *koṉṟai* flowers (which are typically offered to him in worship), and his body glows with a golden light. In addition, he holds the goddess Gaṅgā, the river Ganges, on his head. The second poem most clearly resonates with the poetic landscapes of Caṅkam poetry in which the emotional phases of love are linked with the natural landscape. In *akam* poetry the rainy season is associated with the forests and with patient waiting for the lover. In this poem Śiva's matted locks are likened to the rainy season since Gaṅgā flows over them like the rain, and the *koṉṟai* flowers that crown his head grow only during the rainy season. The allusion to the rainy season also suggests the loving relationship between Śiva and his consort.[20] Śiva carrying the goddess Gaṅgā in his hair is an expression of his grace, as revealed in the story:

> The ancestors of King Bhagīratha angered the sage Kapila by disturbing him during his meditation; the sage burned them to death with his eyes. King Bhagīratha sought to purify his ancestors' ashes with the waters of the celestial river Gaṅgā. He performed severe austerities (*tapas*) so that Gaṅgā would come down to earth; he asked Śiva to break the impact of the mighty river's fall. As Gaṅgā descended, Śiva graciously caught the river in his matted hair and cushioned her impact on earth.[21]

But Śiva's main wife is Pārvatī or Umā; Ammaiyār teases Śiva about having two consorts, and the jealousy that must exist between the two women, a common theme in the mythology of Śiva and the goddess:[22]

> Umā belongs to a good lineage, so She will not leave
> Your side.
> Flowing Gaṅgā is of the same nature.
> You who adorn Yourself with white sacred ash and bone,
> You also won't leave them.
> Between these two here, please say
> Who enjoys Your love? (*Aṟputat Tiruvantāti* 95)

> The blue curls of the woman of Himavāṉ's lineage
> who is one side of the One who keeps the

> beautiful moon on the right side of His matted hair,
> look like the fruits put out by the *koṉṟai* flowers that
> He wears in His matted hair
> have come over to hang there. (*Aṟputat Tiruvantāti* 50)
>
> If we, who always perform sweet service to Him,
> one day ask Him for one thing,
> will He bestow it on us?
> For Umā who has a red mouth like a *toṇṭai* fruit,
> He searched for another one like
> that young white bull which has no equal and which
> supports Him.
> Since He did not find one,
> This Supreme Being keeps Her with Him. (*Tiruviraṭṭai Maṇimālai* 19)
>
> If You are sensible,
> You will see the danger of
> the snake lying like a garland on Your chest.
> That big, ferocious snake that crawls on You
> may one day reach Umā.
> If that happens, it is Your sin. (*Aṟputat Tiruvantāti* 13)

These poems describe more of Śiva's attributes as the yogi meditating in the cremation ground: He is covered with ash, adorned with bone ornaments, and he wears the crescent moon in his hair. His vehicle and constant devotee is his bull Nandi. Umā, the daughter of Himavān or the Lord of the Himalaya Mountains, has a mouth like the fruit of a *toṇṭai*, a kind of vine common in the Tamil land.[23]

In the last three poems, the beautiful, gentle Umā is described as half of Śiva in his Ardhanārīśvara form, the origins of which are told in this myth:

> Brahmā's mind-born sons failed to procreate, so the Creator performed severe penance to Lord Śiva. Śiva was satisfied with Brahmā's penance and appeared before him as an androgyne, united with Śakti, the Goddess. Brahmā praised Śiva, who separated Śakti from his body and made her a separate being. Brahmā asked her to be born as the daughter of his son Dakṣa, so that creation could proceed. Śakti consented, and from the middle of her eyebrows she created a goddess like herself, who became

> Satī, the daughter of Dakṣa. Śakti re-entered Śiva's body, so that he became Ardhanārīśvara again, and vanished. Ever since that time creatures have been made through sexual intercourse.[24]

The heroic god who destroys evil and conquers death gains his power through meditation and practicing austerities. Sometimes Śiva's yogic activities threaten to destabilize the cosmos, as in the story of Śiva burning Kāma (Tamil Matan̲) in anger:

> The terrible demon Tāraka was terrorizing the gods and causing havoc in the world. The gods knew that only a son of Śiva was capable of killing him. The ascetic yogi Śiva was engaged in meditation in a Himalayan forest. Satī had been reborn as Pārvatī, the daughter of the mountain, Himavān, and was performing austerities (*tapas*) in order to win Śiva as her husband. The gods sent Kāma, the god of desire, to pierce Śiva with his flower-arrow to rouse his passion and love for Pārvatī so that they could produce the son that would save the world. But when Kāma came before Śiva with his bow and arrow, Śiva opened his third eye and burned Kāma to ashes.[25]

O You who looked at the powerful Matan̲ with a bright bow
and burnt him to white powder,
then went back to Your meditation with a clear mind.
When the mouth that drank the strong poison looks the same,
how come only Your throat became black?
Explain this to me! (*Ar̲putat Tiruvantāti* 89)

The complex iconographic portrait that Kāraikkāl Ammaiyār constructs includes not only detailed descriptions of Śiva as the paradoxical yogi whose body is shared by Umā and who carries Gaṅgā on his head, but numerous references to his many heroic deeds and victories over demonic beings:[26]

This is your foot that
pressed Rāvaṇa,
who through arrogance lifted the mountain on his
twenty strong shoulders,

and made Māl who always has Lakṣmi with him, and
Brahmā, lament,
because they had not seen it.
But then later they rejoiced, and worshiped it.
And Your foot conquered Yama,
then kicked him. (*Aṟputat Tiruvantāti* 80)

This poem links three myths narrating Śiva's heroic deeds through Śiva's foot, which is worshiped by devotees and gods alike, and which performed two of the deeds. The first lines refer to Śiva's crushing of the demon Rāvaṇa with his toe:

> Rāvaṇa, the ten-headed demon king of Laṅkā, was riding through the air in his chariot; he saw that Śiva's Himalayan abode Mt. Kailāsa was blocking his path. Śiva was sitting with Pārvatī on the mountain. Rāvaṇa began to lift the mountain up to remove it from his path; when the mountain began to tremble, Śiva pressed his big toe down and crushed Rāvaṇā underneath. The frightened demon worshiped Śiva with hymns; in return, Śiva graciously granted him boons.[27]

In the last lines of the poem Śiva's foot kicks Yama, referring to his deeds as *Kālasaṃhāramūrti* ("the Lord who conquers Death"):

> The sage Mṛkaṇḍu was childless and performed austerities to Śiva. Śiva appeared before him to present his boon, and gave him the choice of an evil son who would live a long life, or a pious boy who would live only to the age of sixteen. Mṛkaṇḍu chose the pious boy; when he was born, he named him Mārkaṇḍeya. This boy grew up to be a wise, virtuous, ardent devotee of Śiva. When he entered his sixteenth year he was immersed in meditation before a Śiva *liṅga*; as Yama, the god of death, approached him to take him away, Mārkaṇḍeya embraced the *liṅga*. Śiva sprang out of the *liṅga* and kicked Yama to death. Mārkaṇḍeya was given the boon of immortality and remained sixteen years of age forever; Śiva revived Yama.[28]

The middle of the poem refers to "Māl," an epithet for the god Viṣṇu, whose consort is the goddess Lakṣmi. The poem describes how the gods Viṣṇu and Brahmā first lament, then worship Śiva, referring to one of the central myths narrating Śiva's superiority over the other gods.

> In the darkness and flood before the beginning of a new cosmic age, Brahmā and Viṣṇu argued with each other over who was the supreme divine power in the universe. A massive pillar of fire, a *liṅga* of light, suddenly appeared in the darkness. Brahmā took the form of a wild goose and flew up as high as he could; Viṣṇu took the form of a boar and burrowed into the earth as far as he could go. Neither god could reach the end of the great pillar and came back to the earth's surface. Śiva showed himself inside his fiery *liṅga;* Brahmā and Viṣṇu admitted defeat, acknowledged Śiva as the supreme deity in the world, and worshiped him.[29]

Ammaiyār's poetry champions Śiva as the supreme deity in the world, as the only god who can bring salvation to the devotees who worship him. Many verses convey to the devotee a detailed iconographic portrait of Śiva's attributes and his beautiful form. In the above myth Śiva shows himself inside the fiery shaft of light. The *liṅga is an aniconic image that represents* Śiva as both unmanifest and manifest at the same time (Tamil *cakaḷaniṭkaḷam;* Sanskrit *sakala-niṣkala*), and as mysterious. In this poem Ammaiyār understands that Śiva takes on different forms as part of his divine activity:[30]

> The mind is unique by nature.
> In order to elevate itself, and to receive the highest
> refuge,
> it meditates solely on the One with the long snakes that
> spit hot, fiery poison,
> the One who has taken a body as an ornament,
> and looks glorious. (*Aṟputat Tiruvantāti* 14)

This poem describes Śiva's *līla,* his divine play in which he has taken a body wrapped in threatening snakes as an ornament, giving his devotees a form to meditate on. Ammaiyār persistently exhorts devotees to get beyond terror and revulsion at "the macabre horror in which he clad his transcendence" in order to see that he is the conqueror of death (Kramrisch 1988, 358).

Locating Śiva in the Tamil Land

The figure of the ascetic yogi Śiva seems to find a particularly fertile landscape for taking up a new residence in an area full of fierce and ambivalent forces that haunt Śiva's favorite place, the cremation ground. Śiva's *gaṇa* troupe meshes easily with the *pēys* that populate the Tamil landscape; as one of Śiva's *pēys* Ammaiyār lays out a path of devotion that integrates familiar elements and that ultimately transforms the geography and culture of the Tamil land. Brahmanical ideas from the north such as karma and reincarnation had been making inroads into the Tamil region from at least Caṅkam times, but the mythic, iconographic portrait of Śiva as a personal deity who is all-powerful and who grants liberation from the cycle of birth and rebirth is new.[31]

> Our Lord, without considering anything,
> wanders to all places, begging for alms everywhere,
> and dances in the cremation ground in the middle of the night.
> When we see Him, we will find out why.
> What's the point of asking here? (*Aṟputat Tiruvantāti* 25)

Śiva as the wandering beggar who dances in the cremation ground is a vital story in the Tamil region. In the invocation of the fourth to sixth century Tamil *akam* anthology *Kalittokai*, Pārvatī keeps time while Śiva performs the martial dances *koṭukoṭṭi, pāṇṭaraṅkam,* and *kāpālam*. The *kāpālam* dance specifically refers to Śiva dancing with the *kapāla* or skull of the god Brahma in his hand, which evokes a central myth of Śiva as the ascetic beggar who must do penance for the brahminicide he committed by slicing off Brahmā's fifth head:[32]

> Brahmā haughtily declared himself the highest reality in the universe. Śiva, in his terrifying Bhairava form, sliced off Brahmā's fifth head with his nail, incurring the sin of brahminicide. The skull stuck to his palm, so Bhairava became known as the Kāpālika, the Skull-Bearer. In order to expiate his sin he took a vow to wander naked begging for alms, holding the skull as his begging bowl. In this Bhikṣāṭana form, Śiva wandered all over the world asking for alms; women in the houses he stopped at were enchanted by him. Eventually he came to the Pine Forest where the sages were practicing austerities; they did not recognize Śiva. The

ascetics' wives were infatuated by the naked beggar, which outraged the sages, who angrily demanded that Śiva make his *liṅga* fall off. He did, and vanished. There was chaos in the world, so the sages went to Brahmā, who told the sages that the beggar was the great god Śiva. The sages went back to the Pine Forest and worshiped Śiva.

Śiva continued wandering and came to Viṣṇu's abode. The gatekeeper Viṣvaksena did not recognize Śiva and blocked his entry; Śiva pierced him with his trident and carried his corpse into Viṣṇu's residence as *Kaṅkāla-mūrti*. Viṣṇu offered him gushing streams of blood from a vein in his forehead, but the blood did not fill Śiva's begging bowl. Śiva left Viṣṇu's abode and proceeded to Vārāṇāsī; when he entered the holy city, the skull fell off his hand and he was free of the sin of brahminicide.[33]

Ammaiyār has several poems referring to Śiva as the wandering beggar, including some that are playful or admonitory in tone:

You, the One who wears the moon on Your head,
we have heard the gossip about
the food dropped in the skull You carry, to which flesh
sticks.
If You do not consider it a sin,
You, the One with the hue of burnt, white ash,
You tell me. (*Aṟputat Tiruvantāti* 56)

Even if you beg for alms all over the world,
leave Your bad snake behind and go!
Good women will not come and give You alms
since they will be afraid of the venomous snake on Your
head
that sways all the time with its hood spread. (*Aṟputat Tiruvantāti* 57)

They took water from many big wave-filled oceans to
cook the food,
but they say it was not filled.
So how is it Your broad begging bowl that is a skull
was filled with the alms given
by innocent women who do not want anything in
return? (*Aṟputat Tiruvantāti* 74)

We see in these poems some of the attributes of Śiva the ascetic yogi that pervade Ammaiyār's poetry: the skull for begging for food; the moon in his hair; the ash from the cremation ground that is smeared on his body; and the snake that wraps around him, which Ammaiyār pays particular attention to in her poetry. In the myth of Śiva wandering as a beggar as penance for cutting off Brahmā's fifth head it is said that his begging bowl could not even be filled by the gods, but here Kāraikkāl Ammaiyār plays with this concept by declaring that if one is truly devoted to Śiva, wanting nothing but to be his slave, then like these pure women, one can reach him. These poems evoke the women's enchantment with the wandering beggar that is an important erotic layer in the Sanskrit myths as well as in the hymns of the *Tēvāram* poets, but which is not a focus of Ammaiyār's poetry.[34]

The ascetic practices evoked by the image of Śiva as the wandering beggar appear in Caṅkam literature, which contains descriptions of ascetics practicing *tapas* or austerities in order to attain *mukti* or liberation.[35] Some of these ascetics may have been part of the earliest Śaiva sects whose followers imitated Śiva in his terrible Bhairava form, often in the cremation ground, enacting Śiva's penance for brahminicide, which gave Śiva the beggar the epithets Bhikśātana and Kāpālin the skull-bearer. These early sects were known as Kālāmukhas, Kāpālikas, and Pāśupatas. Later Śaiva poets such as Appar refer to Kāpālika and Pāśupata ascetics worshiping at Śiva's shrines, but the emerging orthodox tradition rejects their extreme devotional mode. Perhaps because the town of Tiruvoṟṟiyūr, near Tiruvālaṅkāṭu, is known to have had a significant Pāśupata presence at this time, Kāraikkāl Ammaiyār's poetry encompasses a more extreme asceticism than the later *nāyaṉmārs* embodied, one that is rooted in a milieu of multiple traditions.[36]

All those other people who do not understand that
He is the real truth,
have seen only His *pēy* form:
His lotus-like body smeared with ash and garlanded
with bones.
See that they ridicule Him? (*Aṟputat Tiruvantāti* 29)

His greatness is such that it is not known by others.
But others know He is the great consciousness.
Our Lord, wearing the bones of others,

happily dances along with the powerful ghouls
in the fire at night. (*Aṟputat Tiruvantāti* 30)

How do I reach Him through love?
Not only does that snake that sways on Him
not allow anyone to come close to Him,
He wears a string of skulls that make noise,
and a garland of white bones;
and, rejoicing, He mounts a bull. (*Tiruviraṭṭai Maṇimālai* 17)

These poems vividly convey the distinction between the devotees who know that Śiva is the ultimate truth, realizing that his ghoul form is not terrible but sublime, and those who are repelled by his ash-smeared body and bone necklace. Bones are a central liberation motif in Kāraikkāl Ammaiyār's poetry; Ammaiyār is an emaciated skeleton of a figure, an assemblage of bones at home in the cremation ground but liberated by it. In the second poem, the first "others" refers to those who do not understand him. The second "others" refers to his devotees, who do realize who he is. The third, "the bones of others," refers to "just anyone": Śiva ornaments himself with a garland of bones he finds in the cremation ground, the bones of everyone and anyone; he does not discriminate, just as he responds to all devotees.

Kāraikkāl Ammaiyār formulates the key *bhakti* doctrine of total surrender to Śiva that continues throughout the development of Śaivism.

My heart!
Give up your bondage, your wife and children.
Saying that you take refuge here at His feet,
think of Him and worship
the Lord of the Immortals,
and of the universe;
my Father,
who is like the red flame of an unextinguished fire,
whose matted hair is not wet, even though a river enters it;
the One who belongs to me. (*Tiruviruṭṭai Maṇimālai* 13)

Not following a false path ruled by the five senses,
we have achieved merits;
because of the love of the slaves for the Lord,

the One who wears the flayed skin of a strong elephant,
being pleased,
He covers His three forms. (*Tiruviraṭṭai Maṇimālai* 16)

In the first poem Ammaiyār is speaking to her heart, yet she speaks as a male ascetic would. This may suggest that renunciation of the world was a contested category, that it was seen as a path open predominately to men, or for those on the margins of society.[37] But it also emphasizes Ammaiyār's asexual, ascetic approach to Śiva, the lack of eroticism in the intimacy that she enacts as one of Śiva's *gaṇas*. In the second poem Ammaiyār emphasizes that the ascetic path of focusing on Śiva generates merits, which brings Śiva's grace. Śiva's three forms refers to his sharing his form with Umā and Tirumāl or Viṣṇu. That he "covers" his three forms alludes to the Śaiva Siddhānta principle that Śiva hides himself until the soul is ready to reach him.[38] Ammaiyār addresses Śiva as Lord and as Father, the heroic father who can eradicate karma and rebirth:[39]

If, with wisdom,
and without ridiculing His body that is garlanded with
bones,
they praise the One who wears a moon on His long
matted hair,
and who conquered the three great cities of the powerful
asuras
who did not respect Him,
they will not be born here in this world in a body with
bones. (*Arputat Tiruvantāti* 37)

This poem is one of several in which Ammaiyār refers to the important myth of Śiva as *Tripurāntakamūrti* when he destroys the three cities of the *asuras* or evil demons:

The demon Tāraka's three sons, Tarakāṣa, Kamalāṣa, and Vidyunmālin, practiced austerities (*tapas*) and won a boon from Brahmā. The three demons asked for immortality, but Brahmā could not give them that. So the demons asked to live for a thousand years in three fortified cities that could move around the universe; they would reunite after a thousand years and combine their three cities into one city. The three cities could only be destroyed by the god who could pierce them all with one arrow. The architect Maya built three cities, of gold, silver, and iron, in which the three demons roamed around marauding and attacking all the beings in the world. The gods complained to Brahmā, but he said only Śiva had the power to destroy the demons because of his yogic practices. Śiva consented to the gods' request to conquer the demons' cities. When the demons reunited after one thousand years, Śiva rode out in a special chariot with a bow and arrow, all composed of divine beings and celestial and terrestrial elements. Brahmā served as his charioteer. Śiva released the fire-tipped arrow and destroyed the three cities.[40]

Śiva's Dance

The story of Śiva's destruction of the three demon cities is linked to his dancing in the cremation ground in early Tamil literature. In the epic *Cilappatikāram,* canto six describes eleven kinds of dances, including Śiva's dance of destruction that he performed when he conquered the three cities of the demons, called both the *koṭukoṭṭi* (or *koṭṭiccētam*) and the *pāṇṭaraṅkam,* which are also mentioned in the Caṅkam anthology *Kalittokai.* Śiva dances in the cremation ground where Kālī danced, with Umā as half of him, and who also keeps time (6.38–45).[41] Śiva as the heroic conqueror of the three cities of the demons resonates with the heroic warrior on the bloody battlefield in Caṅkam poetry.

> The *pēy* with a big, wrinkled mouth sings
> on this big cremation ground You take as Your stage;
> You make the *bhūtas* come to worship You.
> O Meritorious One with the tightly worn hero's anklets,
> lifting Your leg, You perform the dance.
> Have You discharged arrows with Your bow
> in order to burn the three big walls of the *rākṣasas* with
> fire? (*Tiruviraṭṭai Maṇimālai* 15)[42]

This poem brings together three kinds of demonic beings: The *pēy* of the Tamil landscape and the *bhūtas* or *bhūtagaṇas* of Śiva's troupe, accompany Śiva in the cremation ground, where he dances after conquering a third kind of demonic being, the *rākṣasas* or evil demons in their three cities. The *pēy* Ammaiyār is a devotee of Śiva and therefore part of his demonic troupe, as opposed to the evil demons he destroys. Śiva wears the hero's anklets (*kaḻal*) worn by victorious warriors in Caṅkam poetry. He lifts his leg in his fierce *tāṇḍava* dance of destruction that he performs in victory and at the end of each age to usher in the following age. Śiva's *tāṇḍava* dance is first described in great detail in Bharata's *Nāṭyaśāstra* (ca. second to fourth century CE), the classical text that explicates drama and dance.

Bharata and the great fourth-century Sanskrit poet Kālidāsa distinguish the fierce *tāṇḍava* performed by Śiva from the soft, graceful *lāsya* performed by Pārvatī, as suggested by this poem:[43]

> Keeping Umā, with curls on the nape of her neck and
> beautiful bangles,
> gracefully on Your side,
> don't go there to dance in the flaming fires with the
> ghouls
> in the big cremation ground in the middle of the night
> so that
> Your hero's anklets jingle loudly. (*Aṟputat Tiruvantāti*, 51)

In this poem Ammaiyār playfully warns Śiva not to keep the gentler Umā with him when he dances his violent dance in the cremation ground; the implication of Śiva holding Umā "gracefully" is that he is so powerful it is easy for him to hold her.

Above we saw that in one poem Ammaiyār describes Śiva's "streaming hair flying in the eight directions" (*Tiruvālaṅkāṭṭu Mūtta Tiruppatikam* 1.1). There are several other ways in which Ammaiyār conveys the fierceness of Śiva's dance of destruction:

> A *pēy*, not knowing whether the corpse is dead, goes
> close and touches it with a finger.
> Shouting and roaring, it flings the fire away.
> Jumping over the body, it runs away,
> and quivering with fear, hits its hollow stomach,
> making many demons run away.
> Taking the form of a Madman, in this place my Lord
> will dance. (*Tiruvālaṅkāṭṭu Mūtta Tiruppatikam* 2.4)

> Śiva!
> If you lift Your feet,
> the regions of hell will shift.
> If You move Your hair,
> the roof of the world will shatter.
> If You move Your hand with bracelets bouncing up and
> down,

the eight directions will be dislocated.
The stage cannot bear this.
So consider all these things,
then perform Your dance. (*Arputat Tiruvantāti*, 77)

He went around to countries and cities, following a good path,
showing kindness to others.
Now, his shrouded corpse is brought to the cemetery and placed next to an old corpse.
The moment it is put there,
the troupe of ghouls comes together and surrounds the corpse.
The place where He who has a snake which sways with open hood and who has fire in His hand,
dances so that the forest, sea, mountain, earth, and heaven vibrate,
is Tiruvālaṅkāṭu. (*Tiruvālaṅkāṭṭu Mūtta Tiruppatikam* 1.8)

In the cremation ground where you hear crackling noises
and the white pearls fall out of the tall bamboo,
the demons with frizzy hair and drooping bodies shout with wide-open mouths,
and come together and feast on the corpses.
In the big, threatening cremation ground,
when Māyaṉ dances, the Daughter of the Mountain watches Him,
in astonishment. (*Tiruvālaṅkāṭṭu Mūtta Tiruppatikam* 2.8)

These poems vividly convey the violence of Śiva's dance of destruction, and that he is in fact "the cosmos in dance" (Vatsyayan 192).

In the first poem Śiva is described as dancing like a madman, suggesting frenzied movement that defies easy understanding. In the second poem Ammaiyār pleads with Śiva to be careful about how he moves, since his violent dancing can dislocate and even shatter the universe. In the third poem Śiva's destructive dance again causes the universe to vibrate, but here his dance is directly set in the cremation ground where a good person has died, his good deeds in life contrasted with what happens to his body at death as ghouls surround the corpse. In the final poem Śiva's dance is so fierce, Umā, the daughter of the Lord of the Himalayan mountains, watches Śiva in astonishment. Śiva's fierce dance of destruction is also the dance of bliss, the transcendence of the mundane world that points toward liberation. Śiva Naṭarāja, Śiva as the Lord of Dance, is traditionally engaged in his *ānanda-tāṇḍava* or dance of furious bliss, one of seven *tāṇḍava* dances Śiva performs. Kaimal (3) gives a detailed description of Śiva Naṭarāja:

> Shiva stands on his deeply bent right leg while his slightly flexed left leg lifts to waist height and crosses the hips. Parallel to the dramatic transverse line of the lifted leg, one of his four arms crosses the body, its relaxed "elephant hand" (gajahasta) suspended above an equally relaxed ankle. Shiva places one of his right hands just above that loose wrist in the open-palm gesture (abhayamudra). Behind these boldly disposed limbs, the hips twist slightly to Shiva's right, but the torso remains erect. Long, matted tresses alternating with flower garlands stream outward from Shiva's head. On his right and among these locks sits a diminutive personification of the river Ganga (the Ganges), her body human above the waist and piscine below. She presses her palms together in the gesture of respectful address (anjalimudra). A crescent moon, a flower sacred to Shiva (the datura), and a cluster of spiky kondrai leaves crown Shiva's topknot. Shiva stands on a rotund dwarf.

In Ammaiyār's poetry Śiva has long matted hair ornamented with kondrai (*koṉṟai*) flowers; the crescent moon and Gaṅgā are in his hair as well, although Gaṅgā is not described as part human and part fish in the poetry. There is no mention of a dwarf. Śiva has multiple arms, and raises his leg in dance, but Ammaiyār is not specific about exactly what position the raised leg and hands take, with a couple of crucial exceptions that we will examine below.

Kaimal and other scholars believe that this image of dancing Śiva originated in the Tamil region and achieved the full iconographic form in the ninth or tenth century. Since the seventh century, Śiva Naṭarāja has been most explicitly connected to the temple in Chidambaram or Tillai, where according to tradition the *ānanda-tāṇḍava* originally took place.[44] The myth of Śiva's dance of bliss at Chidambaram is a version of the well-known Sanskrit myth of Dārukavana (Tamil Tārakavaṉam) or the Pine Forest, but the Chidambaram version has no Sanskrit counterpart.

> The sages in the Pine Forest were practicing their rituals and austerities without true devotion to Śiva, who enters

the forest as a wandering beggar along with Viṣṇu who has taken the form of a beautiful woman. The two gods seduced the sages' wives. The enraged sages attempted to kill Śiva by making a sacrificial fire out of which emerged several threatening beings and objects: a tiger, which Śiva killed and draped its skin around his waist; an antelope that Śiva lifted in his hand; snakes that he adorned himself with; a skull that he put in his hair; a trident that he grasped in his hand; a drum that he held with another hand; a fire that he held in another hand; a host of demons that he made his servants; and finally an evil dwarf (Apasmāra) that he stepped on top of. Then Śiva made the entire cosmos tremble with his heroic *tāṇḍava* dance, which the sages witnessed and then fell at Śiva's feet. Śiva returned to Mount Kailāsa but continues his *ānanda-tāṇḍava* dance in Chidambaram.

This myth connects Śiva as the wandering beggar with Śiva the dancer, as we have seen in Ammaiyār's poetry. Some scholars speculate that Śiva the dancer evolved from Bhairava, the fierce beggar form.[45] Most of the objects emerging from the sacrificial fire that Śiva takes as his attributes in this myth are central elements in the iconographic portrait Ammaiyār draws in her poetry, with some variations. Śiva carries a begging bowl but does not wear one in his hair; the demons play a variety of drums but Śiva does not play one himself; he holds fire and is surrounded by his troupe of ghouls, but he does not step on the demon Apasmāra;[46] and as seen in the following poem, he is ornamented by the animals that emerge from the sacrificial fire, reminding us that Śiva, as the Lord of Creatures and consort of the goddess Gaṅgā, encompasses in his body a moonlit grove of animals nourished by the sacred waters of his *śakti*:

Since He who has an eye in His forehead
and a golden form with brilliant rays
has brought together the snake, the moon, the gentle
deer, and the ferocious tiger,
and since He has Gaṅgā flowing in His hair,
He deserves the hero's anklets
on His beautiful, sacred feet. (*Aṟputat Tiruvantāti*, 67)

It is also in Chidambaram that Kālī challenged Śiva to a dance contest. As the god and goddess danced, Śiva raised his leg straight up to the sky in his *ūrdhva-tāṇḍava* dance; her modesty kept Kālī from performing the same move, so she admitted defeat and left her shrine in the forest. Although Chidambaram is where the the dance contest between Śiva and Kālī has traditionally been located, there is telling evidence that suggests that Tiruvālaṅkāṭu may be the original site of the contest in which Śiva performs his *ūrdhva-tāṇḍava* dance.[47]

Two of Ammaiyār's poems depict Śiva raising his leg high in the *ūrdhva-tāṇḍava* pose, and both suggest that his posture is forming a circle, which could be an early description of the Naṭarāja position that Kaimal describes above, in which Śiva raises his bent leg and crosses it over the other leg in the air.[48]

> A small fox takes rice from the sacrificial pit and eats it.
> The demons run, clapping their hands, angrily saying,
> "We didn't see it first!"
> There in that burning ground used as a stage,
> He forms a circle, taking the *uḷāḷam* posture;
> He swiftly lifts His leg so that it touches the sky.
> This place where our Lord stands erect and dances is
> Tiruvālaṅkāṭu. (*Tiruvālaṅkāṭṭu Mūtta Tiruppatikam* 1.4)
>
> Demons with flaming mouths and rolling, fiery eyes,
> going around, doing the *tuṇaṅkai* dance, running and
> dancing in the terrifying forest,
> draw out a burning corpse from the fire and eat the
> flesh.
> The place where our Lord raises His leg
> with the hero's *kaḻal* jingling
> and the anklets tinkling,
> dancing so that the fire in His hand spreads everywhere
> and His hair whips around,
> is Tiruvālaṅkāṭu. (*Tiruvālaṅkāṭṭu Mūtta Tiruppatikam* 1.7)

These poems are both set in the cremation ground with *pēy* demons running around as Śiva dances.

In the first poem Śiva raises his leg so high it touches the sky, a clear reference to his *ūrdhva-tāṇḍava* pose.[49] In the second poem the demons are dancing the *tuṇaṅkai dance,* which is associated with Koṟṟavai, the Tamil goddess of war and victory who dwells in forests. It was also danced at festivals, and in fact can mean "festival." It is a type of village dance in which the arms are bent and struck against the sides of the body. *Tuṇaṅkai* is also a kind of *pēy* or demon. These tropes root this text to Tamil soil, as well as to Śiva's band of ghouls.[50] In the second poem the dance contest between Śiva and Kālī is conveyed by the two sets of anklets worn by the dancers: Śiva wears his *kalal* or hero's victory anklets, while Kālī wears the *cilampu*, the anklets worn by women. Śiva dances so violently, his hair spreads out and whips around, suggesting that he defeats Kālī in the divine dance competition.

The Cremation Ground as Śiva's Stage

Kāraikkāl Ammaiyār locates Śiva's stage, the cremation ground, in the Tamil landscape, most particularly in the place called Tiruvālaṅkāṭu or "Sacred Banyan Tree Forest" in the two *patikam* she composed, *Tiruvālaṅkāṭṭu Mūtta Tiruppatikam*.[51] The eleven stanzas of the first *patikam* contain some version of the refrain "The place where my Lord dances is Tiruvālaṅkāṭu." Ten of the eleven stanzas of the second *patikam* describe the Lord dancing in the cremation ground, but do not name the place. As we saw in Chapter 1, the Tamil word *kāṭu* means forest, jungle, or desert, but it also means cremation or burial ground, as well as boundary or limit.[52] Forests are an integral landscape in many Indian narratives, notably in the epics *Mahābhārata* and *Rāmāyaṇa*, each of which contains a "Forest Book." Philip Lutgendorf highlights some of the environmental paradigms forests represent. Forests are the stage for relatively temporary adventures, such as when heroes go hunting, and would-be kings are exiled until they return to the city to rule, but forests can also be the permanent residence of raging *rākṣasas*, as well as peaceful but sometimes scary sages. The forest can also be a state of mind, in that the poet goes beyond the naturalistic to create a stage on which to project an aesthetic mood. Forests are "other" to the city and civilization; they are sacred places where supernatural beings reside, liminal experiences or stages of life take place, and human limitations can be transcended.[53]

Although the name of the area suggests it was a dense forest of banyan trees, which are widely thought to be the abode of gods,[54] the vegetation in Ammaiyār's poetry is that of the burning ground. Her poetry praising Śiva resonates with the earlier Caṅkam *puram* poetry that praises heroes in war and provides detailed descriptions of the battlefield, where demons feast on the corpses lying on the field and dance, garlanded with intestines, evoking the ancient Tamil belief that sacred power emerges in gruesome places of death and sacrifice.[55] Yet these fearful places full of threatening forces are connected to ordinary landscapes and mundane domestic activities, on one level rendering the power of the place accessible.[56] In Kāraikkāl Ammaiyār's poetry there is a vivid juxtaposition of the horrors and desolation of the cremation ground with the abundance of life forms and seemingly ordinary activities it supports.

The *eṭṭi* and *ilavam* trees, and the *īkai, cūrai,* and *kārai*
shrubs, are spread all over.
The burning cremation ground is covered with cactus.
The demon with wide-open eyes like a *paṟai* drum
seizes the dangling intestines of the dead bodies strewn
all over the cremation ground.
The ghoul plays the *muḻavam* drum and sings.
The Beautiful Lord dances there. (*Tiruvālaṅkāṭṭu Mūtta Tiruppatikam* 2.1)

The trees and shrubs here grow commonly in Tamilnadu. The tall *ilavam* or silk-cotton tree, the *īkai,* a species of mimosa, and the *cūrai,* a jujube shrub[57] thrive alongside the *eṭṭi* tree, the seed of which provides the deadly poison strychnine, and the *kārai,* a low shrub with sharp thorns found in desolate places.[58] The two drums here are ancient instruments: *Paṟai* is a generic term for a drum, but is also specifically a drum played in ancient battles by the *paṟaiya* or drum-beating caste.[59] The *muḻavu* is a huge drum played in ancient times when a king attained victory,[60] and is the precursor of the modern mrdangam.[61] The images of death and desolation are starkly contrasted with the abundant plant life that encircles the scene, the center of which is the dance of the Beautiful Lord Śiva.

The thorn bush burns; the wood on the pyre gets charred.
The corpse's brain leaks out in clumps.
The cactus shrivels up; the wood-apple tree is abundant.
In this very hot cremation ground,
wearing the skin of a spotted antelope, and with a tiger
skin on his shoulders,
considering this cremation ground also as His resting place,
the Lord dances. (*Tiruvālaṅkāṭṭu Mūtta Tiruppatikam* 2.5)

The cremation ground is of course a very hot place when a funeral pyre is burning. Here, although one plant, the wood-apple, thrives in the dry soil, the cactus is shriveled by the heat and the thorn bush is scorched by the funeral fire. Thorn bushes are associated with burning grounds in Caṅkam poetry; the scene evokes sacrifice as well as death, yet it is such a place the Śiva considers his resting place, his home.

In the Tiruvālaṅkāṭu poems Kāraikkāl Ammaiyār uses rhythmic, concussive sounds to convey the experience of Śiva dancing.[62]

The seeds in the white dried pods of the spreading *vākai*
tree rattle,

there, in the middle of the night of bewildering darkness,
the rock horned owl and *āṇṭalai* bird screech,
the owl jumps on top of a branch and flaps its wings.
Inside the cemetery, in the shadow of a row of cactus on
which the *iṇṭu* creeper twines,
the funeral pyre is lit.
This place where our Lord dances in the fire with a cool
body is
Tiruvālaṅkāṭu. (*Tiruvālaṅkāṭṭu Mūtta Tiruppatikam* 1.3)

There are several things in this poem that evoke the extraordinary and terrifying place where Śiva lives. The *vākai* tree is a kind of mimosa[63] that has long, narrow pods with seeds inside. In this poem the seeds are dried up and rattle, providing a scary, rhythmic accompaniment to the screeching of the birds. Demons customarily gather at the foot of *vākai* trees,[64] so their presence is implied here. The screeching of birds such as an owl can be a bad omen.[65] But in Tamil poetry owls are traditionally associated with the burial ground, where they keep company with ghouls,[66] shriek the invitation to other owls to feast on the corpses,[67] and hoot the message to the dead that they must add their ashes to those already in the cremation ground.[68] The *āṇṭalai* is a "fabulous bird of prey with a head like a man's." A flag with the *āṇṭalai* on it was used to frighten evil spirits away from the offerings on the altar.[69] The ubiquitous cactus, covered with a vine,[70] provides a backdrop for the funeral fire. The center of this crowded, gruesome scene is Śiva dancing in the fire of destruction, yet his yogi body is cool, not affected by the fire he creates. Kāraikkāl Ammaiyār promotes a vision of Śiva as the beautiful embodiment of the rhythm of life, burning away our illusions with the fire in his hand.

In the big cremation ground filled with the smoke from
the fires of funeral pyres
and white skulls,
surrounded by bamboo groves,
there are vultures, and demons, and monkeys jump around.
When rhythmic music plays,
when the white *tuṭi* drums and the *paṟai* drums beat,
the Great Lord who has the curved, white, teetering
crescent moon
and the rippling Gaṅgā
will dance. (*Tiruvālaṅkāṭṭu Mūtta Tiruppatikam* 2.9)

The *picācu*, wearing a white skull garland tied tightly,
swallowed up the congealed fat.

Having named her child Kālī,
bringing her up with comfort,
she wiped the dust off the child, suckled it, then went
away.
The child, not seeing the mother returning, cried itself to
sleep.
The place where our Lord dances in the cemetery is
Tiruvālaṅkāṭu. (*Tiruvālaṅkāṭṭu Mūtta Tiruppatikam* 1.5)

Kāraikkāl Ammaiyār's close attention to mundane activities confronts the devotee's habitual understanding of the cremation ground as a threatening, marginal, "other" place. It seems that she is consciously associating the powerful forces of the demons occupying Tiruvālaṅkāṭu with the transcendent god dancing in the cremation ground. Here, the *picācu* ghoul is a gentle mother caring for a child.[71] The intimate scene plays out in the same space as Śiva's dance, breaking down the barrier between domestic space and the place of death. The motherly demon in this poem resonates with the many female beings populating the ancient Tamil land.

By becoming one of Śiva's *gaṇas* or ghouls, Kāraikkāl Pēy assumes a kind of power familiar in the early Tamil world, yet adds a new devotional level by connecting the indigenous demon tradition with one of the central myths of Śiva. We have seen that the war goddess Koṟṟavai was integral to Caṅkam poetry; during the post-Caṅkam period (approximately 300–600 CE), Koṟṟavai is increasingly associated with Durgā and Kālī, and therefore with Śiva. In addition, a fierce goddess is connected to the village of Paḻaiyaṉūr, which borders Tiruvālaṅkāṭu, and whose story is told in the epic *Cilappatikāram*. Nīli is a vengeful goddess who, like Kaṇṇaki, the heroine of the epic, becomes divine through her righteous anger at a failure of justice and the revenge she enacts on those who committed the misdeeds. Nīli curses Kōvalaṉ, the hero of the epic, to be murdered unjustly since in their previous births Kōvalaṉ had unjustly killed Nīli's husband. In the twelfth century Cēkkiḻār tells a different version of Nīli's story.[72] Local tradition, as well as stories about the Tiruvālaṅkāṭu temple, continue to tell Nīli's story in connection with Kāraikkāl Ammaiyār and Kālī. Despite the strong goddess tradition in the area and the resonances between Kāraikkāl Pēy and local divine beings, however, Kāraikkāl Ammaiyār does not single out Koṟṟavai or any specific local goddess, nor does she present herself as a goddess-like figure, but only as one of Śiva's demons. Pārvatī appears in several of her verses, but Ammaiyār's single-minded devotion never wavers from the Lord who dances in the cremation ground.[73] Although the story of the dance competition between Śiva and Kālī has been specifically connected to Chidambaram for centuries, the evidence in Ammaiyār's poetry and other early Tamil literature suggests that this divine contest was first located in Tiruvāḷaṅkaṭu. In this competition Śiva subdues Kālī and wins the contest; similarly, when Śiva moves down from the north to take up residence in the Tamil land, the indigenous goddesses are subdued or even driven out.[74]

The harsh landscape so central to Ammaiyār's poetry is used in another sixth-century text located in the coastal area of Tamilnadu; it is a Buddhist text, but one that helps illuminate Kāraikkāl Ammaiyār's conception of Śiva. *Maṇimēkalai* is a Buddhist epic about a courtesan's daughter who becomes a nun. Buddhism was a significant religious and political force during this period, and the author Cāttaṉār composed his work in order to foster the Buddhist community in Tamlinadu.[75] In this epic, the heroine Maṇimēkalai must overcome her attraction to a prince before she can progress on her spiritual path and commit to being a Buddhist nun. Early in the epic, after the prince has tried unsuccessfully to abduct the heroine, is a branch story that conveys central Buddhist ideas about what the world really is and how one should live in it. In this story, the goddess Maṇimēkalai, after whom Maṇimēkalai is named, takes the heroine and her companion to a nearby cremation ground called "The Cosmic Place," which parallels the desolate *pālai* landscapes in Ammaiyār's poetry, including many of the same plants, animals and birds that thrive in Tiruvālaṅkāṭu. "The Cosmic Place" is described in vivid detail: bodies burn in pyres surrounded by dessicated vegetation; ascetics (presumably Kāpālikas) practice penance by collecting skulls and stringing them into garlands; funeral drums sound, vultures shriek, flesh-eating owls screech; ravenous *pēys* gleefully compete with preying wildlife to consume bits of human flesh. This is Kālī's playground, a place of death, where the suffering of impermanence is on full display. Human heads are offered to Kālī, who is attended by her female *pēys*. The author Cāttaṉār shows the audience that this *pālai* landscape is reality, the truth that lies beneath the outer appearance (Richman 70–1). Cāttaṉār uses familiar Tamil elements to convey the Buddhist notion of the transience of all life, setting Maṇimēkalai and the audience up for the truth of salvation. Through her contemplation of the cremation ground, Maṇimēkalai achieves knowledge of life in *saṃsāra* or the cycle of death and rebirth. Maṇimēkalai is encouraged to turn her back on sexual love, renounce the world, and become a nun. Later in the text a great ascetic of the cremation ground (113) tells the prince's father that it is his duty as king to protect women who renounce the world, giving a forceful speech about the power inhering in women who control their sexuality. It seems clear in this epic that the sixth-century Tamil audience was not especially receptive to female renunciation; the author Cāttaṉār carefully acknowledges the respect given to the wife who worships her husband, but claims that female renouncers are worthy of equal respect (118). Later in the epic, Maṇimēkalai will be given a magic begging bowl with which to feed the community, allowing her to practice the Buddhist virtue of unlimited giving, but also marking her as a female who continues to nurture others.

Caṅkam-era *puṟam* poems vividly show that the cremation ground is where all human beings end in death, even the bravest warriors. It is also a fertile place for practices that induce religious insights. *Maṇimēkalai* uses elements of the familiar Caṅkam landscape of the cremation ground to convey the truth that all life is impermanent and in order to achieve liberation from the cycle of rebirth one must renounce the fleeting sensual pleasures of embodied existence and practice the Buddhist path. Meditation on a corpse, particularly a female corpse, is a standard Buddhist practice for monks and nuns to detach themselves from the impermanent life of the body. The goddess Kālī rules over this place of death and horror. *Maṇimēkalai* is a didactic text that aims to construct a community of Buddhists in opposition to other religious practices in the region, including those that involve Kālī. *Maṇimēkalai* demonstrates that it is in the terrifying and repulsive *pālai* landscape of the cremation ground that the true nature of reality can be perceived.[76]

For Ammaiyār as well the cremation ground is the place where the impermanence of life and the path to salvation are revealed, but through meditation on Śiva.

> The person who has died, with muddled intellect and
> cloudy knowledge,
> is put in the cremation ground at the crossroad.
> The eligible person performs the rites, then ignites the
> red fire that makes light.
> As always, the gods sound the drums.
> The place where our Lord performs the great dance at
> twilight,
> so that His anklets jangle and the directions vibrate,
> is Tiruvālaṅkāṭu. (*Tiruvālaṅkāṭṭu Mūtta Tiruppatikam* 1.10)

Here Ammaiyār describes a cremation ritual for a person who has died "with cloudy knowledge," without realizing that Śiva is the ultimate truth. The cremation ground is the stage of Śiva's dance of life and death and salvation, but as the poem suggests, it is available to all who would see that this world is accessible to those who love the Lord. The cremation ground is also the space in the heart of the devotee where the ego is burned up as she surrenders to him. To the devotee who sees, the terrifying place of death is really the beautiful and blissful abode of the Lord, and the sacred grove of liberation from this world.

Creating a Devotional Community

Look!
Having become a slave to the beautiful feet of the
One whose red matted hair has the waves of Gaṅgā,
we have realized Him through scriptures;
we have become suitable for this life and for the other
  world.
Why do others gossip about us behind our backs?
Understand us. (*Aṟputat Tiruvantāti* 91)

Oh! You pitiable people
who are without wisdom.
It is an easy way to live,
thinking of our Lord all the time,
our Father with the gleaming throat,
Who wanders around,
wearing a snake. (*Aṟputat Tiruvantāti* 46)

Even though the gods, meditating on Him, adorn His
  feet with the best flowers,
they will not reach His feet.
I also meditate on Him.
Now what will the One with the radiant, red matted
  hair,
who knows the Vedas,
do to me, who worships Him? (*Aṟputat Tiruvantāti* 15)

Unlike the later *Tēvāram* poets who include hostile diatribes against Buddhist and Jain monks in their poetry, Kāraikkāl Ammaiyār does not refer to any group by name, but lumps together as "others" the people she is defining her spiritual path against.[77] But it is clear in the third poem that part of her conceptual iconography of Śiva is as the Knower of the Vedas, so some of the "others" she is referring to are certainly non-Vedic groups. The many references to these "others" who do not understand Śiva reveals how influential the heterodox communities were. Peterson observes that critiquing Jain asceticism is a central preoccupation of the later nāyaṉmārs. The saint Appar, who had been a Jain monk before converting to the path of Śiva, composed scathing condemnations of his previous life:

> I was a deadly snake, dancing to the tunes
> of evil men, filthy, foul-mouthed, I wandered aimlessly,
> begging for food, eating with both hands, truly a wretch.[78]

Kāraikkāl Ammaiyār's refusal to specify any one community conveys the key point: Everyone who doesn't follow Śiva is equally ignorant. In contrast to the later poets who critique the ascetic ways of Jain and Buddhist monks, Kāraikkāl Ammaiyār's more extreme ascetic emphasis reveals the early, broad roots of the Tamil Śaiva tradition before it is systematized into a temple-based orthodoxy. Kāraikkāl Ammaiyār's transgressive behavior does not go to the extremes of some Śaiva worshippers of her milieu, but she engages in behavior that turns ordinary categories of personal and social perception upside down in order to force a transcendent spiritual awareness, including an understanding of the self as rooted in divine power. Kāraikkāl Ammaiyār transforms the ancient image of the fierce flesh-eating goddess in the cremation ground into the female ghoul that dwells happily in Śiva's world. She embodies what she conveys in her poetry: that Śiva is the Truth, the Absolute, and that knowledge of him brings liberation from *saṃsāra*. Her poetry is not erotically charged but is more intellectual, focusing on the experiential understanding of Śiva as knowledge and the ultimate truth gained through meditation and loving service.

> I have done enough *tapas*.
> My heart is a good heart.
> I decided to eradicate all my births.
> I have become a servant to the
> God who wears an elephant skin,
> has a third eye in His forehead,
> and is smeared with sacred ash. (*Aṟputat Tiruvantāti* 7)

> Even though He does not remove our afflictions;
> even though He does not pity us;
> even though He does not guide us to the path we
> should follow;

for Him—our God in the form of flame,
dancing in the fire, garlanded with bones—
the love in my heart
will never cease. (*Aṟputat Tiruvantāti* 2)

We have covered Hara with the mantle of love.
Because of a special relationship with Him,
we have filled our hearts completely with Him.
We have hidden Him by deception.
So who is able to see Him? (*Aṟputat Tiruvantāti* 96)

In the first poem Ammaiyār emphasizes that she has intentionally performed *tapas* or austerities in order to constantly meditate on Śiva and achieve liberation from rebirth. This poem refers to the myth in which the demon Gajāsura ("Elephant-Demon") continually antagonized the gods. Śiva killed the elephant demon, flayed him, and draped the still-bloody skin around him.[79] In the second poem Ammaiyār declares that whether or not she receives Śiva's grace, her love for him is undying. The third poem is an emotional one in which the devotees' intense love for Śiva (Hara) leads them to extreme possessiveness, to trying to keep him all for themselves by hiding him from others. The word Ammaiyār uses for "deception" or "illusion" is the Tamil *māyam* or Sanskrit *māyā*, which signifies an important aspect of Śaiva Siddhānta cosmology in later centuries.

As part of his activity of manifesting and reabsorbing the universe, Śiva, through his Śakti or Goddess, acts upon the original pure potential substance of the universe, *bindu* or "drop," from which emerges *māyā*; from *māyā* all the elements of the lower material universe are manifested. The cosmos is intimately linked to the degree to which Śiva is concealed.[80] But in this poem the cosmic functions Śiva performs are upstaged by the relationship between the devotee and Śiva. The word Ammaiyār uses to convey the special relationship Śiva has with his devotees is *tāyam*, which connotes family inheritance, share of wealth, and a paternal relationship, all suggesting that the devotee has essentially a "right" to a share of Śiva's grace since he is the divine father who responds to his worshipers' devotion. This intense love and fear of separation from the beloved is a stock trope in Caṅkam *akam* or love poetry, but in *bhakti* poetry the love object with whom the devotee wants to be is God.[81]

You who say you want to go into the happiness of
  liberation without falling,
having crossed the flooding sea of base miseries:

without getting tired, pleading,
with humility, with focused concentration,
always worship the Hero who saw that the cities of the enemies were destroyed,
the One with eight shoulders,
and with pure gold hero's anklets. (*Tiruviraṭṭai Maṇimālai* 9)

The poetry is filled with vivid images of Śiva as the heroic god whose grace rescues his devotees from the sorrows of the world. Ammaiyār's poetry is the vehicle for individual devotional experience, yet it is clear that worship of Śiva should be practiced in a community of devotees. Ammaiyār conveys a detailed visual iconography of her lord that unites the emerging Śaiva community and links it to the broader Indian traditions surrounding Śiva. It seems clear that even at this early date Kāraikkāl Ammaiyār and the emerging community of worshipers were seeing iconographic images of Śiva in temples, whether those temples were actual structures or open-air shrines.[82] The later Śaiva poets describe their pilgrimages to hundreds of specific shrines and temples that link the Tamil region in a sacred geography.[83] In contrast, Ammaiyār links her worship of Śiva only to the cremation ground at Tiruvālaṅkāṭu. Ammaiyār's ascetic milieu is balanced by her descriptions of such central, orthodox rites of worship as bowing to Śiva's feet and offering flowers:

If the karmas will not endure when they see
the shadow of those who have seen and worship with desire
the red feet that wear the hero's anklets,
when they see us worshiping with pure flowers in our hands
our Lord who is without compare,
whose body glows red like the embers of a fire,
will the old karmas that come and afflict us endure?
(*Tiruviraṭṭai Maṇimālai* 11)

Hara stands as the first principle of the ancient universe.
He has the nature of One who might not appear to those
who look for Him.
To those who see, worshipping with love and folded hands, He appears.
To those who see, He appears as a light in their minds.
(*Aṟputat Tiruvantāti* 17)

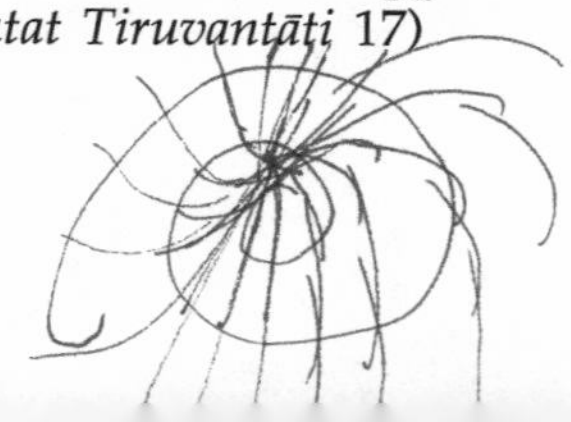

In another poem (*Tiruviraṭṭai Maṇimālai* 8) Ammaiyār refers to Śiva "who has the auspicious day of Ātirai," which is the lunar asterism in the Tamil month of Mārkaḻi (December–January). The *Tēvāram* poet Appar describes this important festival, which suggests it is possible that Ammaiyār was also referring to a festival performed for Śiva on this day.[84] Ammaiyār lays out important aspects of this community's devotional path that will persist in later Śaiva poetry, an important part of which is the devotion to the earlier devotees of Śiva.[85]

Ignorant mind,
worship the feet of the devotees, again and again,
focusing on them, and praising them with words.
Leave that group of people who do not think about
the One who wears a moon as a small garland,
which no one else wears. (*Aṟputat Tiruvantāti* 40)

This poem contains two imperatives: to worship those servants who are truly devoted to Śiva, and to avoid those people who do not worship him. Through vivid descriptions of the Beautiful Lord Śiva, multiple mythic references to his deeds, and regular references to a host of ignorant "others," Kāraikkāl Ammaiyār delineates a spiritual path and creates a community that centers on a self-conscious understanding of Śiva as the ultimate truth and the only path to liberation. As Ammaiyār says:

Strong ghouls without face paint come together,
beating each other, shouting with joy, and
spread out in a circle.
A partridge dances; next to it a jackal plays the lute.
Those who are able to recite the ten verses in classical
  Tamil
by Kāraikkāl Pēy with uncombed hair,
on the feet of the Lord
who is in the auspicious Tiruvālaṅkāṭu,
will attain the bliss of reaching Śiva. (*Tiruvālaṅkāṭṭu
  Mūtta Tiruppatikam* 1.11)

Unlike the later Śaiva poets who consistently praise the Tamil language, Ammaiyār makes only this one reference to the literary language in which she has composed her poetry.[86] Her poetry expresses in literary Tamil a life of perpetual, spontaneous worship of Śiva in which all thought and action fuse in a ritual offering of pure awareness of god. Ammaiyār delineates the only realm of action that has ultimate meaning: sublimating herself as one of Śiva's adoring, *pēy* attendants in the cremation ground. In Kāraikkāl Ammaiyār's poetry, the path becomes the goal. Earlier in this chapter I talked about Lutgendorf's paradigm of the forest as a state of mind, as a place not delimited by what is natural, what is actually there. Kāraikkāl Ammaiyār expands that paradigm; she lives as one of Śiva's demons and witnesses his dance, and through the power of her poetry she attempts to shatter the illusions of ordinary awareness and show that ultimately, the cremation ground is a state of mind, where the true devotee who meditates on Śiva experiences him as the Beautiful Lord.

Kāraikkāl Ammaiyār's renunciation of domestic life to live in the cremation ground praising Śiva is an example of "ritualization," a term used by several theorists, and defined by Catherine Bell as ritual as lived practice, as a way of acting that uses diverse strategies to differentiate meaningful, powerful, or sacred action from ordinary behavior (Bell 1992, 88–93). Ritualization creates a spatial/temporal environment in which an individual embodies and enacts structures of personal and social meaning within a perceived field of possibilities. Bell writes:

> Ritualization always aligns one within a series of relationships linked to the ultimate sources of power. Whether ritual empowers or disempowers one in some political sense, it always suggests the ultimate coherence of a cosmos in which one takes a particular place. This cosmos is experienced as a chain of states or an order of existence that places one securely in a field of action and in alignment with the ultimate goals of all action. (Bell 1992, 141)

Kāraikkal Ammaiyār delineates a world in which all actions are performed in love and service to Śiva, the cosmic hero localized in a Tamil landscape. The order of existence she conveys in her poetry allows all devotees to meditate on Śiva's beautiful form and to serve him and gain his ultimate grace, salvation from the cycle of rebirth. Ammaiyār's path is more ascetic than the later Śaiva poets in that she exists as a demon in Śiva's cremation ground, away from ordinary household life. There are no details about places other than the descriptions of the cremation ground at Tiruvālaṅkāṭu. But the devotion to Śiva takes place in a community of devotees, whose relationships are not based on the traditional social categories of caste or gender, but on heartfelt service to Śiva and to his true devotees. The rituals of meditating on Śiva, bowing to his feet, praising him, and offering flowers that Ammaiyār prescribes are fundamental temple rites but are not connected to particular temples, which the later poets will praise. Śiva's cosmos in the cremation ground replaces the normative social categories with a simple hierarchy of the Lord and his servants. Ammaiyār's poetry evokes the early stages of a community that is evolving from a renouncer's focus on liberation outside of ordinary social life, to devotion to Śiva in a sectarian community that worships in a temple. Ammaiyār lives as a *pēy*, performs *tapas* or austerities, and cries "My heart! Give up your wife and children" (*Tiruviraṭṭai Maṇimālai* 13). These are the activities of a *sannyāsin* or renouncer that critique the normative Brahmanical social world in which rituals are defined in a hierarchical and temporal order, i.e., specific people must perform prescribed rites at particular times. Ammaiyār performs her devotion to Śiva all the time, which is one of the hallmarks of *bhakti*. This devotion is based on, and further develops, the knowledge of Śiva as the truth and the foundation of the cosmos.[87]

In her poetry Ammaiyār performs her own devotion by building a vivid iconographic portrait of Śiva as a means of praising and focusing on him. At the same time her iconographic portrait serves to construct the emerging community of devotees and "creates a tradition-specific subjectivity. This subjectivity is not individualistic but is itself a sign of the community and an expression of tradition. So while there is undoubtedly the development of interiority through text and ritual performance, this is not the development of a private self in contrast to a public self" (Flood 2004, 221–222). The *bhakti* subjectivity that Ammaiyār projects in her poetry is constructed when the path becomes the goal, when the devotee lives everyday in perpetual service to Śiva in a community of devotees.[88]

Ammaiyār's perpetual devotion to Śiva as one of his *pēys* suggests a Tantric orientation in her devotional path. The fundamental practice of Tantric traditions is the divinization of the body through various means.[89] Ammaiyār does not engage in the more extreme practices of cremation ground ascetics such as the Kāpālikas and Pāśupatas, who deliberately transgress social norms in their imitation of Śiva's ferocious Bhairava form. Nor is Ammaiyār's relation to Śiva erotic; he is always her Lord and Father. Ammaiyār has received a supernatural demon body through Śiva's grace, a body the poetry shows she helped to construct through her unwavering devotion to the lord dancing in the cremation ground: singing his praises, visualizing and meditating on his beautiful form, offering him flowers, and bowing to his feet. The ritualization of her life, the perpetual performance of devotion, has brought her a *pēy* form that has made her a bit more Śiva-like. Ammaiyār's poetry is a record of her communion with Śiva that serves as the medium for other devotees to participate in devotion, constituting a "process of divination. . . . Through an all-consuming enjoyment of the sacred hymns, one experiences bhakti, and the experience of bhakti itself transforms the experiencer. Devotion engenders divinity in the devotee; thus the perfected devotee or saint is treated as a divine being" (Cutler, 51).

In her poetry Ammaiyār is always Śiva's *pēy* devotee, a status that she considers the most exalted status of all.[90] Ostensibly she is still female, yet for Śiva's ghouls gender is irrelevant. The *pēy* status is open to everyone, regardless of gender or caste status. Ammaiyār conveys a detailed iconographic portrait of Śiva who is localized in the familiar Caṅkam *pālai* landscape. She uses a trope of the heroic warrior to describe Śiva as the conqueror of death for the devotee, and the ultimate sovereign of the universe. Ammaiyār shows that the cremation ground in which Śiva dances is the central stage of all life, where the mundane and spiritual worlds merge.

Kāraikkāl Ammaiyār's poetry is an early attempt to construct a community of devotees who are united by their love of the god Śiva, who is made iconographically present through the poems. Some of her poems suggest an ascetic withdrawal from the domestic world in order to focus on liberation from rebirth through Śiva's grace, the discipline of devotion. But many of the poems set out the path that devotees should follow collectively, including rituals to be performed. Ammaiyār does not sing the praises of the Tamil land as the later poets do, nor celebrate shrines and temples, but she clearly delineates a community devoted to the heroic god Śiva dancing in the cremation ground, located in the Tamil land. The god who is the foundation of the cosmos is also the loving god whose grace will save his devotees from rebirth in the mundane realm. Kāraikkāl Ammaiyār's poetry bridges the earlier Caṅkam world of powerful, demonic beings inhabiting dessicated landscapes like the cremation ground with the emerging world of devotion to the heroic god Śiva. It is through Ammaiyār's poetry that the yogic god of Sanskrit myths dances in the Tamil landscape and in the hearts of Tamil devotees.

> I thought of only One.
> I was focused on only One.
> I kept only One inside my heart.
> Look at this One!
> It is He who has Gaṅgā on His head,
> a moonbeam in His hair,
> a radiant flame in His beautiful hand.
> I have become His slave. (*Aṟputat Tiruvantāti* 11)

3

Kāraikkāl Ammaiyār Through Her Stories

The Śaiva saints or nāyaṉmārs were first listed by Cuntarar (in appropximately the late eighth or early ninth century) in an eleven-stanza poem called *Tiruttoṇṭattokai*, "The List of the Holy Devotees," in which he names sixty-two saints. In this hymn Kāraikkāl Ammaiyār is referred to only as "Pēyār" meaning "the one who is a demon." In the eleventh century the poet Nampi Āṇṭār Nampi compiled the hymns of the Śaiva devotional poets, and told the stories of the sixty-three nāyaṉmārs or saints, including Cuntarar; these hymns and stories formed the first eleven books of what would later be called the *Tirumuṟai*, or "Sacred Text." When Nampi describes Kāraikkāl Ammaiyār he does not mention the name "Pēy" at all; his story describes her birth in the town of Kāraikkāl, and her ascension of Mt. Kailāsa to see Śiva and Pārvatī, where Śiva affectionately calls her "Ammai" or "Mother" and hence the poet becomes known as Kāraikkāl Ammaiyār, "the mother/woman from Kāraikkāl."[1]

The most important hagiographer of the nayaṉmārs was the twelfth-century poet Cēkkiḻār, whose *Periya Purāṇam*, or "Great Story," forms the twelfth and final book of the Śaiva canon *Tirumuṟai*. Kāraikkāl Ammaiyār is the twenty-fourth saint in this *Purāṇam*, one of only three women and the only female poet. Cēkkiḻār describes her life in sixty-five stanzas, providing a compelling biography that influences all subsequent stories of Ammaiyār as well as of the other saints.[2] Below is a synopsis of Cēkkiḻār's story.[3]

Cēkkiḻār's Story

Kāraikkāl is a prosperous coastal town full of merchants. When the wealthy merchant Taṉatattaṉ performed austerities, his daughter Kāraikkāl Ammaiyār was born and originally named Puṉitavati. She was a beautiful girl who seemed to be an incarnation of Lakṣmī, the goddess of fortune. But she was not only beautiful, she was from the beginning of her life a devotee of Śiva. When she was still a baby, as soon as she could walk and talk, she worshipped Śiva. Her father Taṉatattaṉ showered her with affection and material comforts. As she grew up both her beauty and her devotion to Śiva increased. (vv. 1–5)

When she was of age Puṉitavati's family began inquiries into an alliance with an appropriate family. She was married in a lavish ceremony to the rich merchant Paramatattaṉ from the town of Nākapaṭṭiṇam. Because Puṉitavati was his only child, Taṉatattaṉ persuaded Paramatattaṉ not to take Puṉitavati back to Nākapaṭṭiṇam, but to live in a house he built next door to his in Kāraikkāl. Puṉitavati was a faithful wife, and maintained the household with assiduous care. She continued to be an ardent worshipper of Śiva, meditating on his feet. She gave food, clothes, and even luxurious things to the Śaiva devotees who came to her door. Supported in this loving and orderly domestic milieu, Paramatattaṉ prospered. (vv. 6–15)

One day Paramatattaṉ received two mangoes from a customer, which he had delivered to his house for Puṉitavati to serve him for his midday meal. But before he returned home for lunch, a famished Śaiva holy man came to the door for alms; the curry was not yet ready, so Puṉitavati gave him one of the mangoes with his rice. When her husband came home she gave him his meal along with the remaining mango. (vv. 16–23)

Paramatattaṉ thought the mango was delicious and asked for the other one. A worried Puṉitavati went to the kitchen and thought about her Lord Śiva, who responded immediately to his distraught devotee; through his grace another mango appeared, which Puṉitavati served to her husband. This one was so much more delicious than the first, her husband was suspicious and asked his wife where she had gotten it. Knowing that a good wife should neither stay silent nor lie to her husband, she meditated on Śiva and reluctantly told her husband about the grace of the Lord, but he doubted her story and asked the auspicious goddess in front of him to repeat the miracle in his presence. Again

Puṉitavati prayed to Śiva, and another mango appeared, to her husband's amazement. When she handed the fruit to her husband, it immediately vanished. Her husband was terrified of her power, seeing her as a frightening goddess (*aṇaṅku*) rather than as a human (v. 31), and fled without releasing her from her wifely duties. He sailed away on a ship. (vv. 24–33)

Paramatattaṉ set up another household in another city, prospered there, and married a Lakṣmī-like woman, not revealing to anyone that he had deserted an *aṇaṅku*-like woman. When a daughter was born, he named her after the wife he had left behind and now considered a family deity. Meanwhile, Puṉitavati continued to live as a chaste wife, keeping up the house and her appearance in anticipation of her husband's return. Eventually her parents found out where Paramatattaṉ was and took their daughter to him. When Paramatattaṉ heard that his first wife had arrived in his town, he was immediately afraid, but he proceeded to meet her. Paramatattaṉ and his second wife and daughter fell at Puṉitavati's feet and worshipped her; Paramatattaṉ told her he desired her divine grace. The relatives who had come with Puṉitavati were shocked that a husband would worship his wife, and asked Paramatattaṉ why he was worshipping Puṉitavati. (vv. 34–46)

He replied that his wife was not human but a goddess, and he fled from their house because of his fear of her. When Puṉitavati learned that her husband did not see her as a wife anymore, through her spiritual wisdom she begged Śiva to take away the beauty she no longer needed and give her a *pēy* (demon) form. Through his grace Śiva granted her wish and Puṉitavati attained the goal of her spiritual path and became a demon; the celestials rejoiced, but her relatives, after paying homage to her, fled in fear. (vv. 47–51)

Out of her expanding knowledge of Śiva she sang the *Aṟputat Tiruvantāti*, then the *Tiruviraṭṭai Maṇimālai*. In response, Śiva graced her with permission to approach his abode on Mt. Kailāsa. When people around her were afraid and began moving away, she said, "If Śiva recognizes me, why is my form important to these people?" She then made a pilgrimage to the Himalayas to see Śiva and Pārvatī, walking on her hands up Mt. Kailāsa so as not to defile

> the god's heavenly abode with her feet. (vv. 57–65) When Pārvatī saw this amazing being coming up the mountain and asked Śiva who she was, he replied, "She is a devoted mother who cherishes us." Śiva was so moved by her devotion he called her "Ammai," or "Mother," to which she replied "Father." Śiva asked her what she wanted, and she replied that she wanted to escape rebirth, but that if she had to be reborn, she never wanted to forget him but wanted to joyously sing at his feet forever. Śiva told her to go to Tiruvālaṅkāṭu, where she would witness his dance and sing at his feet forever. She went to Tiruvālaṅkāṭu on her head, watched Śiva's cosmic dance, and sang the two *Tiruvālaṅkāṭṭu Mūtta Tiruppatikaṅkaḷ*. (See Figure 3.1.) She remained in Tiruvālaṅkāṭu at Śiva's feet, as he performed his *tāṇṭava* dance, forever his adoring slave. (vv. 52–56)[4]

In many obvious ways, this story about Kāraikkāl Ammaiyār seems to have little connection to the poetry, other than listing the

Figure 3.1. Kāraikkāl Ammaiyār Walking on Her Hands on Mt. Kailāsa. *Painting by Ben Sloan*

works that she composed and describing Śiva's grace in granting her the *pēy* form she desires. As we have seen, the only concrete biographical detail in the poetry is that the author calls herself Kāraikkāl Pēy. In contrast, Cēkkiḻār emphasizes Puṉitavati's great beauty, the wealth of her family, how well she is brought up, and that she is married at an appropriate time in a beautiful and proper marriage ceremony. The details of a wealthy but socially normative life balance Puṉitavati's ardent devotion to Śiva; her worship is performed in the household and ensures the prosperity of her husband. This story highlights traditional notions regarding a married woman's role: she should be chaste; devoted to her husband and serve him diligently; maintain an orderly home within the husband's means; be hospitable to guests; and observe religious duties. A virtuous wife is, in essence, the foundation of a prosperous household and an orderly world; she is a Lakṣmī on earth. These ancient ideas are found in the *Tirukkuṟaḷ*, the famous Tamil ethical treatise written by the poet Tiruvaḷḷuvar, most likely in the sixth or seventh century, roughly contemporaneous with Kāraikkāl Ammaiyār.[5]

> She whose husband is her only God
> Says, "Rain" and it rains.
>
> A true wife never tires guarding
> Herself, her husband and their name.[6]

Puṉitavati is a virtuous wife, but her ardent love for Śiva threatens to disrupt the domestic harmony of her household. When the Śaiva ascetic arrives at her door, she cannot bring herself to give him only rice, too meager a meal for a servant of God. Yet when her husband demands the second mango she is genuinely distraught that she cannot give him what he wants, which a sincere wife should be able to do.[7] When her husband demands to know where the ambrosial mango from Śiva has come from, Puṉitavati hesitates; a good wife should always tell her husband the truth, but her duties to her husband should not be compromised even by devotion to God. For some time Puṉitavati balances her devotion to her husband and to Śiva, but the boundaries of her domestic realm ultimately prove to be porous. Nevertheless, she does not forsake her wifely role until her husband has officially renounced her. When her husband flees from her in a ship, Puṉitavati continues to uphold her chastity, behaving as if her husband could return any day. It is only when she confronts him in his new city that, in a dramatic role reversal that shocks the onlookers, Paramatattan̲ acknowledges Pun̲itavati as a goddess and worships her. Cēkkil̲ār describes how when Paramatattan̲ witnessed the miraculous appearance of the mangoes, he was afraid of his wife's power, yet once he has set up a new household and his daughter is born, he has come to regard Pun̲itavati as a family deity (v. 38). But since he does not consider Pun̲itavati human (v. 47), he can no longer accept her as a wife, so Pun̲itavati is freed from her duties to her husband and can fully immerse herself in devotion to Śiva. Pechilis notes (2006, 178) that Cēkkil̲ār signals Paramatattan̲'s changing view of his wife from a frightening being when she miraculously receives more mangoes, indicated by the Tamil word *aṇaṅku*, to a benign deity or *teyvam*, the Sanskrit term for divinity, when he has set up another household away from Pun̲itavati. The fierce local goddess is domesticated. When Pun̲itavati asks Śiva for a *pēy* form and is granted her wish, Cēkkil̲ār frames it as a moment when her life of devotion has yielded true knowledge of Śiva, which she now embodies as his perpetual servant. This complete surrender to Śiva gives her the spiritual insight to compose her first two works of poetry. Her understanding of Śiva is contrasted with the ignorance of the people around her who are frightened by her appearance, and her superior understanding and love are given the ultimate recognition when Śiva himself calls her "Mother!" and she responds by calling him "Father." When Śiva calls her "Mother," he reinscribes the skeletal demon with a feminine gender, softening her with nurturing qualities.[8]

Cēkkil̲ār's story highlighting Pun̲itavati's devotion to Śiva reveals the ideal of *bhakti* or devotion that had developed over the centuries between Kāraikkāl Ammaiyār's life and the composition of the *Periya Purāṇam*. But the divine power of a virtuous woman predates the devotional movement. The power of a woman's chastity, or *kar̲pu*, is an ancient theme in the Tamil country, dating back at least to the Caṅkam age.[9] The preeminent example of the powerful, chaste woman is the heroine Kaṇṇaki in the famous epic *Cilappatikāram*, discussed in Chapter 1. When Kaṇṇaki finds out that her husband Kōvalan̲ has been unjustly accused of a crime and put to death by the king of Maturai, Kaṇṇaki goes to the palace and proves that her husband was innocent. She then tears off her left breast and throws it at the city of Maturai; the power of her chastity burns down the unrighteous city, in which only the innocent are spared. Kaṇṇaki journeys west to the Cēral country where the local hill dwellers witness the gods taking her up to heaven. When Kaṇṇaki's story is told to the Cēral king, he installs a memorial stone (*naṭukal*) for Kaṇṇaki in a temple, where she is now known as the goddess Pattin̲i ("chaste woman").

Kaṇṇaki's unwavering chastity and eventual retreat from the world when her husband is gone echoes the same trajectory in Puṉitavati's life. This chastity can be seen as a kind of asceticism, as George Hart has observed, requiring a woman to not only avoid any immodest behavior, but to purge herself of any thoughts or desires beyond serving her husband, controlling herself no matter what situations arise.[10] The power that chaste women generate through controlling their sexuality can be auspicious or destructive. One of the words used to connote sacred female power in ancient Tamil is *aṇaṅku,* which is associated with girls and women, sometimes thought of as residing in their breasts, and with goddesses; but it can also mean "fear" or "malevolent deity" and therefore a fierce goddess.[11] In Cēkkiḻār's story, when Puṉitavati receives another mango from Śiva, her husband sees her as an *aṇaṅku* or frightening goddess (v. 31). When Kovalaṉ is executed for a crime he did not commit and Kaṇṇaki comes to the king's palace to demand justice, she is compared to the goddess Aṇaṅku, one of the Seven Virgins, as well as Kālī and Koṟṟavai, the Tamil goddess of victory who is associated with Durgā.[12] In the *Cilappatikāram* Koṟṟavai is described as the consort of Śiva, and the goddess to whom men sacrifice their heads in extreme states of devotion.[13]

Cēkkiḻār's text represents a late stage in the displacement of ancient Tamil local goddesses and other supernatural beings by the localization of the worship of Śiva. Cēkkiḻār was a minister in the court of the Cōḻa ruler Kulōttuṅka II (1133–1150) and therefore composed his hagiographies of the Śaiva saints several centuries after the time of the *Cilappatikāram* and Kāraikkāl Ammaiyār's life and work. His text is the twelfth and final text of the Śaiva canon, the *Tirumuṟai,* and reveals a highly developed tradition defining itself among competing religious paths. Cēkkiḻār's text emphasizes the exemplary devotion of the saints, and shapes a Śaiva theology that will continue to have a significant influence on the tradition in the succeeding centuries. Monius argues that Cēkkiḻār paints a new portrait of Śiva as the heroic father in contrast to earlier poetic depictions of him as an erotic lover or charming but ash-covered dweller in the cremation ground, and asserts that Cēkkiḻār is shaping an image of Śiva at least partly in reaction to the representations of the Śaiva tradition in Jain and Vaiṣṇava texts. The Jains were a significant religious and literary presence in Tamilnadu for centuries and an important community against which the Śaivas formed their identity. Jain texts such as the ninth- to tenth-century *Cīvakacintāmaṇi* promote the ascetic Jain path by satirizing the erotic love extolled by classical Tamil love poetry as well as the intensely emotional, devotional love and longing for god sometimes conveyed in overtly erotic language. The three *Tēvāram* poets composed hymns with explicitly erotic imagery of Śiva as a consort to his divine lovers, and as a lover to his devotees. Śiva as the chaste, heroic father in Cēkkiḻār's text resembles the Śiva in Kāraikkāl Ammaiyār's poetry; although he is playfully portrayed as the consort of two goddesses, Umā and Gaṅgā, and as the paradoxical erotic ascetic who although married remains a yogi in the cremation ground. Ammaiyār's relationship with Śiva is asexual; she consistently calls him "Father" and "Lord."[14]

There is also a parallel between Cēkkiḻār and Ammaiyār in the heroic myths they include in their texts. The *Tēvāram* poets localize the pan-Indian myths of Śiva's eight heroic deeds or *aṭṭavīraṭṭāṉam* at specific temple sites in the Tamil land. The four most common myths of Śiva's heroic deeds in the *Periya Purāṇam* are the destruction of the three demon cities, the flaying of the rutting elephant, the kicking of Yama, and the incineration of Kāma, all of which are deeds that Ammaiyār refers to frequently in her poetry. Cēikkiḻār refers to the destruction of Dakṣa's sacrifice only once, a myth that Ammaiyār does not reference. Neither Cēkkiḻār nor Ammaiyār refer to the two myths in which Śiva destroys the demons Andhaka and Jalandhara. Monius points out that these two myths are filled with sexual imagery: Andhaka lusts after Umā; Jalandhara invokes dancing girls to divert Śiva in battle, and takes on Śiva's form to try and seduce Umā. These myths do not support the chaste father figure that dominates the *Periya Purāṇam*.[15]

Cēkkiḻār never refers to Śiva's beheading of the god Brahmā, which leads to his wandering as a beggar in penance for committing brahminicide and which undermines Śiva's superiority to the other gods. In this myth Śiva takes on his fierce Bhairava form, which also contradicts Cēkkiḻar's emphasis on Śiva as loving father. Kāraikkāl Ammaiyār refers to Śiva as the wandering beggar in several poems, but she only vaguely suggests the sexual allure the wandering beggar has for the sages' wives in the Pine Forest. In her poetry Śiva is fundamentally the ash-covered ascetic, begging for alms or dancing in the cremation ground with his troupe of ghouls.[16] In his hagiography of Kāraikkāl Ammaiyār, Cēkkiḻār refers to Śiva's heroic conquering of the three demon cities, and as the meaning of the Vedas. He also describes Śiva as possessing many of the attributes that are in her poetry: He rides a bull, he has a third eye and matted hair, he wears a snake and a crescent moon, and his throat is dark from swallowing poison. Śiva's dance is briefly described as beautiful and bliss-inducing, but he is not the frightening, ghoulish figure he is in the poetry.[17]

In "sanitizing" the figure of Śiva in his text, Cēkkiḻār shifts the violence from Śiva to his devotees, whose total immersion in profound devotion to the Lord is expressed through extreme acts of violence. Such acts signify that love (*aṉpu*) of and selfless service to Śiva are the only things that matter, and form the highest ideal of the devotional path. At least one-third of the saints commit acts of violent devotion. Some of the most popularly known saints are Ciruttoṇṭar, who beheads and cooks his son when Śiva in the guise of a Śaiva ascetic requests this meal; the hunter Kaṇṇappar, who gouges out his own eye with his arrow to replace the bleeding eye of a Śiva image he finds in the forest; and Caṇṭēcurar, who cuts off his father's feet when he disrupts his worship of Śiva in the form of a sand *liṅga*.[18] These saints embody the heroic devotion to Śiva that is love in action, a love that is purified by *tapas*, the discipline of austerities. The *Tēvāram* poets criticized the Jains for their extreme and seemingly pointless self-denial; in contrast the asceticism of the saints has as its goal the total surrender to Śiva in a community of devotees. In Cēkkiḻār's devotional path, *tapas* fires love and love motivates *tapas*.[19]

Yet the *tapas* that has produced the saints' single-minded love of Śiva was performed in previous lives and prepared the saints for the lives of complete devotion that Cēkkiḻār documents. In his story of Kāraikkāl Ammaiyār, he emphasizes that she was born devoted to Śiva, echoing the first poem of her *Aṟputat Tiruvantāti* when she describes how she has worshiped Śiva since she could speak. Cēkkiḻār portrays Ammaiyār, as well as many other saints, as an incarnation of the divine form she has achieved already through Śiva's grace. Cēkkiḻār's use of the term *avatāram* (Sanskrit *avatāra*) is the first in a Tamil text, a term that is most often used in stories of Viṣṇu's earthly descents. Traditions connected to Kṛṣṇa were becoming increasingly popular during the twelfth century in the Tamil region. And the Vaiṣṇava poets the Āḻvārs criticized Śiva for being inaccessible to his devotees, living as an ash-covered ascetic in the wretched cremation ground, unlike their god who incarnated himself repeatedly. Cēkkiḻār's claim that many of the Śaiva saints are *avatāras* seems "to argue for Śiva's enduring presence in the world; although he never takes full incarnational form, his favored devotees and holy ash do" (Monius 2004b, 165). Cēkkiḻār says that Kāraikkāl Ammaiyār is the *avatāram* or incarnation of Lakṣmī, the goddess of fortune (v. 2). He emphasizes the importance of human birth on the devotional path—that humans are uniquely able to love and understand Śiva. But by characterizing Ammaiyār and the other saints as avatars, he also points to their extraordinariness—their special ability to receive Śiva's grace because of their many lifetimes of devotion.[20]

In Kāraikkāl Ammaiyār's poetry, as in the hymns of the other Śaiva poets, devotees reach Śiva through intense struggle: practicing austerities, serving, yearning to be with him, feeling deep despair that they will never experience the bliss of his grace, yet never flagging in the absolute devotion to him that finally leads to the bliss of realization and liberation. Ammaiyār's poetry is an early appeal for community-based devotion to Śiva in its references to worship rites and adoring Śiva's servants, but it does not provide any details about specific temples or participation in normal social life. In the poetry Ammaiyār embodies her absolute devotion to Śiva in the cremation ground, which she represents as the only true world. Cēkkiḻār's story preserves Ammaiyār's *pēy* form in which she composes her devotional poems to Śiva, but it is counterbalanced by her being born as an avatar of the benevolent goddess Lakṣmī. Unlike many of the other Śaiva saints, Kāraikkāl Ammaiyār does not perform horrific acts of violence out of devotion to Śiva, but her demon form embodies the macabre aspects of Śiva and his entourage that she conveys in her poetry and which Cēkkiḻār seeks to minimize. In contrast to the poetry, Cēkkiḻār's story of Kāraikkāl Ammaiyār, along with the stories of many other saints, portrays the consequences for an ordinary householder of all-consuming devotion to Śiva.[21]

In her poetry Ammaiyār maintains that she is an emaciated, shriveled *pēy* among Śiva's troupe of *gaṇas*; she never claims any other role, surrendering herself to live in complete devotion to the Lord. Her relationship with Śiva is not erotic and therefore does not violate the rules of chastity; and her devotion to the Lord differentiates her from the demons on the battlefield in Caṅkam literature. But the fact that she has taken on a *pēy* form and lives in the cremation ground with a ghoulish Śiva shows that she has rejected the normal household life in order to live as a complete devotee, a role that threatens the social order.[22] In the poetry a ghoulish body is justification in itself, the anatomy of devotion. In Cēkkiḻār's text Ammaiyār's absolute devotion is sanctioned by Śiva himself when he calls her "Ammai," but her ghoulish renunciation is balanced by the fact that she was first a dutiful wife with a beautiful body—a Lakṣmī on earth—who does not transgress social norms until her husband rejects her. Unlike the ninth-century Tamil Vaiṣṇava saint Āṇṭāḷ who outright rejects marriage to a human husband in order to secure a divine marriage with god, Puṉitavati struggles to confine her devotion within the household.[23]

In Ammaiyār's poetry the asceticism of a life completely focused on serving god carves out a new concept of divinity and reveals the path of *bhakti* or devotion that is open to all devotees. Ammaiyār's *pēy* form and status allow her to be close to Śiva, affirming his accessibility to his devotees. Ammaiyār's voice as a *pēy* with virtually no social indicators marks the devotional path as free of social constraints. But in his text Cēkkiḻār shapes a Śaiva theology that moves away from the asceticism of the Jains and emphasizes full participation in the social realm. There is a tension in Cēkkiḻār's text between acknowledging the necessity of a body suffused with devotion in order to experience Śiva, and the patriarchal imperative for women to maintain their social roles.

Cēkkiḻār's *Periya Purāṇam* has remained enormously influential since its composition; numerous editions have been published, including abbreviated and illustrated versions. The stories are included in the pamphlets of Śaiva temples. In the next chapter we will see how Cēkkiḻār's story of Kāraikkāl Ammaiyār is included in the literature of the two temples with which she is associated. Cēkkiḻār's stories have also been made into films, including one about Kāraikkāl Ammaiyār.[24]

Contemporary Cultural Images

Film

The 1950s Tamil film "Kāraikkālammaiyār"[25] encapsulates some of the key points of the story that has become dominant over the centuries. In this film Puṉitavati has a friend, Pallavi, echoing early Tamil *akam* poetry in which the heroine has a close friend in whom she can confide, as well as typical Tamil film plots. At the beginning of the film Śiva and Pārvatī are looking down from Mt. Kailāsa at the world; Puṉitavati is singing to Śiva in a temple. Śiva and Pārvatī discuss who is good in the world, and talk about Puṉitavati.

Puṉitavati's parents want to get her married; several members of the Chettiār (merchant) community discuss it. Puṉitavati's friend Pallavi also wants her to marry, but Puṉitavati confesses that she only wants Śiva; from birth she has only wanted him. She and Pallavi go to the temple, and see a woman there singing devotional songs; Puṉitavati asks the woman whether it is best to stay single and worship Śiva, or to marry and worship Śiva. The woman replies that it is best to marry. In the meantime, the man who will become

Puṉitavati's husband has come to the temple with his male friend; the two pairs talk, the "sidekicks" playing the comic pair. Puṉitavati tells her future husband her interpretation of the Tamil word for god, *kaṭavuḷ*, dividing the word into its two parts: *kaṭa* meaning "to cross over," and *uḷ* meaning "inside." Puṉitavati tells her future husband to say the word very fast. Then Puṉitavati and Pallavi worship in the temple: They see a cobra behind a small *liṅga;* Puṉitavati is not afraid and worships it. She thinks that Śiva has left her a small *liṅga* for her worship, which she picks up to take home.

The parents of the two young people have arranged for them to meet. Puṉitavati comes home to install her *liṅga,* not knowing about the parents' meeting. She bumps into the man from the temple, her future husband, who has been invited to the house; she accidentally pours flowers on his feet, an act of worship. Her parents tell her who he is, so she brings him milk and they talk. The marriage arrangements proceed and the two are married. (Meanwhile, Pallavi and the male sidekick also marry.) On the wedding night Puṉitavati's husband asks her why Śiva has Gaṅgā on his head. She replies, "If a child falls and gets dirty, the mother needs a pot of water to clean it. So Śiva needs a lot of water to cleanse the sins of the world." She tells him that she is his slave; he tells her that she is his goddess—traditional "first night" lines.

In the film the mango scene and the husband's fearful flight to another city are enacted faithfully according to Cēkkiḻār's story, with a few cinematic additions. When Puṉitavati's husband asks her to prove that she received the mango from Śiva, she prays to the Lord and receives another mango, and her husband sees Śiva appear and give her the mango. He is awed and becomes a worshiper of Śiva, thinking that his wife is a scary devotee, more like a goddess than a woman. He departs, leaving a palm leaf note saying that he has gone on a business trip. But in reality he has left Puṉitavati and marries again. When a daughter is born to him and his second wife, he names her Puṉitavati.

In the meantime, Puṉitavati is extremely distraught; her husband's friend goes to find her husband, and meets his daughter in a temple. The entire story is revealed. When Puṉitavati realizes that she is released from her wifely role, she prays to Śiva and becomes old (not demonic). She sings devotional songs (not her own verses) and visits many temples (which Kāraikkāl Ammaiyār does not do according to her stories and poetry). Then she visits Mt. Kailāsa: As she is about to ascend, the mountain becomes covered with *liṅgas;* where can she put her feet without defiling the ground?[26] So she walks on her head. Śiva calls her "Ammai" and goes to receive her. Then as Ammaiyār is on her way to Tiruvālaṅkāṭu, Kālī comes to her and tells her that she must worship her first before seeing Śiva; that is the tradition now in the Tiruvālaṅkāṭu temple. When Ammaiyār gets to the cremation ground, skeletons come out. She sees Śiva and Pārvatī dance (they perform *Bharata Nāṭyam*), and she attains *mokṣa* or liberation.

The film's plot is closely based on Cēkkiḻār's story of Kāraikkāl Ammaiyār, encompassing the major points in the hagiography and adding cinematic details to support the themes. The film focuses on Kāraikkāl Ammaiyār as an ardent Śiva devotee as well as a devoted wife, although in the film Puṉitavati's husband is also portrayed as a devotee when they first meet as strangers in a Śiva temple. God and husband are linked as divine beings worthy of Puṉitavati's devotion through her accidental pouring of flowers meant for Śiva onto her husband's feet. But she is shown as the more spiritually enlightened of the two of them, deconstructing *kaṭavuḷ*, a Tamil word for god, for him, and then on their wedding night explaining why Śiva bears Gaṅgā on his head. In the beginning of the film Śiva and Pārvatī look down from Mt. Kailāsa and discuss how good and devoted Puṉitavati is. And her spiritual power shines through when Śiva delivers the mango her husband demands, and her husband realizes that she is more of a goddess than a wife. Yet the film also emphasizes the importance of marriage and the household. Puṉitavati claims that she would rather stay unmarried and devote herself to Śiva, who she has worshiped since she was born, echoing both the first verse of Ammaiyār's long poem *Aṟputat Tiruvantāti* as well as Cēkkiḻār's emphasis on Puṉitavati's innate devotion to Śiva. But her friend, Pallavi, and a woman singing devotional songs in the temple both tell her it is better to marry, and ultimately she does.

This film is an exemplary part of the tradition in Tamil cinema of revering the "good" woman who is "chaste, intelligent, motherly and divine. The bad woman is a coquette, a temptress and a loudmouth who finally gets her dues" (Lakshmi 16). Images of good women are supported by references to Tamil literature; the heroine Kaṇṇaki in the epic *Cilappatikāram* is a popular symbol of chaste Tamil womanhood. From ancient times to the present, purity or chastity has been associated with sacredness or spirituality, which is in turn linked with Tamil language and Tamil womanhood. Just as Tamil language must retain its purity or chastity to retain its sacredness or spirituality, Tamil women should retain the purity or chastity to retain their sacredness or spirituality (Pandian 1992, 90, quoted in Chinniah 30).[27]

Puṉitavati, played in the film by the beautiful young actress Lakshmi, is clearly a chaste, beautiful, and intelligent woman, as well as divine in the sense of receiving Śiva's grace in return for her unswerving devotion. Although she is not a biological mother, in a culture that sees motherhood as an important duty, she is shown as tender and nurturing as a young woman. But it is in her transformation from the beautiful young wife into an old woman that she truly becomes a motherly figure, yet paradoxically free of male control. The story of Kāraikkāl Ammaiyār strains at the conventions of Tamil cinema that make women secondary to men; Puṉitavati is a good wife and does not reject her husband, but he does not come across as heroic and ultimately she is the heroine of the story.

In the film Puṉitavati is not given the form of a demon when her husband rejects her, but she becomes an old, grandmotherly woman who walks slowly with a staff, played by the venerable Tamil actress K. P. Sundara Ambal. She is dressed like a widow in a white sari, and wears the three parallel white lines across her forehead that signify she is a devotee of Śiva. She looks kindly, not frightening, like someone many would call "Ammai" or Mother. According to the traditional stages of life, older persons who no longer have pressing household duties can devote themselves to their own spiritual pursuits. The 1950s production techniques in Tamil films were quite low-tech, with scenes set on a stage with moveable props (the cremation ground does not look forbidding but more like a stage in a concert hall) where Śiva and Pārvatī perform their *Bharata Nāṭyam*. In the film, Kāraikkāl Ammaiyār is an ardent devotee of Śiva but she is motherly, not frightening. As in Cēkkiḻār's story, she attains liberation through loving service and devotion, performed in an ordinary household setting, not through renunciation, as in the poetry.

A Contemporary Short Story

The image of the blameless wife who is an ardent devotee of god still resonates in Tamil society. The story of Kāraikkāl Ammaiyār continues to be told in popular publications.[28] The popular Tamil writer Bālakumāraṉ has written many works based on Śaiva literature and history; in 1995 he published *Periya Purāṇak Kataikaḷ (Periya Purāṇa Stories)*, focusing on fourteen of the *nāyaṉmārs*, including Kāraikkāl Ammaiyār. Bālakumāraṉ "introduces a modern repertoire of urban gestures, hitherto unknown in Tamil prose: partners touch, weep and actually embrace; men sweat and slap each other on the back. . . . This language, very widely and intentionally borrowed from English, is more direct and daring and it has a sensual and sexual articulation which, through the 1980s, brought him a sizeable public amongst the urban middle classes. [In addition] Balakumaran introduces self reflective characters, conscious of themselves as social beings" (Gros 355).

In narrating his tale of Kāraikkāl Ammaiyār, Bālakumāraṉ closely follows Cēkkiḻār's story, but reframes it as a narrative that Paramatattaṉ is telling a friend in flashback from his new life in Nākappaṭṭiṉam, where he fled when he left his wife. Although he separated from her as a wife, Puṉitavati has never left him: She is the source of Paramatattaṉ's life, of his prosperity; she is his new family's deity. Bālakumāraṉ vividly describes the events that rupture their ordinary household lives: events that do not result from any particular fault of either character, but evolve out of the true devotion that is a supreme cultural value. When Paramatattaṉ asks for the second mango that Puṉitavati has given to the Śaiva saint, her heart beats with anxiety at not being able to satisfy her husband's demands. She remembers that "[a]fter marriage her mother had told her only one thing. 'Live your life without making your husband angry.'" Until now she had not made anyone angry. But now the devotion that has been the foundation of her orderly domestic life has brought her to a crisis, revealing the tensions underlying the competing demands of husband and God (21–22). Where does her responsibility fall? When Puṉitavati confesses that Śiva has sent the second mango she serves her husband, Paramatattaṉ reminds himself that she is a good devotee with no blemishes, but he cannot fathom that a devotee could have this kind of power. Orderly devotion needs to stay within proper boundaries. When Puṉitavati receives yet another mango from Śiva, in his amazement Paramatattaṉ thinks,

> Is my wife such a devotee that without even giving voice, calling God inside her heart and extending her hands, she got the fruit? She is my father-in-law Tanatattaṉ's daughter. Or is she God's lamp, is she a human woman? Or is she the goddess that conquered the buffalo demon? Is she half of God? . . .
>
> Oh God . . . What kind of girl is she? If I say this to someone in the village, will they believe me? Who is able to do what happened here in my hall?
>
> Oh goddess . . . Paramatattaṉ's heart trembled. I met you as my wife . . . How many things . . . His heart shook. Making her bathe, serve rice, rub his legs while he slept, fold betel leaf . . . Wrong things . . . Wrong things . . . Can I bear

> this? What is all this, all these days I didn't know that my wife is a divine woman . . . His heart again trembled . . . He washed his hand and went out. Memories churned and pricked his heart. Leaving the village without telling anyone, he came to Nākappaṭṭiṉam.[29]

From Nākappaṭṭiṉam, Paramatattaṉ sails away to start a new life and a new family in another town. The story follows Cēkkiḻār's narrative, with the addition of interior dialogue. Paramatattaṉ thinks about Puṉitavati all the time; he is sad and torn and attributes all of his success to her. When Puṉitavati's family bring her to him, he and his new wife and daughter worship her. When the people watching the reunion are shocked that a husband would worship his wife, he tells them, "Puṉitavati is not my wife. She is not human. Through god's grace she received a holy birth. She is a powerful goddess (*yōkiṉi*) who can do anything due to the grace of the all-powerful Śiva . . . I separated from her because I could not bear the miracle. . . ." (27). Everyone worships her.

Puṉitavati meditates on Śiva, receives her *pēy* form, becomes Kāraikkāl Ammaiyār and a worthy poet. The gods and beings on earth rejoice. She goes to Mt. Kailāsa, then to Tiruvālaṅkāṭu to watch Śiva's dance of bliss. She achieves liberation and undying fame.

The story resonates with the film about Ammaiyār in several ways. In the film Ammaiyār becomes a kindly old woman when her husband rejects her; in the story when Ammaiyār becomes a *pēy* her form is not described at all, nor is there a cremation ground. As in the film, the story stays focused on family and community life in a town, and emphasizes that Puṉitavati is good wife who happens to also be a divine being, not a ghoulish ascetic. Her husband is torn about rejecting her, but he just wants an ordinary wife, not a powerful goddess in his home. Paramatattaṉ wonders if his wife is the goddess Durgā, who killed the buffalo demon, or Umā, who is half of Śiva. Bālakumāraṉ makes even more explicit than the film the inherent tension in the devotional path between good but ordinary people and fervent devotees whose spiritual power transgresses ordinary human boundaries. In his story Bālakumāraṉ poignantly depicts the anguish Paramatattaṉ feels when he realizes the categories of his life have changed, that his world has been turned upside down by a woman who tried to be a perfect wife. His internal dialogue allows us to inhabit his situation, to imagine what it would be like to be married to a divine being. The characters' self-reflexivity gives the narrative a "modern" feel, but Bālakumāraṉ's story eloquently affirms the power and influence of Cēkkiḻār's several-hundred-year-old story.

The contemporary images of Kāraikkāl Ammaiyār are based on Cēkkiḻār's story that became the standard narrative of this poet. This narrative focuses on a chaste wife who is a pure-hearted devotee of Śiva. She does not intentionally neglect her duties to her husband, but her unswerving devotion to Śiva derails the ordered domesticity that should be the center of her world. These images reflect the dominant devotional paradigm in Tamil Śaivism, as well as the continuing tensions between complete devotion and ordinary domestic life. On many levels these contemporary images bear little resemblance to the devotional path or to the poet herself as seen in Kāraikkāl Ammaiyār's poetry. It is in the temples associated with Ammaiyār where the story of her life and her poetry are more closely united.

4

The Temples and Their Festivals

There are two towns that are closely associated with Kāraikkāl Ammaiyār and that contain temples that specifically honor her. Kāraikkāl (or Karikal) is the medium-sized coastal town south of Puducherry (Pondicherry) in which Kāraikkāl Ammaiyār was born. Tiruvālaṅkāṭu is the small village approximately 50 kilometers west of Chennai in which the temple where Ammaiyār watched Śiva perform his dance is located. These two temples each celebrate Ammaiyār in annual, but very different, festival celebrations.

The Kāraikkāl Temple and Festival[1]

In the town of Kāraikkāl there is a fairly modest-sized but lovely Kāraikkāl Ammaiyār temple in which she occupies her own shrine, as the goddess in a Śiva temple would.[2] Her image is that of a beautiful, ornamented, married Tamil woman, holding a mango in her left hand and a scroll in her right.[3] In 1972 the artist Kārai Ē. Ē. Alīm painted Cēkkiḻār's story about Kāraikkāl Ammaiyār on the outside of the walls surrounding her shrine.[4] The panels begin with her birth and end with her walking up Mt. Kailāsa on her head to see Śiva and Pārvatī. Next to her shrine is a hall at the end of which is a large painting of her marriage to Paramatattaṉ. Behind this hall is the largest part of the temple, dedicated to Śiva Comanātar; the central image is a *liṅga*. The sixty-three *nāyaṉmars* are lined up around the walls. But in this temple the most important form of Śiva is as the Beggar, in Tamil *Piccāṇṭavar*, the form that he takes when he comes to Puṉitavati's house, as if he is a devotee of Śiva. On the wall outside of the Comanātar shrine is an image of Ammaiyār with Śiva as the Beggar. Śiva is also depicted emerging from the *liṅga*, with Pārvatī, as Dakṣinamūrti, Bhairava, and Nandikeśvarar, the Lord of the *gaṇa* troupe. Next to Nandikeśvarar is an image of Durgā standing on the buffalo demon. There are shrines to Murukaṉ, Lakṣmī, and Vināyakar (Ganesh). Across the street is the Kailāsanātha temple that plays an integral role in Ammaiyār's festival.[5]

The chapbook sold at the temple, *Kāraikkāl Talapurāṇamum Kāraikkālammaiyār Aruḷ Varalāṟum*, begins with all of Ammaiyār's poetry, then gives the *talapurāṇam* or story of the temple, followed by two versions of Ammaiyār's story: a short synopsis followed by a longer narrative based on Cēkkiḻār's hagiography. The book ends with a discussion of the time period in which Ammaiyār lived and her works. Here is a synopsis of the story of how Śiva, Pārvatī, and Viṣṇu came to Kāraikkāl (here Kāraivaṉam):[6]

> Caunakar and the other sages were living in the hermitage. Seeing Cūtamuṉi who is an expert in reciting the *purāṇam*, they asked him to explain how Ampāḷ was given the name Cākampari from among the thousand names for Parāśakti. Cūtamuṉi told the story of the goddess Cākampari.
>
> As the gods Brahmā, Viṣṇu, Indra and the other gods were worshiping Śiva who was sitting on Mt. Kailāsa, the great sage Nārada told Śiva that since the earth had been without rain for a long time, the astrologers predicted many creatures would die. He requested that Śiva protect the creatures. Śiva told Pārvatī to go down to earth and live in order to protect the sages and other beings. He told her to go to Kāraivaṉam, where the Ari river and the sea join, which is a sacred place with a sacred river—bathing in the Ari river brings more blessings than bathing in the Kāvari.
>
> According to Śiva's command, Pārvatī took the form of a girl and came to Kāraivaṉam. A sage doing *tapas* in the forest had worshiped in that forest to make it appropriate for a *liṅga*. In front of Pārvatī a *liṅga* sprang up; she worshiped it and *śakti*; she named the images Kailāsanāthar and Cuntarāmpāḷ. Because God was happy with her worship, he emerged from the *liṅga* in the form of an old man. He told her that those who bathed in the sacred river and those who worshiped him along with Ampāḷ would be liberated. Because of the rain and the rays of light coming from her crown, many trees, fruits, and other plants would grow. Because she was protecting them her name would be "Cākampari"; after bestowing this boon on her the old

man disappeared back into the *liṅga*. This food-giving goddess protected and saved all those who came to the forest from other parts of the earth. She invited many sages and their disciples to live there in the forest. The great sage Puṇṭarīka came there and did penance, worshiping Viṣṇu. Mahāviṣṇu came down in a huge vehicle with the Vedas, the epics, and Śrī Dēvī, Bhu Dēvī, and Nīlā Dēvī. Treated by Cākampari as a guest, they lived there. Cākampari named Viṣṇu "Nitya Kalyāṇa Perumāḷ." In Kāraikkāl today there is a separate Nitya Kalyāṇa Perumāḷ temple in the center of the city.

This temple is famous for the mango festival it celebrates every year during the month of Āṉi, June–July, at least since 1890.[7] (See Figure 4.1.) The festival is celebrated on Paurnami, or the full moon day of the month, and lasts for three days. Here is a brief description:[8]

The mango festival celebrates the day that Śiva came to Kāraikkāl Ammaiyār's house. On the first day the flag at Ammaiyār's temple is raised; then is the procession; on the second day the marriage is celebrated; then on the third

Figure 4.1. Sculptures on Entrance to Kāraikkāl Ammaiyār Temple in Kāraikkāl.
Photo by the author.

day there is *darśan* or vision of the deity. On the first day in the evening in the Kailāsanāthaswamy Temple, Śiva is worshipped. There is a chariot which has five horses decorated with colorful lights, and that night, accompanied by nagaswaram music, it goes to invite Paramatattan̲ Chettiār from the Śakti Vināyakar Temple as bridegroom, and brings him to stay in the Kailāsanātha Temple.[9] In the same temple Vināyakar will come in procession, stopping at each house to give pūjā.

The next morning, the second day, the Subrahmaṇya procession will be conducted with pūjā.[10] At that time in Kāraikkāl Ammaiyār's temple, Pun̲itavati will be taken to the tank where she is bathed (*tīrttavāri*). That same morning at 8:00 Paramatattan̲ Chettiār will be taken on the king's horse through the Raja Street with the music of nagaswaram, from Kailāsanātha Temple to the marriage hall in Pun̲itavati's house. The groom brings *varicai* or marriage offering of fruits, flowers, silk cloth and the like to the bride. Paramatattan̲ Chettiār and Pun̲itavati's wedding is conducted during the day, complete with the *yākakuṇṭam* or sacrificial fire. After the marriage ceremony the bride and groom sit in the swing. People receive blessings from the new couple. After the ceremony the bride and groom go in procession around the town. Members of the Chettiār community are represented by painted doll-like masks worn by people in the procession. But in the evening at 6:30 Śiva Perumāl takes the form of a beggar—Bhikṣātanamūrti (Piccāṇṭavar).[11] He is covered in white ash. From heaven he comes to earth with a joyful dance. At 8:00 in the sacrificial hall, pūjā for Piccāṇṭavar is performed. At 10:00 Pun̲itavati and Paramatattan̲ Chettiār come in procession in the pearl-decorated cart. From Pun̲itavati's temple the cart goes through Raja Street with all the traditional music and dance. People present mangoes and other offerings.

The third day, early morning at 3:00, in the Kailāsanātha temple's spring mandapam mahā pūjā is performed to Piccāṇṭavar and to five other forms of Śiva (Pillaiyār or Ganesh, Murukan̲, Pārvatī, Nandi, Śiva).[12] The same morning at 9:00 Paramatattan̲ Chettiār goes to the Poyātumūrti Vināyakar temple to start a money-lending shop. Some people he does business with give him two mangoes and he sends them with his worker to his house. Until it is time to serve food Ammaiyār will stay at the Kāraikkāl Ammaiyār temple. At 10:00 after the pūjā is over, Piccāṇṭavar, in the coral chariot, will carry a begging bowl; he has taken this form for Kāraikkāl Ammaiyār. With all sorts of soldiers, elephants, flags and music in front of them, along with the ghosts (*bhūtas*), he comes in procession. Many Śiva devotees come to this part of the procession carrying begging bowls. From morning until evening on Raja Street, the devotees come like a flood. People are given mangoes.[13] All along the road the devotees give water and food.

At 6:00 in the evening at Puṉitavati's temple, Puṉitavati brings Piccāṇṭavar to her house and serves food; she serves a mango with curd. Paramatattaṉ Chettiār comes from the money shop and Puṉitavati serves him food. At that time she gives him the remaining mango. After he eats that, the Chettiār asks his wife for the other mango; Puṉitavati miraculously receives another mango. When he sees that, Paramatattaṉ is shocked. He goes away in the ship to the Pandiya country. This part of the festival is enacted in the Śakti Vināyakar temple.

At 9:00 in the same temple Paramatattaṉ performs his second marriage. At 11:00 the same night, Puṉitavati goes with her relatives in the flower palanquin from the Kāraikkāl Ammaiyār temple to the Śakti Vināyakar temple. She reaches there at 3:30. Paramatattaṉ Chettiār comes toward her with his second wife and daughter, then circumambulates her and worships her. Then Puṉitavati thinks whole-heartedly about God and asks him to remove her body. She takes the *pēy* form, and sings *Aṟputat Tiruvantāti*, and *Tiruviruṭṭai Maṇimālai*.[14] Then in her *pēy* form she moves in procession down the street in the dark; all the street lights have been turned off and she is accompanied by only one torch. People chant *"Pēy! Pēy!"* When she reaches the Pillaiyār (Ganesh) temple, she sees the Pañcamūrtis (five forms of Śiva) and pūjā is performed. Then in the North Street Śiva Kailāsanātha appears and grants her *mukti* or liberation. After this the Pañcamūrtis process to Raja Street. Ammaiyār goes into her temple where Śiva Comanātar is, and the doors are closed. This means that she has reached Mt. Kailāsa.

In Cēkkiḻār's story a Śaiva devotee comes to the door asking for alms, and Puṉitavati gives him one of the mangoes her husband has brought home. Here in Kāraikkāl it is Śiva himself who comes to Puṉitavati's door, interacting directly with his devotee and making the Lord's accessibility vividly concrete. The overwhelming consensus at the temple and during the festival is that Ammaiyār's devotees consider her to be a goddess.

The Kāraikkāl temple is famous locally for the mango festival. Kāraikāl and Tiruvālaṅkāṭu are geographically far apart and are very different places, but there are some parallels in the annual Ammaiyār festivals they each celebrate.

The Tiruvālaṅkāṭu Temple[15]

Kāraikkāl is a small city, but Tiruvālaṅkāṭu, approximately fifty kilometers west of Chennai, is a very small village in a rural area; it still evokes something of the desolate forest area Ammaiyār describes in her poetry. The Tiruvālaṅkāṭu Śiva temple is quite old; some of the walls were built during the Pallava dynasty (sixth–ninth centuries). The Tēvāram poets Appar, Campantar, and Cuntarar wrote about this temple.[16] Major renovations on the temple were completed after 1960.[17] "Tiruvālaṅkāṭu" means "sacred banyan tree forest," as we have seen. The temple tree is still a banyan, on which people hang small cloths in the form of cradles to petition for children. The temple is famous as one of the five *sabhais* or halls in which Śiva Naṭarāja performs his dance. Here, Śiva performs his fierce *ūrdhva tāṇḍava* dance in the Ratna Sabhai (Tamil *irattiṉa capai,* jeweled hall).[18] In Sanskrit "banyan forest" is *vatāranyam;* Śiva (Iśvara or Lord) here is called Vaṭāraṇyēśvarar, Lord of the Banyan Forest. Śiva performing his *ūrdhva tāṇḍava* dance with Kāraikkāl Ammaiyār singing at his feet is represented in one of the sculptures above the entrance gopuram (gateway). Other images at the entrance are Kālī dancing and Śiva and Umā on Nandi the bull. Past this first entrance on the second wall encircling the temple is a sculptured diorama of scenes from Ammaiyār's life: her marriage, the Śaiva devotee holding a mango, and her walking on her hands to see Śiva and Umā on Mt. Kailāsa. The diorama opposite this one shows the wedding of Śiva and the goddess Mīnākṣī in Maturai. Above the entrance to the main temple are sculptures of Śiva performing his dance in the five *sabhais* or halls: In addition to his *ūrdhva tāṇḍava* in Tiruvāḷaṅkāṭu, the other dances are performed in Chidambaram, Maturai, Tirunelveli, and Kutralam. Just outside this main temple Umā has her own small temple. She is called Vaṇṭārkuḻali, which means "the one who has bees swarming around her hair," a reference to when the gods brought such sweet-smelling flowers to worship her, the fragrance brought a swarm of bees around her.[19]

In the main part of the temple, just inside the entrance to the right, Śiva performs his *ūrdhva tāṇḍava* dance in the Ratna Sabhai with Śivakāmī (Pārvatī) to his side and Kāraikkāl Ammaiyār singing at his feet. Behind these images is Ammaiyār's *samādhi* or shrine, where she is said to have attained liberation. Ammaiyār's Tiruvālaṅkāṭu poems are written on the walls enclosing this shrine and the images, along with *Tēvāram* poems about the temple. Past this shrine on the left, dancing Bhadrakālī is installed in a separate shrine. Just past Bhadrakālī's shrine is a doorway to the back section of the temple where the inner sanctum containing the *liṅga* is located. In front of the inner sanctum on the right are moveable images of Śiva Naṭarāja and Śakti; through a doorway on the left, Ammaiyār and the four major Śaiva poets Appar, Campantar, Cuntarar, and Māṇikkavācakar are positioned in a row from which they can watch Śiva dance. These four are the only saints installed in this temple.[20] Near the saints are the sages Muñcikēcar, Kārkkōṭakaṉ, and Agastya, who are important in the temple myth.

To the west of the temple is a large temple tank, called the Muktitīrtha; on the northeast bank is a separate temple to Bhadrakālī. This Kālī temple is considered to be Tiruvālaṅkāṭu's *mūlasthāna* or oldest shrine. On the other side of the tank is the Muktīśvarar (Śiva) temple. (See Figure 4.2.) Close to the Śiva temple are small temples to the sages Kārkkōṭakaṉ and Muñcikēcar.[21]

Figure 4.2. Entrance to Śiva Temple in Tiruvālaṅkāṭu.
Photo by the author.

The ancient town of Paḻaiyaṉūr is approximately three-quarters of a kilometer from Tiruvālaṅkāṭu; one can easily walk from one village to the next. According to inscriptions found at Tiruvālaṅkāṭu, the Cōḻa king Rajendra I made a land grant in the sixth year of his reign, 1018, to the beautiful Śiva temple in Paḻaiyaṉūr, the village which today is called Tiruvālaṅkāṭu.[22] In the town of Paḻaiyaṉūr is the Kailāsanātha temple to Śiva; the God here is also known as "Ammaiyappa" ("Mother-Father") because it is believed that here Kāraikkāl Ammaiyār hugged Śiva; he called her "Ammai" and she called him "Appa." The temples and the two towns are intertwined throughout history, which is most evident during the festivals. There is a cremation ground in Paḻaiyaṉūr, as well as shrines marking events from the story of Nīli, which continues to be told in the temple pamphlets. (See Figure 4.3.)

In the *talapurāṇam* or story of how the Tiruvālaṅkāṭu temple was established, the main theme is that Tiruvālaṅkāṭu is the place where Śiva and Kālī dance. Although the Chidambaram temple is today the most famous place associated with Śiva as the Lord of the Dance, and Tiruvālaṅkāṭu's *talapurāṇam* reveals the influence of the Chidambaram tradition, Tiruvālaṅkāṭu may be the original site of

Figure 4.3. Sculptures on Tiruvālaṅkāṭu Temple Mandapam; L to R: Kālī, Ammaiyār, Śiva, Umā, Sages Muñcikēcar and Kārkkōṭakaṉ.
Photo by the author.

the dance contest, as discussed in Chapter 2.[23] Both David Shulman and Mahalakshmi R. have observed that the *talapurāṇam* localizes the Sanskrit *Devī Mahātmya* myth in which Kālī and her army of Śaktis defeat the demons that have conquered the gods. In the Tiruvālaṅkāṭu myth, Kālī takes up residence in the banyan forest, linking her to the ancient Tamil Caṅkam goddess Koṟṟavai and the fierce female beings that occupy forests and wastelands.[24] The following is a rendition of the Tiruvālaṅkāṭu *talapurāṇam*:[25]

> The two demons Cumpaṉ and Nicumpaṉ (Sanskrit Śumbha and Niśumbha) came to Tiruvālaṅkāṭu and caused trouble for the gods, sages, people, and everyone else. The gods and the sages came before the Lord and pleaded for help. Devī took pity on them and along with the Seven Mothers and Cāmuṇḍī came down and conquered the demons. But then the demon Raktabīja began to fight; from each drop of his spilled blood more demons appeared. Out of Umā's rage Kālī was born. Śiva himself came down and along with Kālī's armies they did battle and conquered the demons. Kālī drank all of Raktabīja's blood and destroyed the rest of the demon army. Śiva made Kālī the leader of the Tiruvālaṅkāṭu forest and returned to Mt. Kailāsa. But because of drinking the demons' blood, Kālī became intoxicated and began to commit many cruel deeds. When he saw these things, the sage Nārada went to Mt. Kailāsa and informed Śiva of what was going on. The Lord assumed his fierce form from among his ancient forms; Śiva along with his troupe of *gaṇas* went to Tiruvālaṅkāṭu.
>
> Seeing Śiva in his fierce form, Kālī was afraid and thought of a scheme in order to defeat him. "If you are able to defeat me in a dance contest, then you can rule this banyan forest," she said. Śiva agreed. Nārada, Nandi, Viṣṇu, Brahmā and the other gods came and played instruments, and Pārvatī presided. Muñcikēcar, Kārkkōṭakaṉ and all the other sages came to watch. Śiva performed many kinds of dances with Kālī, who imitated his moves and did not grow weary. Then finally Śiva performed the fierce *ūrdhva tāṇḍava* dance. He dropped one of his jeweled earrings onto the ground. Then Śiva lifted his left leg straight up to the sky so that it touched his ear, dancing his *ūrdhva tāṇḍava* dance. Because she could not do that dance, Kālī appeared to faint. Śiva said, "Apart from me, no others are

> your equal. You will live by my side." He graced her with the boon of being worshiped first. He also gave the sages Muñcikēcar and Kārkkōṭakaṉ the boon of always remaining in his temple where they can see the Lord.

Śiva knows that Kālī will not lift her leg that high because it is an immodest move for a female dancer, so he outwits her in the dance contest. But after proving his superiority, Śiva grants Kālī the boon of living at his side in Tiruvālaṅkāṭu, and of receiving worship from devotees first, before him. In the temple today Kālī's shrine is in front of the main Śiva *liṅga* in the inner sanctum, so she is worshiped first. In one version of this story a *svayambhu liṅga* or "self-begotten" *liṅga* appeared under a banyan tree; whoever saw this *liṅga* would achieve *mukti* or liberation. Word of this *liṅga* spread among the celestial beings, who had to contend with demons in order to worship the *liṅga*. This version posits the constant presence of Śiva in Tiruvālaṅkāṭu through his most common image.[26] Śiva had previously sent the sages Muñcikēcar and Kārkkōṭakaṉ to the forest of Tiruvālaṅkāṭu to await his divine dance. Muñcikēcar had prayed to Śiva for the boon of witnessing his dance, so when Śiva sent him to Tiruvālaṅkāṭu, he undertook austerities until the Lord appeared. He maintained such a deep state of meditation that he was covered by an anthill, on top of which reeds grew; "muñci" means "reeds." Kārkkōṭakaṉ was a snake king who at one time adorned Śiva's arm as a bracelet. One day Kārkkōṭakaṉ accidentally squirted poison on the Lord's arm, so Śiva angrily sent him to Tiruvālaṅkāṭu to do penance until he came there to dance. It was after Śiva established his *ūrdhva tāṇḍava* form in Tiruvālaṅkāṭu that he sent Kāraikkāl Ammaiyār there to watch his dance. According to Śri Sabharathina Gurukkaḷ, her *pēy* form was appropriate for the forest, since the forest is where the ghosts live.

The image of Ammaiyār at Śiva's feet in the Ratna Sabhai is a beautiful bronze sculpture of her *pēy* form with emaciated limbs, shriveled breasts, ribs sticking out, and hair like the shredded leaf of a *tāḷi* palm, as she describes a demon in the cremation ground in one of her Tiruvālaṅkāṭu poems (2.6).

She is sitting with her knees bent, playing the cymbals; her lovely face is calm, a slight smile on her lips, her gaze directed inward. Sculptured images of Ammaiyār in her *pēy* form appear at least as early as the eleventh century, predating Cēkkiḻār (first half of the twelfth century). Images of Śiva dancing, often with his *gaṇas,* are seen on Pallava temples as early as the seventh century. On the wall of the eleventh-century Cōḻa temple Gaṅgaikoṇḍacōḻapuram is a sculpture of

Śiva dancing, with Kālī dancing behind him; at his feet Ammaiyār is shown in her seated *pēy* form playing the cymbals alongside several *gaṇas*. Sculptured images of Ammaiyār in her resplendent, seated *pēy* form, sometimes shown at Śiva's feet, proliferated and diversified in the succeeding centuries, testifying to her recognition and esteem in the Śaiva tradition. Some of the images emphasize the serenity of her meditation, others her macabre fierceness, and still others combine her ghoulish and calm attributes. When she takes her place among the *nāyaṉmārs* in Śiva temples she is a seated *pēy*.[27]

The image of Śiva performing his *ūrdhva tāṇḍava* dance in the Ratna Sabhai is quite similar to the typical image of Śiva Naṭarāja described in Chapter 2, with the position of his left leg being the major difference. He is surrounded by a ring of fire; his right foot stands on a dwarf, his left foot is extended straight up into the air; his matted hair flies outward, a mermaid-like Gaṅgā is in his hair, and he is entwined with snakes. He has eight arms, five of which hold objects: fire, the drum, cymbals, the trident, and the noose. One hand points in a relaxed way toward the ground in the "elephant-hand gesture" (*gajahasta*), one hand is raised in the open-palmed "do not fear" gesture (*abhayamudra*), and the final hand is held above the raised left leg. His face is calm, his gaze directed inward.

Dorai Rangaswamy (456) believes that Śiva's *ūrdhva tāṇḍava* of Tiruvālaṅkāṭu is at least as ancient as Kāraikkāl Ammaiyār, based on her poetry. Shulman believes that the story of the dance contest at Tiruvālaṅkāṭu is older than the tradition at the Chidambaram temple.[28] What is clear is that the stories connected to the Tiruvālaṅkāṭu temple reflect the marginalization of the local goddesses of the Tamil land as Śiva took up residence and became the focus of a major devotional movement. Shulman connects Kālī with Koṟṟavai, the local Tamil goddess of war.[29] Shulman (1980, 161) and Ramaswamy (2003, 163) consider Kāraikkāl Ammaiyār to be a form of Nīli, another powerful female figure from the town of Paḻaiyaṉūr, which is today a separate village next to Tiruvālaṅkāṭu but is the ancient name of the town that once included the present-day Tiruvālaṅkāṭu.

Nīli harkens back to ancient Tamil themes as well as to the epic *Cilappatikāram*. In the *Cilappatikāram* Nīli is the wife of Caṅkamaṉ, who is unjustly executed in front of the king. After her husband's murder Nīli wanders around the city raving about the king's injustice, and curses Caṅkamaṉ's murderer to share her husband's fate in a future life. Caṅkamaṉ's murderer is reborn as Kovalaṉ, Kaṇṇaki's husband and the hero of the epic.[30] Nīli is mentioned in a poem by Campantar that praises "Our Lord in Paḻaiyaṉūr Ālaṅkāṭu,/home of men who feared for their honor/when they heard of the woman/who took her lover's life by foul means . . ."[31] In the approximately tenth-century Jain epic *Nīlakeci*, Nīli is a bloodthirsty goddess living in Paḻaiyaṉūr. In this epic a Jain sage resides near a cemetery and persuades the local people to stop making blood sacrifices to the village goddess, which displeases the *pēys* in the cemetery. They complain to the goddess Kālī, who sends Nīli to get rid of the sage. Nīli is unable to scare off the sage, and ends up listening to his polemics about the consequences of harming sentient beings. She is converted to Jainism and spreads Jain principles all over India.[32] In Cēkkiḻār's *Periya Purāṇam* and in the *Cēkkiḻār Purāṇam* Nīli is referred to as a fierce *pēy* who comes to Paḻaiyaṉūr for revenge, and through deceit kills a merchant and causes seventy Vēḷāḷars to enter the fire.[33] The story of Nīli continues to be popular in oral and literary tales, and is presented by folk theater and dance troupes such as the *villu paṭṭu* or bow song tradition.[34] The Tiruvālaṅkāṭu temple books include long, detailed narratives about Nīli, affirming her continuing importance to the area. Here is Nīli's story:[35]

> A Brahmin lived in Kāñcipuram. His son Puvaṉapati wanted to go to Kāśi, so he went there. Every day he bathed in the holy Gaṅgā, and he worshipped Kāśi Viśvanātar. A Brahmin named Cattiyaññāṉi also lived in Kāśi. He had a son named Civakkiyāṉi and a daughter named Navakkiyāṉi. The father was attracted by Puvaṉapati's character and activities, so he offered his daughter Navakkiyāṉi to him in marriage. Puvaṉapati did not reveal that he was already married, and out of lust for this woman he married again. After he stayed in Kāśi for some time, he decided to return to Kāñcipuram. When Navakkiyāṉi found out, she said that she and her brother Civakkiyāṉi would accompany him, and they started out. Puvaṉapati agonized about going with them, but he couldn't do anything about it, so with a worried heart he agreed. The three of them went toward Kāñcipuram. As they got closer and closer, Puvaṉapati thought about how he could take his second wife to his village; as he was thinking about this, they arrived in the middle of Tiruvālaṅkāṭu and stayed there.
>
> Thinking that he would be subjected to his first wife's scolding, he sent his brother-in-law to fetch water and killed his second wife Navakkiyāṉi by hitting her on the head with a rock before he returned. He then walked quickly

to Kāñcipuram. When Civakkiyāṉi came back and saw his younger sister had been killed, his heart could not bear it. He cried and mourned, and because of his love for the one who had been born with him, he could not think of living, and hung himself with a rope. Because of their untimely deaths, they took *pēy* forms to take revenge on Puvaṉapati: Civakkiyāṉi became Nīlaṉ, and Navakkiyāṉi became Nīli. They wandered in the forest of Tiruvālaṅkāṭu.

The Brahmin who killed his wife was reborn as a Chettiār in Kāñcipuram and named Taricaṉaṉ. When he attained puberty and his horoscope was cast, it said that in his previous birth he had killed a girl; she had become a *pēy* and wandered to the north of the city, waiting to take revenge on him. Taricaṉaṉ's father was worried about the consequences of his son's sin and asked the astrologer what to do. The astrologer gave him a knife in which he put a mantra, saying that no harm would come to the son as long as he carried the knife. The astrologer told the father not to let his son go north. When Taricaṉaṉ got married, his father gave him the knife and told him not to go north. Then the father died.

In Paḻaiyaṉūr there was a Vēḷāḷar whose wife had no children. She prayed for children and became pregnant; the *pēys* Nīlaṉ and Nīli entered her womb and were born as twins.[36] During the day these children lay quietly in their cradles, but at night they took on their old *pēy* forms and entered sheds and killed and ate goats and cattle, then resumed their forms as babies and slept. The owners of the goats and cows saw the animals disappearing and punished the watchmen. The watchmen wanted to know how the animals were being destroyed, so they hid and watched. They saw two *pēys* enter the shed and kill and eat the goats and cows. They followed the forms back to their father's house. The father did not believe his babies were ghosts, but while he was watching one night, his children came from his house, changed into *pēys*, and killed and ate goats and cows. After seeing this, the father thought it would be a good thing if the children were killed, but realizing that killing them would be a sin, he left the babies under a tree near the Naṭarāja temple.

The two children realized they had taken their old forms. Nīli said, "If we both stay here we will be killed, so you stay here alone and I will go to Tirucceṅkōṭu and wait at a babul tree." Nīlaṉ alone stayed in Tiruvālaṅkāṭu at a babul tree. One day the Vēḷāḷars from Paḻaiyaṉūr cut down the babul tree in order to plow, and left. When Nīlaṉ saw that the tree was cut down, he thought about taking revenge on the Paḻaiyaṉūr Vēḷāḷars. One day the Paḻaiyaṉūr Gurukkaḷ came to do pūjā in Tiruvālaṅkāṭu. When the Gurukkaḷ was going home to Paḻaiyaṉūr, Nīlaṉ beat him badly and took the food offerings from the pūjā. The Gurukkaḷ complained about his troubles to Śiva Naṭarāja, who sent his *gaṇa* Kuṇṭōtaraṉ to kill Nīlaṉ. In Tirucceṅkōṭu Nīli came to know of her brother's death, and realized that the Paḻaiyaṉūr Vēḷāḷars were responsible. Nīli wanted to take revenge on the husband who had killed her, and on the Vēḷāḷars, so she waited in Tiruvālaṅkāṭu.

In Kāñcipuram, Nīli's husband had been reborn as Taricaṉaṉ. He went to many places to do business. He heard that Paḻaiyaṉūr was doing very well, so he wanted to go to that village to trade. His mother and his wife reminded him that his father had told him not to go north, and Paḻaiyaṉūr was north. Taricaṉaṉ responded that he had a knife containing a mantra to protect him. He set off for Paḻaiyaṉūr, telling his wife that he was going to do business, so it would be hard to take her and their child along. Without being invited, his wife went with him anyway. On the way, in the middle of the night while his wife was sleeping, Taricaṉaṉ left her and continued his journey alone. When his wife woke up the next morning, she looked all over for him but did not find him. Some people in the area helped her and sent her back to Kāñcipuram.

As Taricaṉaṉ was going through Tiruvālaṅkāṭu, Nīli was watching him, waiting to take revenge for the actions of his previous birth. Through magic Nīli set up a business and invited Taricaṉaṉ to stay there and trade. Taricaṉaṉ knew that a woman wouldn't have a business in the forest alone, and held out his knife; the business and the woman disappeared. Taricaṉaṉ ran in fear. Nīli knew that she wouldn't get near Taricaṉaṉ as long as he had his mantric knife. As Taricaṉaṉ ran he got thirsty. Nīli took the form of a girl with a water stand and offered him water. Taricaṉaṉ was also suspicious of this girl and got more frightened; he ran toward Paḻaiyaṉūr. Nīli took her own *pēy* form and blocked Taricaṉaṉ. She said to him, "No matter where you go, tonight I am going to take revenge on you, and tomorrow I will take revenge on the Vēḷāḷars." Taricaṉaṉ ran to the Paḻaiyaṉūr Vēḷāḷars and told them what had happened, and they promised to protect him.

In the meantime Nīli took the form of Taricaṉaṉ's wife who he had left behind. She took a branch from the *kaḷḷi* tree and when she placed it on her hip it became a baby. She walked into Paḻaiyaṉūr and saw Taricaṉaṉ with the Vēḷāḷars. "Aiyo! The elders and the astrologers told you not to come north, but without listening you set off. You left the child and me in the middle of the night and came here. You've been wandering around, but I have found you. Such is the strength of my marriage *tāli*." Taricaṉaṉ replied, "She is not my wife! This is not my child! She is a demon who is here to take revenge on me; don't believe her." Taricaṉaṉ told the Vēḷāḷars what had happened up to that time. Nīli said, "You are calling me a demon?" and she began to cry. The Vēḷāḷars' hearts melted at her tears; they said it was a sin to say things like that about your wife. Then Nīli put the child down on the ground; the child went directly to Taricaṉaṉ and hugged him, and began to chatter to him. The Vēḷāḷars believed Nīli; how could a small child tell a lie? So they said to Taricaṉaṉ, "Sir, you stay with her tonight. We will talk tomorrow morning." Taricaṉaṉ was afraid and told them that he might not be alive tomorrow. The Vēḷāḷars were devotees of Śiva; they were trying to do the right thing. They put them together in a house. Nīli told the Vēḷāḷars that her husband was very angry with her and might try to kill her and the child; if he kills them, then the sin will go to them. So she asked the Vēḷāḷars to take his knife away. The Vēḷāḷars asked the Chettiār for his knife, but he would not give it, saying that if they took it away he would surely die. In response, the Vēḷāḷars said, "Your wife has spoken correctly. If you lose your life tonight, then we seventy people will give our lives tomorrow." They took this vow on the *liṅga* called Cāṭcipūtēcuvarar. The Vēḷāḷars took the knife, saying they would return it tomorrow. They gave them food, and left them in the house.

In the middle of the night Nīli took her own form and killed Taricaṉaṉ, taking revenge for the actions of

> his previous birth. Then she put the baby on the ground and crushed it to death with her foot. The next morning sixty-nine of the Vēḷāḷars came to the house and found Taricaṉaṉ dead. They said, "We have committed a sin. He told the truth, and we did not protect him." In front of Cāṭcipūtēcuvarar they made a fire, jumped into the fire and killed themselves. The last Vēḷāḷar had gone to plough his field. Nīli took the form of his wife, went to the field and said to him, "Sixty-nine people have jumped into the fire. You alone have escaped with your life." Hearing this, the Vēḷāḷar took his plough blade and stabbed himself, giving up his life. In this way Nīli completed her revenge on Taricaṉaṉ and the seventy Vēḷāḷars. But because the Vēḷāḷars were honest, trustworthy devotees, Śiva granted them liberation.

In the epic *Cilappatikāram,* Nīli and Kaṇṇaki are powerful female figures who take revenge for the unjust deaths of their husbands: Nīli curses her husband's murderer to share the same fate in a later life, and Kaṇṇaki burns the city of Maturai and purges it of sinful inhabitants. Kaṇṇaki ascends to heaven and becomes a goddess. In successive stories about Nīli, she avenges her own death, as well as the death of her brother, which includes the gruesome sacrifice of the seventy truthful Vēḷāḷars. In some versions of this myth, Nīli and Taricaṉaṉ are locked up in a Kālī temple, which could be the Kālī temple located on the bank of the temple tank discussed above.[37] In all of the later stories Nīli is firmly rooted in Tiruvālaṅkāṭu.

In Tamilnadu when a woman cries fake tears, people say that she is crying *Nīli kaṇṇīr* or "Nīli's tears." Today, near the Paḻaiyaṉūr bus stand, there is a small enclosure surrounding a preserved footprint and the caption on the back wall that says in Tamil "Footprint of Nīli pressing her child [to death] with her foot." The inside of the enclosure has a small niche for lamps, which has been decorated with kumkum. Not far from this footprint is a monument to the seventy Vēḷāḷars who died. In the center of the stone mandapam is the statue of a Vēḷāḷar with his hands above his head, standing in a flaming fire so that only his upper body is visible. Carved in relief on the stone walls surrounding the statue are the sixty-nine Vēḷāḷars who jumped into the fire. In the roof above the shrine is a relief sculpture of Śiva performing his *ūrdhva tāṇḍava* dance. Across the road from the shrine to the Vēḷāḷars is a temple to Cāṭcipūtēcuvarar, the *liṅga* in front of which the Vēḷāḷars took their vow and built the fire to immolate themselves. *Cāṭci* means witness. Nearby in the cremation ground is a memorial stone to Nīli of three large split slabs of stone (*pāṟai*), two standing up and one laid horizontally on top, piled with small stones; it is called the Nīlippāṟai.[38] (See Figure 4.4.)

Kāraikkāl Pēy is not vengeful or bloodthirsty, as Nīli and Koṟṟavai are, but her fierceness and demonic appearance link her to these powerful female divine beings located in this forest area, as well as to Śiva. The first direct connection to Kāraikkāl Ammaiyār's poetry in Cēkkiḻār's story is when Puṉitavati asks Śiva for the *pēy* or demon form, which he grants her, and she sings her first two compositions. Cēkkiḻār states that she is able to compose the poetry at this moment, in her demon form, due to her increasing knowledge (*jñānam*) of Śiva; the demon form has given her closer access and deeper understanding. The Tiruvālaṅkāṭu Gurukkaḷ, Śri Sabarathina, emphasized that she was not a "natural" poet, but that her ability to sing hymns came from Śiva.[39] In the story the fact that Puṉitavati was a beautiful, virtuous wife who deliberately gives up her enviable form to be a frightening demon makes her devotion vividly astonishing. In her demon form, Puṉitavati travels to Mt. Kailāsa to be in the presence of Śiva and his wife Pārvatī; Śiva calling her "Ammai" or mother resurrects the

Figure 4.4. Nīlippāṟai.
Photo by the author.

feminine, nurturing form she intentionally discarded, and which is absent from the poetry. In Cēkkiḻār's story, when Śiva tells Pārvatī that Puṉitavati is a "mother that cherishes us," the verb he uses, *pēṇu*, also means nurturing.[40] Here Kāraikkāl Ammaiyār embodies competing roles: She is both a nurturing mother and a ghoulish being who is unafraid of places of death, connecting ancient Tamil ideas with the emerging understanding of devotion to Śiva. It is in the festival at the Tiruvālaṅkāṭu temple that Ammaiyār's competing roles come together most completely.

The Temple Festivals

For the past several decades the festival for Ammaiyār has been celebrated as part of the temple's annual major festival, the *brahmā utsavam*, which takes place in the month of Paṅkuṉi, March–April. This is a multiday festival that includes concerts and other entertainment.[41] Some days the festival is centered in Paḻaiyaṉūr, other days in Tiruvālaṅkāṭu.

The climax of this festival is the procession in which Śiva and Pārvatī are pulled through the village streets in a temple car. During the seventh day of the 2006 festival the car was painted and elaborately decorated with flower garlands and cloth ornaments. At 7:30 in the morning of the following day Śiva and Pārvatī were installed in the car with *pūjās*, or devotional rites People crowded around the car to get *darśan* or a vision of the deities. Many people—men, women, and children—took turns pulling the car through the streets with ropes. The car stopped at nearly every house; when a green flag was thrown up, the people pulled the car; when a red flag was thrown, the people stopped pulling the car. Partway through the morning important members of the Vaṇiyar community were garlanded; this is the community that sponsors this part of the Tiruvālaṅkāṭu festival.[42]

At the front of the procession was a truck spraying water on the road (it is brutally hot during this month in Tamilnadu). Behind the truck two people carried a beautifully painted screen. Behind the screen walked a horse, which is symbolic of the Vaṇiyar community. The horse carried two drums, one on each side; two older women were beating the drums. A beautifully decorated elephant walked behind the horse. Behind the elephant ten men and boys dressed in yellow danced. At the end of the procession was the car carrying Śiva and Pārvatī. As the procession made its way around the villages, people in the houses would give water or buttermilk to the devotees. At noon the procession stopped in front of the Kālī temple for awhile, then it continued around the villages until it returned to the Tiruvālaṅkāṭu temple around 5:30 in the evening. Later that night there was a concert and fireworks.

Usually the festival for Kāraikkāl Ammaiyār comes right after the festival for Śiva and Pārvatī. This festival has not been celebrated for as long as the *brahmā utsavam*; it was started only a little over fifty years ago by Mrs. Mā. Caṇpakavalli Ammaiyār. Her granddaughter, Mrs. Hema Chandrasekhar, told me that her grandmother was a famous orator who traveled all over the world to give religious discourses.[43] One day when she was giving a discourse on Kāraikkāl Ammaiyār, someone in the audience told her that at Tiruvālaṅkāṭu there is no celebration of her *mukti* or liberation. Her grandmother pursued this celebration and had to go through many hardships in order to establish the festival. She even had to get Kāraikkāl Ammaiyār's image out of the closed room it had been kept in for years. But she gained the support of very devoted Śaiva followers. She worked with the heads of the temple and some of the elders in Tiruvālaṅkāṭu to develop the rituals that are now followed during the festival. The *jyoti* or light ritual that is the culmination of the festival, symbolizing Ammaiyār's merging with Śiva, was developed by Mr. Sachidanandam Pillai, a learned and ardent devotee of Śiva. Mā. Caṇpakavalli Ammaiyār's daughter continued the tradition of sponsoring the festival, and now her granddaughter, Mrs. Hema Chandrasekhar, plays the major role. With a large group of dedicated relatives and friends, she starts preparing for the festival about two months before it is to begin.

In the year 2006, Kāraikkāl Ammaiyār's festival day (under the star *swasti*) came at a different time from the car festival for Śiva and Pārvatī, falling on March 17 and 18, almost two weeks before the Śiva festival (on the day of Paṇkuni *uttiram*). The following description is based on my experience of the two-day festival, during whch I was accompanied by Mr. Thavamani.

At about 6:00 on the evening of the first day Mrs. Chandrasekhar's family arrived at the temple carrying many plates of fruits and other items for the *abhiṣeka*, or consecration. The *abhiṣeka* took place at the image of Kāraikkāl Ammaiyār among the four *nāyaṉmārs* and Seven Mothers to the side of the *liṅga* shrine, where she looks directly at a movable image of Śiva Naṭarāja, watching him dance. The Gurukkaḷ brought the main Kāraikkāl Ammaiyār image from the *ūrdhva tāṇḍava* shrine and put it next to her *nāyaṉmār* image. The electricity had gone off due to the heavy rain, so most of the ritual took place in darkness. The Gurukkaḷs with their assistants performed the full *abhiṣeka* to both

Ammaiyār images, during which the images were bathed with various substances like milk, ghee, sandal paste, and *pañcamṛtam*, or the five ambrosial substances, here five kinds of fruit. The family sat directly in front. As the ritual continued, more and more devotees came in. At the end of this ritual, they also did pūjā to Naṭarāja.

Later that evening there was a storyteller and devotional songs were performed on a stage set up in front of the temple.[44] Around 10:00 that night the next phase of the celebration began. Mrs. Hema Chandrasekhar graciously came up and offered us her hospitality (since I had traveled so far to see this festival!). She brought us straight into the temple in front of the festival image of Kāraikkāl Ammaiyār, which had been installed in a small room near the Ratna Sabhai shrine where Śiva performs his *ūrdhva tāṇḍava* dance and Ammaiyār sits at his feet keeping time and singing. We stood with the family right in front of the image as the Gurukkaḷs finished the pūjā, then several men carried the image outside of the temple and around the main shrine, dancing and halting at spots, with the *mēḷam* or group of drummers, nagaswaram players, and other musicians accompanying the procession the entire way. After circumambulating the main shrine, the image was carried out to the mandapam in the outer courtyard where Ammaiyār was installed in a cobra swing. Mrs. Chandrasekhar's family went to an old house just across from the temple, where the *varicai*, or offerings to the bride, were spread out on plates. A group of women, including Mrs. Chandrasekhar and other members of her family, processed with all these offerings a short way around the streets that circle the temple, accompanied by the musicians; then they came into the temple courtyard. They brought the offerings up to the swing, where Gurukkaḷs helped to distribute them to people in the crowd. The Gurukkaḷ from the Paḻaiyaṉūr Kailāsanātha temple put mangoes on the front of the image, while other offerings from the plates the women brought continued to be handed out. (See Figure 4.5.) At this point in the festival Ammaiyār is still Puṉitavati, the devoted wife. This process takes a long time. The crowd in the courtyard was large at this time. The entertainment on the stage outside the temple continued.

On Saturday, March 18, at 11:30 in the morning, the Gurukkaḷs were finishing decorating Ammaiyār. The previous night she had been carried on a simple palanquin by a few men, but today she was installed on a cart with wheels and a generator to keep all the lights going. Men pulled the image, and a Gurukkaḷ walked along at the side of the car reading Kāraikkāl Ammaiyār's story from the *Periya Purāṇam* and poems from the *Tēvāram*. The procession stopped at all

Figure 4.5. Kāraikkāl Ammaiyār Festival in Tiruvālaṅkāṭu.
Photo by the author.

the houses where people were waiting with pūjā plates, which took several hours.

At approximately 2:00 in the morning the procession had gone around the villages and returned to the front of the temple. The main Gurukkaḷ was doing pūjā. We followed him into the main shrine of the temple. Many people had been sleeping in and around the temple while the car made its slow way around the villages; as people realized it was time for the main event, they rushed to the doorway of the temple. Everyone lined up on either side of the *ūrdhva tāṇḍava* shrine, forming crowded rows from the shrine steps across the temple to the doorway directly opposite. A large crowd was pushing and trying to get to a place to see the shrine. I saw several Śiva *bhaktas* wearing saffron clothes and *rudrākṣa* beads. The previous evening's events in the temple courtyard had an almost casual air, but tonight the atmosphere was electric; everyone was excited and expectant and amazingly quiet for such a large crowd. Although Mrs. Chandrasekhar's family is based in Chennai, the Gurukkaḷs at the temple said that most of the people who attend the festival are local people; this is their festival. As we were standing there, Ammaiyār was carried on a palanquin to the door opposite to and facing the *ūrdhva tāṇḍava* shrine, so that Ammaiyār and Śiva looked directly at each other across this part of the temple. While we were there waiting, several men were placing disks of camphor in a row all along the hall from Ammaiyār to Śiva, making sure there were no gaps between the pieces of camphor. Mr. K. Aruḷānantam, the *ōtuvār* or traditional singer of Śaiva devotional songs, put on the *parivaṭṭam*, the silk cloth that is first put around the divine image then tied around the head of distinguished guests or participants. He then sang all of Kāraikkāl Ammaiyār's Tiruvālaṅkāṭu songs.[45] One of the Gurukkaḷs sang all of them with him. When they finished singing the songs everyone became completely silent and waited for the main event (everyone else clearly knew what to expect). After doing pūjā to each image, the Gurukkaḷs and their assistants lit the camphor. It flamed up, forming a line of fire between Śiva and Ammaiyār, and the air got hot and smoky. We all stayed very quiet as we watched the camphor burn completely away, symbolizing Kāraikkāl Ammaiyār's *aikkiyam*—her merging into Śiva and achieving *mukti*, liberation. When the camphor had burned away Ammaiyār was carried back into the small room where the sponsoring family was giving respect to the Gurukkaḷs, presenting them with offerings such as fruits and garlands. When the family finished presenting their offerings, the devotees rushed madly toward the room to receive the flowers the Gurukkaḷs were taking from the image to give as *prasād* or the blessed gift from the deity, including enormous garlands. The officials had to keep more people from trying to squeeze into the small area. As people got flowers the crowd slowly got smaller. It was all over at about 3 a.m. This is one of the most amazing events I have ever witnessed.

This awesome, moving festival encapsulates and reflects centuries of the development of a Tamil tradition of devotion to Śiva, and the place of Kāraikkāl Ammaiyār in that developing tradition. She was the first to express devotion to Śiva in Tamil, to locate his heroic deeds in the Tamil land, and marks the beginning of the tradition that would develop over the succeeding centuries. Her life has been celebrated in Kāraikkāl, her birthplace, for more than a century at least. But the fact that up until about fifty years ago there was no special celebration of the first Tamil Śaiva saint in the temple in Tiruvālaṅkāṭu, where she witnessed Śiva's dance, perhaps reveals the continuing predominance of Cēkkiḻār's narrative over the poetry. Her story is simple and portrays the ardent devotion to Śiva that many followers feel; her poetry is more austere and macabre than the hymns of the later *Tēvāram* poets, which are more popular and integral to Tamil Śaivism than Ammaiyār's poetry.[46]

In the Tiruvālaṅkāṭu festival, Kāraikkāl Ammaiyār's poetry and life story come together in an orthodox temple ritual set in a landscape full of ancient traditions and supernatural beings. Ammaiyār's *pēy* form resonates with powerful local female beings like Nīli, whose story connects the modern villages of Tiruvālaṅkāṭu and Paḻaiyaṉūr with the area's ancient roots. But Ammaiyār's *pēy* form gives her access to Śiva's grace, an experience she expresses in her poetry to delineate the powerful devotional path she embodies, bridging the Caṅkam world with the budding devotional movement that would spread throughout the subcontinent. This fascinating festival and the motivation and devotion it took to bring it about reveals a core of dedicated Śiva devotees who were, and are, familiar with Kāraikkāl Ammaiyār's devotional poems. It also reveals the continued power and vitality of the Tamil Śaiva tradition that Kāraikkāl Ammaiyār helped set in motion.

5

The Poems

Aṟputat Tiruvantāti

1.
Ever since I was born in this world, and learned to speak,
with overwhelming love I have always remained at
Your beautiful feet.
O God of the gods, whose blue-suffused throat
shines incandescently,
when will You take away my sorrows?[1]

2.
Even though He does not remove our afflictions;
even though He does not pity us;
even though He does not guide us to the path we should follow;
for Him—our God in the form of flame,
dancing in the fire, garlanded with bones—
the love in my heart
will never cease.[2]

3.
For all seven births we will be only His servants.
We will always love only Him—
the One who wears the crescent moon in His thick, matted hair.
We will never be slaves for anyone except Him.[3]

4.
O God who has already taken us as Yours,
we have become Your slaves.
So, if we plead with You to understand our troubles,

why don't You listen?
Is it because You have a tall red body,
but a sacred throat of another color?

5.
Only God creates all beings.
Only God destroys this world.
And if great misery befalls us,
only God removes it,
when we cry out "O Father!"[4]

6.
Let those who say He lives in the sky say that.
Let others who say the King of the gods lives in this world
say that.
With spiritual wisdom I say
that the One with the radiant throat previously darkened
by poison
lives in my heart.

7.
I have done enough *tapas*.
My heart is a good heart.
I decided to eradicate all my births.
I have become a servant to the
God who wears an elephant skin,
has a third eye in His forehead,
and is smeared with sacred ash.[5]

8.
That day I became a slave to the One who has taken me as His.
On that day I became precious.
The One who supports the pure river Gaṅgā,
who is like a golden mountain,
who holds fire and a skull in His hands—
His grace is like that.[6]

9.
It is grace that controls the whole world.
If God's grace can eradicate births,
then I am destined to see the truth only through that grace.
At all times, all things are mine.

10.
I have always kept the Lord,
the God who is sweet to me
as a precious treasure in my heart.
I took Him.

11.
I thought of only One.
I was focused on only One.
I kept only One inside my heart.
Look at this One!
It is He who has Gaṅgā on His head,
a moonbeam in His hair,
a radiant flame in His beautiful hand.
I have become His slave.

12.
That is the way He has become my Lord.
That is the way He has taken me as His slave.
If we come to know Him further, we realize
that is the nature of the One
who wears a flower garland,
who is afraid of the cold waters of Gaṅgā,
and who has a single eye in His bright forehead.

13.
If You are sensible,
You will see the danger of
the snake lying like a garland on Your chest.
That big, ferocious snake that crawls on You
may one day reach Umā.
If that happens, it is Your sin.[7]

14.
The mind is unique by nature.
In order to elevate itself, and to receive the highest refuge,
it meditates solely on the One with the long snakes that spit
hot, fiery poison,
the One who has taken a body as an ornament,
and looks glorious.[8]

15.
Even though the gods, meditating on Him, adorn His feet with the best flowers,
they will not reach His feet.
I also meditate on Him.
Now what will the One with the radiant, red matted hair, who knows the Vedas,
do to me, who worships Him?[9]

16.
Now we have been elevated;
we have reached God's feet.
Now we do not have any troubles.
O my heart!
You will see that we have now crossed over the turbulent sea of inescapable births
that causes an ocean of karma.[10]

17.
Hara stands as the first principle of the ancient universe.
He has the nature of One who might not appear to those who look for Him.
To those who see, worshipping with love and folded hands, He appears.
To those who see, He appears as a light in their minds.

18.
Today I am not able to understand the nature of Him, my Lord, the One who crushed Rāvaṇa so that his power was destroyed with just one toe.
Should I call him Hara?
Should I call him Brahmā?
Should I call him Hari, the beautiful Supreme Being?[11]

19.
Today the knowledge has come easily to us,
so that we see Him:
The One who became immeasurable that day to Viṣṇu and Brahmā,
the One who wears the crescent moon,
the One who is the three-times-seven worlds.[12]

20.
He is the One who knows.
He is the One who makes us know.
He is the knowledge that knows.
He is the truth that is to be known.
He is the moon, sun, earth, sky, and all the other elements.[13]

21.
He is the sun, moon, fire, and space;
He has become earth, water, air.
He is the One who is the soul,
and who has taken eight forms.
He has come and revealed Himself as knowledge.

22.
You are our Lord;
You have come with a throat as dark as a rain cloud.
Realize the intention of that snake with teeth as sharp as a sword
to grab the crescent moon on the top of Your head,
and watch out!

23.
Even if the God adorned with the crescent moon, Gaṅgā, and the snake with fiery poison
does not show us compassion,
I will live saying over and over, that
I have always been a slave to our Lord with the dark throat.
This is my loving mind.

24.
This is the sacred form of the Lord;
this is my refuge.
You appeared as a flash of light, and disappeared.
It keeps on whirling in my mind.

25.
Our Lord, without considering anything,
wanders to all places, begging for alms everywhere,
and dances in the cremation ground in the middle of the night.
When we see Him, we will find out why.
What's the point of asking here?[14]

26.
The curls of His matted locks hang down,
shining like a golden mountain.
On the golden chest of the One with the throat like darkness,
a snake hangs closely around Him,
glittering near His garland of bones.

27.
For many days we have worshipped, praised, and
pleaded with You:
O You who shot down with one arrow
the three walls of Your enemies to destroy their power,
do not adorn Your body with a snake with such relish,
put on a gold necklace instead![15]

28.
Wearing one snake as an ornament,
wearing one comfortably as a shiny belt on Your tiger skin,
and wearing a poisonous snake on Your golden hair—
what effect will all this have on me,
who is so innocent?[16]

29.
All those other people who do not understand that
He is the real truth,
have seen only His *pēy* form:
His lotus-like body smeared with ash and garlanded with bones.
You see that they ridicule Him!

30.
His greatness is such that it is not known by others.
But others know He is the great consciousness.
Our Lord, wearing the bones of others,
happily dances along with the powerful ghouls
in the fire at night.[17]

31.
O ignorant heart, you have attained a great refuge—rejoice!
Shine among humans!
Nurture still more the great love that comes from being the slave
to the One who wanders,
wearing the bones of all, without contempt.

32.
If you analyze the sacred thread which is on the chest of
the Primordial One who burned the three cities that day,
the One who has an eye in His immortal forehead:
It is like one ray of the young crescent moon
that is on His brightly shining, red matted hair
has come sliding down.

33.
Those who speak about bookish knowledge,
who do not have real knowledge of the truth,
let them wander.
The nature of the One whose throat is like a blue jewel
is beyond limits.
To those who practice any kind of austerities,
who imagine Him in any form,
He will appear in that form.[18]

34.
The strong karmas that do not consider the result
will destroy those who do not go close to God—
the One who burned with one arrow the three aerial cities of those who did not praise Him
and become His servants.[19]

35.
Afraid that the white moon would kill it,
the dark band of the beautiful gem-like throat
of the One who shakes the snake with the hood, beautiful throat, and gaping mouth
went into the darkness and made its abode there.

36.
Will the crescent moon grow?
It suffers, calling "Ah! Ah!"
and wanes.
It is afraid that the snake on the long, matted hair of
the One with the dark-banded throat
having reached it, will run over it, and kill it.

37.
If, with wisdom,
and without ridiculing His body that is garlanded with bones,

they praise the One who wears a moon on His long matted hair,
and who conquered the three great cities of the powerful *asuras*
who did not respect Him,
they will not be born here in this world in a body with bones.

38.
The sharp tusk of the black boar
shining with luster on the chest of the One adorned with a snake as a garland,
looks like the moon that rose in the bright sky
and shrank when it was bitten by a bright snake.

39.
The beautiful, red coral body of the Beautiful One
who has taken the tender, shoot-like Umā as one side of Himself,
looks at first like the gem-like, red-gold mountain;
then, if He smears Himself with ash,
He again looks like the crystalline, silvery mountain.[20]

40.
Ignorant mind,
worship the feet of the devotees, again and again,
focusing on them, and praising them with words.
Leave that group of people who do not think about
the One who wears a moon as a small garland,
which no one else wears.[21]

41.
If one says that
one side is Māl who has measured the world,
and the other side is Umā,
in neither side do we find Your aspect.
If we look carefully at You,
is your form Māl?
Or is your form Umā?[22]

42.
What is the nature of this tender young moon?
Did it shrink because the snake came near to grab it,
or did You put it on after You chipped it to the size You wanted?
Hereafter, will such a prosperous child not grow?

43.
We pleaded with Him,
"Our Lord, having adorned Yourself with the moon,
in order to get paltry alms,
don't wander around the place."
If the celestials that shine with great luster do not stop You,
will we be able to prevent You?
He knows everything by Himself.[23]

44.
A generous person is sweet to think about.
You are Gaṅgā's husband,
a great person with a red body,
Lord of the gods.
I have taken refuge in You and live as Your servant.
Why have You not bestowed Your grace on me?

45.
To those who follow the great path of focusing on Him, the Lord,
desiring the Lord's great grace,
and who ask, "Where has He, the Lord, gone?"
He is very easy to see:
He is even here, in the mind of
people like me.

46.
Oh! You pitiable people
who are without wisdom.
It is an easy way to live,
thinking of our Lord all the time,
our Father with the gleaming throat,
who wanders around,
wearing a snake.

47.
The fortune of attaining the beautiful feet of
the One who has given one side of Himself to
Umā, whose bright eyes are like two halves of tender mango,
can only come about by your own efforts,
O ignorant mind.
Is there any other way to obtain Him,
ignorant person?[24]

48.
Looking first at the well-developed boar's tusk on
His beautiful chest,
then looking at the Lord's crescent moon—
until today this stupid snake has not decided for sure
which is the real moon!

49.
The dense rays of the crescent moon which
seems to have been filed into a smooth curve
spread everywhere,
suffusing the matted hair of the
One who can only be compared to Himself,
as if gold and silver strands have been twisted together.

50.
The blue curls of the woman of Himavān's lineage
who is one side of the One who keeps the
beautiful moon on the right side of His matted hair,
look like the fruits put out by the *koṉṟai* flowers that
He wears in His matted hair
have come over to hang there.[25]

51.
Keeping Umā, with curls on the nape of her neck and
beautiful bangles,
gracefully on Your side,
don't go there to dance in the flaming fires with the ghouls
in the big cremation ground in the middle of the night so that
Your hero's anklets jingle loudly.[26]

52.
The crown of flowers worn on the red matted hair of the
One who has red-eyed Tirumāl on one side,
looks like the full moon which rose in the broad, red sky,
its rays spreading beautifully everywhere.[27]

53.
For those who look,
the golden matted hair of our Lord
who has tied a snake around His head,

with its crown of beautiful, flourishing *konrai* flowers
and the Gaṅgā river, flowing abundantly from heaven,
looks like the rainy season.

54.
In ancient times,
our Lord, with an eye on Your forehead and a throat like
a dark cloud,
where did You hide yourself so that
the One who wanders with You as one form,
whose body looks as if it is made of black, water-laden clouds,
who is half of You,
could not see You?[28]

55.
In ancient times, when You drank the poison in the ocean
so that the gods were scared,
not only did Your throat become dark,
but in the white moon which is on the red matted hair of the One
who wears snakes,
there is also a scar that appears like a black gem.

56.
You, the One who wears the moon on Your head,
we have heard the gossip about
the food dropped in the skull You carry, to which flesh sticks.
If You do not consider it a sin,
You, the One with the hue of burnt, white ash,
You tell me.[29]

57.
Even if You beg for alms all over the world,
leave Your bad snake behind and go!
Good women will not come and give You alms
since they will be afraid of the venomous snake on Your head
that sways all the time with its hood spread.

58.
The flower-like curls of Umā who is one half of His golden form
and the red matted hair of the One with a crimson-hued body
look as if a roaring fire and the inky darkness are united.

59.
O You with an eye in Your forehead and a dark throat,
mounted on a bull,
which of Your forms wears the holy ashes?
The form that has Umā?
Or the form that has Māl?
I do not understand Your nature.
You please enlighten me Yourself.

60.
That day when our Lord wrapped His holy body with the
black skin of the intoxicated elephant with the erratic trunk,
it looked like majestic clouds had come together and
covered the radiance of the golden mountain.[30]

61.
On that day I became Your servant without seeing
Your divine form.
Even today I have not seen Your sacred form.
To those who ask,
"What is your Lord's permanent form?"
What can I tell them?
What is Your form?[31]

62.
With what can His form be compared?
With what can His form not be compared?
What will He be? What will He not be?
What can You be compared with? Who knows these things?
In the past He took the form of a strong hunter,
on that day when he fought with Arjuna,
as a hunter with a bow.[32]

63.
On top of Your head is the crescent moon.
In the daytime is it shining, spreading for a long time
because it is competing with the beautiful sun?
You who are beyond words,
You who are like a flame,
tell me!

64.
Like the one roaming around looking for the
white moon that is shining with brilliant rays,
like the wind Your snake also enters Your divine matted hair,
which is like the red sky with the moon in it.[33]

65.
His body glows like the bright morning,
the white ash on His body gleams like the midday sun,
His matted hair looks like the hue evening has taken;
moreover, His throat is like the pitch-black darkness.

66.
You who have poison in Your throat,
is this snake dancing on Your chest with its hood spread
because it got poison in its throat from licking Your throat?
Or because it turned black in color
like the inky darkness inside your throat?

67.
Since He who has an eye in His forehead
and a golden form with brilliant rays
has brought together the snake, the moon, the gentle deer,
and the ferocious tiger,
and since He has Gaṅgā flowing in His hair,
He deserves the hero's anklets
on His beautiful, sacred feet.

68.
In order to avoid the sulkiness of Umā who wears anklets,
He who wears the crescent moon has
smeared the red lac which is on Umā's feet on His hair,
which has made His appearance even more lustrous than
the red sky.

69.
Having taken on our head the benevolent feet of
the Three-Eyed Lord with the curved moon in His hair,
we rejoice that we are capable of being His slaves and
we serve Him here on earth.
We will not pay attention to Yama;
will there be suffering for us anymore?[34]

70.
This is our great desire which will never go away:
Our Lord, one day will You show us
the place where You jump into the leaping flames and dance
in the middle of the night?

71.
If you put the moon which rises in the sky
on the left side of modest Umā,
then we will not see any part of the daughter of Himavān,
who has the left side of You.
O Three-Eyed One,
You look into the matter![35]

72.
O You who wears a piece of the moon that rules the sky,
You who are very dear to all the beings in the seven worlds,
if I cannot serve You by seeing You,
and worshipping You by saying "Our Father,"
even if I get the whole world,
I do not want it.
This is my opinion.[36]

73.
You, my mind,
I told you firmly that
whatever you have thought,
you can achieve it immediately.
My mind, with great love
always praise the lotus feet of
the One who supports the flooding water with swelling waves.

74.
They took water from many big wave-filled oceans to cook the food,
but they say it was not filled.
So how is it Your broad begging bowl that is a skull
was filled with the alms given
by innocent women who do not want anything in return?[37]

75.
If you look at the One who has matted hair that
spreads everywhere,

because of the movement of snakes,
and because of the flowing of Gaṅgā's turbulent waters,
and because of the movement of the shining moon on the tall crown of the Benevolent One,
He looks like the sky.[38]

76.
The beautiful, lotus-like feet of my poor Father
are bruised and scarred all over
by the rubbing of the gleaming, gold, gem-encrusted crowns
of those destined to live in the sky,
and who bow down to Him.

77.
Śiva!
If you lift Your feet,
the regions of hell will shift.
If You move Your hair,
the roof of the world will shatter.
If You move Your hand with bracelets bouncing up and down,
the eight directions will be dislocated.
The stage cannot bear this.
So consider all these things,
then perform Your dance.[39]

78.
O poor mind,
if He who dances in the cremation ground which demons use as a stage
pities all those souls who do not make any effort,
what will He not do for those who ask for pity,
and worship Him always?
What world will He not give?

79.
Bowing to the One with matted hair,
adorning His feet with flowers,
resolving to praise the One who is adorned,
and always being a slave to Our Father—
is the pride in the mind of such a person because of all these things?[40]

80.
This is your foot that
pressed Rāvaṇa,
who through arrogance lifted the mountain on his
twenty strong shoulders,
and made Māl who always has Lakṣmi with him, and
Brahmā, lament,
because they had not seen it.
But then later they rejoiced, and worshiped it.
And Your foot conquered Yama,
then kicked him.[41]

81.
By becoming dependent on and taking refuge in the
lotus feet of
the One who shot the arrow of hot fire to burn and destroy the
ones with the beautiful fortress,
we have conquered even Yama,
overcome the worst hell,
and eradicated the two karmas we have accumulated so far.[42]

82.
If you consider the One who has the complexion of the red rays of
the setting sun
and of a smoldering fire,
and whose matted hair hangs down,
you would say that to those who have surrendered to Him,
He shines like a golden flame;
but to those who move away from Him without taking
refuge in Him,
He has the nature of blazing tongues of fire.[43]

83.
If you ask,
If the One with matted hair who is like lightning comes together
with Māl,
how will He look to people like me?
Then I would say,
He who is the Incomparable One
is like a golden mountain and a blue-jeweled mountain standing
tall together.

84.
Even though you have seen the three walls of the terrible enemies
being destroyed in the raging fire,
the fire that leaps high up,
the cool moon,
and the visibly intense, scorching rays of the sun,
are all three Śiva's eyes.[44]

85.
If I get the opportunity to see the Lord,
I will rejoice always
by calling the One who lives in the sky, and who dances in the fire,
by thinking about Him to my heart's content,
by worshipping Him to my heart's content,
by looking at Him to my heart's content.

86.
The One who has kept another eye on His forehead,
has made me understand a little of Him.
I am one of the *pēys* among His good *gaṇas*.
Whether or not this grace lasts,
I don't want anything else.[45]

87.
Putting flower garlands on the golden feet of Our Lord
and adorning Him with praises,
if, with love, we hold to that real Truth,
the darkness which is the scorching karmas—
how, with what means, will it torment us?

88.
You who gives us grace in abundance and
who has a white moon which shines brightly on
Your red matted hair,
can I say that the luster of Your throat is like darkness,
or can I say it is like a huge dark cloud,
or can I say it is like a flawless blue jewel?

89.
O You who looked at the powerful Mataṉ with a bright bow
and burnt him to white powder,

then went back to Your meditation with a clear mind.
When the mouth that drank the strong poison looks the same,
how come only Your throat became black?
Explain this to me![46]

90.
If the watchful snake with the sharp teeth crawls,
hissing menacingly,
and pulls down the moon,
if the roaring, rushing waves of Gaṅgā
destroy Your cool, matted hair
and swell and overflow,
My Lord, You tell me,
what will You do?

91.
Look!
Having become a slave to the beautiful feet of the
One whose red matted hair has the waves of Gaṅgā,
we have realized Him through scriptures;
we have become suitable for this life and for the other world.
Why do others gossip about us behind our backs?
Understand us.[47]

92.
He is the One who possesses me.
He stands as the One.
He does not need to know Himself.
His pure matted hair looks like coils made of gold.
He is the place where the gods get their grace.[48]

93.
You see! He is the Lord of the gods.
He has a complexion like beautiful red coral.
He is the dark-throated One.
Therefore, good heart,
be devoted to Him with true love.

94.
You who have a bull like a beautiful cloud,
is it because of desire that You will not part from
the Daughter of the Mountain?
Or is it because You do not have any other place to go?

Or is She scared of living away from You in a different place?
You tell me.

95.
Umā belongs to a good lineage, so She will not leave Your side.
Flowing Gaṅgā is of the same nature.
You who adorn Yourself with white sacred ash and bone,
You also won't leave them.
Between these two here, please say
who enjoys Your love?[49]

96.
We have covered Hara with the mantle of love.
Because of a special relationship with Him,
we have filled our hearts completely with Him.
We have hidden Him by deception.
So who is able to see Him?[50]

97.
That blazing fire with red flames that you caused to burn fiercely everywhere,
and that entered the three worlds and engulfed them—
have You kept it hidden in the seven worlds,
or with force,
have You kept it in Your hand?[51]

98.
Has Your beautiful hand become red because of the fire dancing in Your hand?
Or because of the beauty of Your beautiful hand, did the fire become red?
You who perform an awesome dance in the forest where ghouls dance,
Your hero's anklets shaking, holding fire in Your hand,
You tell me this![52]

99.
You who possess a five-headed cobra spitting fiery poison from its gaping mouths,
the dance that You perform,
is it for the One with young, tender breasts shaped like a round pot to see?
Or is it for the troupe of ghouls in the burning cremation ground to see?
You tell me once.

100.
If it walks, the earth trembles.
If it looks, all the directions are burnt.
If it roars, the whole world is afraid.
Is it a lion fighting the mountain, or is it a bull?
Is it Your bull which sounds like thunder?
You who look like gold,
tell me for certain.

101.
Those who say the words of this garland of *antāti veṇpā* verses
uttered by Kāraikkāl Pēy, melting with love,
and worship with everlasting devotion
will reach the Lord and praise Him with unceasing love.[53]

Tiruviraṭṭai Maṇimālai

1.
When great misery arises and makes you suffer,
your mind is afraid.
Avoid sitting here in despair.
Unceasingly worship the Lord,
who has on His head the swelling, overflowing Gaṅgā,
the young, white, curved crescent moon in the sky,
and *erukku* flowers.[54]

2.
Thinking that without Him, the Lord, there is nothing,
feeling timid, having Him in their heart—
the Lord will protect those who live without forgetting Him,
who praise Him,
by keeping them from birth in this world.

3.
That Brahman who has long, red-gold matted hair
with a dense cluster of *koṉṟai* flowers probed by a swarm of quarreling bees
and a snake with a pouch of venom in his mouth that suddenly comes out hissing—
know Him as the Lord,
who will not tolerate the distress of

those who worship Him for many days,
praising Him by saying "You are my Lord."

4.
Those who become the slaves of that Brahman,
saying, "We take refuge in You,"
do not drown in the sea of births.
He is the Powerful One who is capable of coming close to them,
protecting, bestowing grace.
If He sees a lump of gold, He will not put it on,
but instead puts on a poisonous snake.
What do you think of Him now, my heart?

5.
O our Śaṅkaraṉ,
with a bow in your hand, shooting one incomparable arrow,
You burnt the three cities of your enemies that day
so that they were engulfed by cruel fire.
Now if the Daughter of the Mountain who speaks sweet words
and who is half of Your body
sees the One called Gangā in your tall, matted hair,
what will You do?[55]

6.
O heart, without ceasing, always praise Śaṅkaraṉ,
the Meritorious One who has matted hair hanging down,
who rejoices at having a hissing snake on His head,
and who will protect us from drowning that day when we cry
"Ah! Ah!" in distress.

7.
O Brahman who wears on Your head
Gaṅgā whose crashing waves come flooding down and
spread everywhere,
honey-laden *koṉṟai* flowers,
and *vaṉṉi* flowers that suffuse Your red matted hair with fragrance,
if you ask me, there is one thing to tell You:
Do not ever touch the hissing snake
that is above the moon in the red sky.[56]

8.
In order to test this Brahman,
who is the meaning of the Vedas,

the foundation of the Vedas,
and who has the auspicious day of Ātirai—
having taken the form of a strong boar and entered the earth,
even Tirumāl said from below,
"Ah! I am not able to know Him."[57]

9.
You who say you want to go into the happiness of liberation without falling,
having crossed the flooding sea of base miseries:
Without getting tired, pleading,
with humility, with focused concentration,
always worship the Hero who saw that the cities of the enemies were destroyed,
the One with eight shoulders,
and with pure gold hero's anklets.

10.
Having achieved the five supreme things,
bowing down,
those who have realized He is the supreme Sovereign of the whole world,
the One with the throat darkened by drinking poison
and who has the auspicious day of Ātirai,
will see His red-gold hero's anklets.[58]

11.
If the karmas will not endure when they see
the shadow of those who have seen and worship with desire
the red feet that wear the hero's anklets,
when they see us worshiping with pure flowers in our hands
our Lord who is without compare,
whose body glows red like the embers of a fire,
will the old karmas that come and afflict us endure?

12.
Before the old karmas come and surround you,
without delay, quickly,
worship the One who has gentle-natured Umā on one side,
who got angry over Yama,
who shines brightly, smeared with holy ash.
My heart, think of Him.

13.
My heart!
Give up your bondage, your wife and children.
Saying that you take refuge here at His feet,
think of Him and worship
the Lord of the Immortals,
and of the universe;
my Father,
who is like the red flame of an unextinguished fire,
whose matted hair is not wet, even though a river enters it;
the One who belongs to me.[59]

14.
That day, why did You destroy with Your foot
Rāvaṇa's twenty shoulders and his heads?
On Your matted hair Gaṅgā flows;
You dance in the fire that always burns;
You smear Yourself with ash from those flames;
You dance in the fire of ghee.[60]

15.
The *pēy* with a big, wrinkled mouth sings
on this big cremation ground You take as Your stage;
You make the *bhūtas* come to worship You.
O Meritorious One with the tightly worn hero's anklets,
lifting Your leg, You perform the dance.
Have You discharged arrows with Your bow
in order to burn the three big walls of the *rākṣasas* with fire?[61]

16.
Not following a false path ruled by the five senses,
we have achieved merits;
because of the love of the slaves for the Lord,
the One who wears the flayed skin of a strong elephant,
being pleased,
He covers His three forms.[62]

17.
How do I reach Him through love?
Not only does that snake that sways on Him
not allow anyone to come close to Him,
He wears a string of skulls that make noise,

and a garland of white bones,
and, rejoicing, He mounts a bull.

18.
My Lord has bright, matted hair where
Gaṅgā flows in Her full form,
and He swallowed the poison
that was emitted by another snake in the vast sea
which was once surrounded by the Immortals.
For Him, there is no other bull to mount.[63]

19.
If we, who always perform sweet service to Him,
one day ask Him for one thing,
will He bestow it on us?
For Umā who has a red mouth like a *toṇṭai* fruit,
He searched for another one like
that young white bull which has no equal and which supports Him.
Since He did not find one,
This Supreme Being keeps Her with Him.[64]

20.
When you who live prosperously die,
before the relatives pile up the dead wood to burn you—
listen in the depth of your heart to the fame of the
Noble One who ate the poison in the huge sea
and who dances in the fire of ghee,
and be exalted.[65]

Tiruvālaṅkāṭṭu Mūtta Tiruppatikam[66]

Patikam 1; paṇ or musical scale: Naṭṭapāṭai

1.
A female ghoul with withered breasts, bulging veins,
hollow eyes, white teeth, shriveled stomach,
red hair, two fangs,
bony ankles, and elongated shins,
stays in this cemetery, howling angrily.
This place where my Lord dances in the fire with a cool body,

His streaming hair flying in the eight directions,
is Tiruvālaṅkāṭu.[67]

2.
Lifting her leg between the two arms of a cactus,
she pulls out the charred piece of firewood, extinguishes it,
grinds it into collyrium,
and paints her eyes conspicuously,
shrieking with laughter.
Seeing an animal, she gets frightened, jumps onto the
burning corpse in the cremation ground,
and is burned.
She gets very angry, and gathers dust to extinguish the fire.
This place where our Lord dances is Tiruvālaṅkāṭu.

3.
The seeds in the white dried pods of the spreading *vākai* tree rattle,
there, in the middle of the night of bewildering darkness,
the rock horned owl and *āṇṭalai* bird screech,
the owl jumps on top of a branch and flaps its wings.
Inside the cemetery, in the shadow of a row of cactus on which the
iṇṭu creeper twines,
the funeral pyre is lit.
This place where our Lord dances in the fire with a cool body is
Tiruvālaṅkāṭu.[68]

4.
A small fox takes rice from the sacrificial pit and eats it.
The demons run, clapping their hands, angrily saying,
"We didn't see it first!"
There in that burning ground used as a stage,
He forms a circle, taking the *uḷāḷam* posture;
He swiftly lifts His leg so that it touches the sky.
This place where our Lord stands erect and dances is
Tiruvālaṅkāṭu.

5.
The *picācu*, wearing a white skull garland tied tightly,
swallowed up the congealed fat.
Having named her child Kālī,
bringing her up with comfort,
she wiped the dust off the child, suckled it, then went away.

The child, not seeing the mother returning, cried itself to sleep.
The place where our Lord dances in the cemetery is Tiruvālaṅkāṭu.[69]

6.
The *pēy* with dry, cloven feet and long nails
gives birth to its young,
along with the eagle, the rock horned owl, the partridge and the owl who lay their eggs.
The owl, demons, and small fox go to the terrifying
cremation ground where they dance,
running so fast their legs kick up in back.
They turn over the corpse that has been left in the cemetery.
There, the place where our Lord dances so that all eight directions reverberate,
is Tiruvālaṅkāṭu.[70]

7.
Demons with flaming mouths and rolling, fiery eyes,
going around, doing the *tuṇaṅkai* dance, running and dancing in the terrifying forest,
draw out a burning corpse from the fire and eat the flesh.
The place where our Lord raises His leg
with the hero's *kaḻal* jangling
and the anklets tinkling,
dancing so that the fire in His hand spreads everywhere and His hair whips around,
is Tiruvālaṅkāṭu.[71]

8.
He went around to countries and cities, following a good path, showing kindness to others.
Now, his shrouded corpse is brought to the cemetery and placed next to an old corpse.
The moment it is put there,
the troupe of ghouls comes together and surrounds the corpse.
The place where He who has a snake which sways with open hood and who has fire in His hand,
dances so that the forest, sea, mountain, earth, and heaven vibrate,
is Tiruvālaṅkāṭu.

9.
The second, third, sixth, seventh, fourth, fifth and first notes are sung melodiously.

The small kettledrum, the conch, the two-sided drum, kettledrum, and *muracu* drum,
along with the cymbals and *vīṇai*,
the *mattaḷam, karaṭikai* and *vaṉakai* drum with soft skin, the *uṭukkai*, the loud drum, and
the one-eyed drum, all play.
The place where our Lord dances, accompanied by all these instruments
is Tiruvālaṅkāṭu.[72]

10.
The person who has died, with muddled intellect and cloudy knowledge,
is put in the cremation ground at the crossroad.
The eligible person performs the rites, then ignites the red fire that makes light.
As always, the gods sound the drums.
The place where our Lord performs the great dance at twilight,
so that His anklets jangle and the directions vibrate,
is Tiruvālaṅkāṭu.

11.
Strong ghouls without face paint come together,
beating each other, shouting with joy, and
spread out in a circle.
A partridge dances; next to it a jackal plays the lute.
Those who are able to recite the ten verses in classical Tamil
by Kāraikkāl Pēy with uncombed hair,
on the feet of the Lord
who is in the auspicious Tiruvālaṅkāṭu,
will attain the bliss of reaching Śiva.[73]

Patikam 2; paṇ: Intaḷam

1.
The *eṭṭi* and *ilavam* trees, and the *īkai, cūrai,* and *kārai* shrubs, are spread all over.
The burning cremation ground is covered with cactus.
The demon with wide-open eyes like a *paṟai* drum,
seizes the dangling intestines of the dead bodies strewn all over the cremation ground.

The ghoul plays the *muḻavam* drum and sings.
The Beautiful Lord dances there.[74]

2.
The fat melts, wetting the ground.
The demons with sunken eyes and long teeth,
dancing the *tuṇaṅkai* dance, look all around.
The troupe of ghouls comes together, extinguishes the funeral fires everywhere, and
joyously feasts on the corpses.
In the terrifying cemetery, the Beautiful Lord dances holding fire in His hand.[75]

3.
The jackal grabs the skull with flesh that has been punctured by birds.
The owl flaps its wings and hoots.
Next to it a small *kūkai* owl stares menacingly, and
the *ūman* owl frightens the others.
An old jackal howls, tearing pieces everywhere.
This is the big cremation ground where God moves around, dancing all the time.

4.
A *pēy*, not knowing whether the corpse is dead, goes close and touches it with a finger.
Shouting and roaring, it flings the fire away.
Jumping over the body, it runs away,
and quivering with fear, hits its hollow stomach,
making many demons run away.
Taking the form of a Madman, in this place my Lord will dance.

5.
The thorn bush burns; the wood on the pyre gets charred.
The corpse's brain leaks out in clumps.
The cactus shrivels up; the wood-apple tree is abundant.
In this very hot cremation ground,
wearing the skin of a spotted antelope, and with a tiger skin on His shoulders,
considering this cremation ground also as His resting place,
the Lord dances.

6.
The small, beautiful rock horned owl with a bright, curved, white beak,
swallows the brain, head, and corpse, and
screeches in the old cremation ground.
Having fiery eyes, glowing mouths, and hair like the leaves of the *tāḷi* palm
the demons and the ghouls sing to the sound of the flute.
The Beautiful Lord dances.[76]

7.
In the dessicated cremation ground,
the little *pēy* gropes, but finds no food to eat.
It sits there awhile thinking, then goes to sleep.
In the cemetery where the small demons suffer,
when, as always, the gods sound the *muḻavin* drum,
at twilight, the Beautiful Lord dances with fire in His hand,
without missing a beat.

8.
In the cremation ground where you hear crackling noises
and the white pearls fall out of the tall bamboo,
the demons with frizzy hair and drooping bodies shout with wide-open mouths,
and come together and feast on the corpses.
In the big, threatening cremation ground,
when Māyaṉ dances, the Daughter of the Mountain watches Him,
in astonishment.[77]

9.
In the big cremation ground filled with the smoke from the fires of funeral pyres
and white skulls,
surrounded by bamboo groves,
there are vultures, and demons, and monkeys jump around.
When rhythmic music plays,
when the white *tuṭi* drums and the *paṟai* drums beat,
the Great Lord who has the curved, white, teetering crescent moon and the rippling Gaṅgā
will dance.

10.
In the dark burning ground with *iṇṭu* creeper spreading everywhere
are round-bellied, short, small, tall, and mountain-like demons.
The demon with fierce teeth and fiery mouth
embraces and strokes its child, and then threatens it.
When rhythmic music plays,
the One Without Blemish
who has shining, dense, matted hair hanging down,
will dance.[78]

11.
For those who dance and sing these ten verses by Kāraikkāl Pēy
who has sharp teeth and a fiery mouth,
by the abundant grace of the Lord who wears a swaying snake around His waist,
and who wears the moon on His matted hair,
and rotates in His divine dance—
their sins will be destroyed.

Notes

Notes to Introduction

1. No single English word captures the meanings and evocations of the Tamil word *pēy*. "Demon" conveys the supernatural aspect, but often also means "evil" which is not always applicable to the Tamil milieu. "Ghoul" captures the sense of the macabre and often connotes a being who haunts graveyards, but is also more limited than *pēy*. I consistently employ the untranslated Tamil word, but also substitute various English words to try and convey the range of meanings.

2. On the back cover of one of the Tiruvālaṅkāṭu temple's official history books is an upside-down picture of Mt. Kailāsa, which is the view Kāraikkāl Ammaiyār had as she walked down from Mt. Kailāsa to Tiruvālāṅkāṭu on her hands.

3. Mahalakshmi R, 37–40. See Khandelwal; her study of contemporary women renouncers reveals continuing complexities concerning gender and asceticism.

4. Karavelane, 96. See also Gros, 176.

5. Dr. Vijayalakshmy and I based our translations on the Tamil texts *Kāraikkālammaiyār Pirapantaṅkaḷ*, Commentary by Śri Ārumukattampirāṉ; *Tiruvālaṅkāṭṭu Talavaralāṟum Tiruppatikaṅkaḷum*; and *Kāraikkālammaiyār Tirumuṟai*, Commentary by Tiru. Vi. Kalyāṇacuntaraṉār. We also consulted Karavalene and Ramachandran.

Notes to Chapter 1

1. Tamil is the most ancient of the four major Dravidian languages spoken in South India. The two different types of Tamil, spoken and written, continue to characterize modern Tamil. The first detailed description of the three academies or *caṅkams* is in Nakkīrar's eighth century commentary on Iṟaiyaṉār's *Akapporuḷ*, a series of 60 short verses that forms an early classification of Tamil poetic conventions. The first *caṅkam* took place in southern Maturai (*Teṉmaturai*) with 549 members and lasted 4,440 years; the second

took place in Kapāṭapuram with 59 members and lasted 3,700 years; and the third took place in northern Maturai, considered to be the current city of Maturai, with 49 members and lasting 1,800 years. This last academy may have a historical basis of some kind. For a detailed overview of the history of Tamil literature, including problems of dating and discussions about the oral and written properties of the poetry, see Zvelebil 1975, 1–130; 1974, 2–51; 1973, 1–171. See also Hart 1975, 7–158; Hart and Heifetz 1999, xv–xxxvii, 4–6; Ramanujan 1994, 97–108; 1985, ix–xv, 269–297; Nilakanta Sastri 1975, 104–117; Pillay 1979, 185–232; Buck and Paramasivam 1997, x–xiv; Kailasapathy 1968, 1–3; Subramaniam 1992, 11–17.

The corpus of Tamil classical literature was superseded by devotional poetry beginning in the sixth to seventh century. Eventually the Caṅkam literature was "forgotten," and was rediscovered in the late nineteenth century primarily by the great Tamil scholar U. Vē. Cāminātaiyar, who edited the texts and wrote commentaries on them. The Fourth Tamil Caṅkam was established in Maturai in 1901, which published texts and a journal, *Centamiḻ*. The rediscovery of lost works of literature partly inspired the connection made in the early twentieth century between two legends: the Caṅkam legend describing the catastrophic loss of people and literature to oceanic floods, and the legend of the lost land of Lemuria, a land mass thought to have existed in the Indian Ocean. See Pillay 1979, 32–37; Sumathi Ramaswamy 2004, especially 97–136; Zvelebil 1975, 5–21; 1974, 7–8; Ramanujan 1999b; Cutler 2003a, 272–292; Parthasarathy 1993, 346–351; Selby 2000, 10.

2. Hart and Heifetz (1999, xxix–xxx) note that the *puṟam* anthology *Puṟanāṉūṟu* includes eleven *tiṇai*, six of which overlap with the *Tolkāppiyam* list. It seems that the *Puṟanāṉūṟu* poets are following a different classification system, but the poems still focus on kings and heroism. For a more detailed analysis of the *tiṇai* and characteristics of *akam* and *puṟam* poetry, see Zvelebil 1973, 85–110; Ramanujan 1985, 231–297; 1994, 97–115; 1999c; Hart 1975, 211–257; Hart and Heifetz 1999, xxviii–xxxi; Selby 2000, 26–61; Kailasapathy 1968, 1–54. There are numerous subcategories or themes subdividing each *tiṇai*; an example of an *akam tuṟai* is "the guarding of the millet" (Selby 2000, 19), and of a *puṟam tiṇai* is "the feasting and dancing of warriors after victory" (Kailasapathy 1968, 24). The main ideals and values of *Caṅkam* poetry are echoed in the *Tirukkuṟaḷ*: The first group of verses focuses on virtue; the second on economic, social, and political life; and the last on love.

3. Ramanujan 1985, 182, 286–295; Hart 1975, 13–20; Hart and Heifetz 1999, xvii–xxii; Nilakanta Sastri 1975, 120–124; Selby 2000, 56–58; Kailasapathy 1968, 265–271; Pillay 1979, 153–154. The *Tirukkuṟaḷ* affirms the necessity for women to maintain their chastity and the good name of their household, and for men to uphold their honor in the public realm; see especially sections 6, 39–79, 92, 97–100. Section 115 claims that rumors can actually push two lovers together.

4. *Puṟanāṉūṟu* 278, Hart and Heifetz 1999, 165.

5. Nilakanta Sastri 1975, 122; Hart 1975, 99–109; 1980, 116–118; Kailasapathy 1968, 235–237; Hart and Heifetz 1999, 144, *passim*; Pillay 1979, 235–236.

There seems to have been an indigenous tradition of suicide, including a rite called *vaṭakkiruttal* ("sitting [facing the] North") in which a king whose honor has been lost starves himself to death; see Hart 1975, 35–36, 88–93; Ramanujan 1985, 290–291, 294; Hart and Heifetz 1999, 50, *passim*. A woman who immolated herself upon her husband's funeral pyre became known by as a *satī*, or "virtuous wife" in Sanskrit. See Hart 1975, 35–6, 42, 92, 107; Buck and Paramasivam 1997, 15–16. Satī is a wife of the god Śiva; her father, Dakṣa, holds a sacrifice and invites all the gods except Śiva. When Satī attends the sacrifice, her father insults Śiva. In response to this insult, Satī iimmolates herself. The grieving and enraged Śiva destroys the sacrifice, mutilates the divine guests, and cuts off Dakṣa's head, replacing it with a goat's head. There are many versions of this myth; I have based this brief synopsis on Peterson 1989, 345. Hart (1975, 26) claims that "[t]he concept of divinity actually residing in the stone was transferred later to the *śivaliṅkam*, which seems to have taken over many of the functions of the naṭukal."

6. One of the bards was the Pāṇaṉ, whose name comes from the Tamil word for musical scale or mode, *paṇ*. He was a bard who sang songs and played the lute (*yāḻ*), and whose wife, called a Viṟali, sang and danced. The Pāṇaṉ seemed to hold a higher position than the other musicians as the bard to the kings, based on his close interactions with rulers; he wandered from court to court, praising victorious kings and generous patrons, spreading the fame of heroes, serving as genealogist and historian, and transmitting news and important information. He also played particular drums during battle. In addition to the bards, different groups of drummers are specified. There is the Tuṭiyaṉ, who plays the *tuṭi*, an hourglass-shaped drum, and is said to live in wilderness areas; in one poem, for instance, the Tuṭiyaṉ is drumming while the memorial stone is being worshiped. Another drummer is the Kiṇaiyaṉ, who played the *kiṇai*, another small hourglass-shaped drum. It seems that the Kiṇaiyaṉs were also called Paṟaiyaṉs, from *paṟai*, a generic word for drum.

This is a necessarily brief overview of caste and kinds of musicians in the Caṅkam period; in addition there are many more drums mentioned in the poetry. For a discussion of caste in the Caṅkam period, including bards and musicians, see Hart 1988; 1975, 138–158; Ramanujan 1985, 269–295; Kailasapathy 1968, 55–134; Nilakanta Sastri 1975, 122–125; Hart and Heifetz 1999, xxi–xxv, *passim*; Pillay 1979, 148, 199; Hardy 1983, 128–149. "Paṟaiyaṉ" is the source of the English "pariah," meaning outcaste. The Tamil word *kuṭi* means "family," "lineage," "citizens," "house," and "village," as well as caste; see the *Tamil Lexicon* 1982, vol. II, 968. Both the *tuṭi* and *kiṇai* drums are hourglass-shaped; it is unclear whether and how they are different drums, although they are distinguished by different names. The Tuṭiyaṉ drums before the memorial stone in *Akanāṉūṟu* 35.

7. For festivals, dances, and the *tuṇaṅkai* dance see Hart 1975 23–24, 45–47; Kailasapathy 1968, 98–99, 104, 179, 260–261; Nilakanta Sastri 1975, 123–124; Hardy 1983, 136. For Murukaṉ see Clothey 1978, 1–43; Hardy 1983, 131–149; Kailasapathy 1968, 61–69; Hart 1975, 22–23, 28–29, 72, 110, 119–124, 135–136, 193–195, 255; Hart and Heifetz 1999, 12, *passim*.

8. From *Puṟanāṉūṟu* 62; Hart and Heifetz 1999, 48. A section of the *Tolkāppiyam* describes the theme of a wife guarding her husband's body from the ghosts, or *pēys*; Sasivalli 1984, 61.

9. For the definition of *pēy*, see the *Tamil Lexicon*, vol. V, 2893; in addition to beings such as devils, goblins, and fiends, the word connotes wildness and frenzy. In contemporary Tamil the word continues to have associations of evil; see *Kriyāviṉ Taṟkālat Tamiḻ Akarāti*, 772–773. *Pēys* can be malignant beings who possess people and must be exorcised by specialists; see Nabokov 2000. Prentiss (1999, 38–39) discusses the orientalist pitfalls of describing South Indian culture as terrifying. I argue here that threatening forces do not define Tamil culture, but are part of particular landscapes connected to death that remain important in early devotional poetry.

10. From *Puṟanāṉūṟu* 370; Hart and Heifetz 1999, 211–212.

11. From *Puṟanāṉūṟu* 356, Ramanujan 1985, 191. See Hart and Heifetz 1999, *passim*; and Hart 1975, 69–70, 82–86, for translations and discussions of poems describing cremation grounds.

12. *Tamil Lexicon* vol. II, 855. I frequently encountered the distinction between the settled area of the village and planted land from the wild areas beyond while doing research on village goddesses in Tamilnadu; for one example, see Craddock 2001, 145. The distinction between the forest and the village in modern Tamilnadu is a large and rich topic; Mines (2005) provides a recent and extensive study of a village in southern Tamilnadu in which this distinction shapes many of the beliefs and practices.

13. Ramanujan 1985, 51–66, 263–265; 1994, 105–106; Hart 1975, 221–229; Zvelebil 1973, 97–105. See also Shulman 1985, 279–292.

14. Concerning the debate about North Indian versus Tamil cultural elements, see, for example, Nilakanta Sastri 1975, 19–20, 117–118, 309–310, 330–333; Hart 1975, 10–80; 1976; Hart and Heifetz 1999, xxxi; Thapar 1966, 75, 103–105, 167–193.

15. Nilakanta Sastri 1975, 308–312; Iyengar 1995, 463–486; Hart 1975, 51–80, 149; Pillay 1979, 39–53; Hart and Heifetz 1999, xxxi, *passim.*; Ayyar 1974, 101–109. The poems do not explicitly mention Buddhism or Jainism, but several poems seem to express the influence of these religions. According to Tamil inscriptions, Buddhism and possibly Jainism had penetrated South India as early as the fourth century BCE; Pillay 1979, 40–41; Hart 1975, 69; Ahir 1992, 115–148; Richman 1988, 157–166; Monius 2001, 3–7.

16. Hart 1975, 56–59; Pillay 1979, 46–48; Clothey 1978, 62–63; Hardy 1983, 119–238.

17. Hart 1975, 56–59; Hart and Heifetz 1999, xxxi, 7, 41–43, 65, 107, 259, 260; Ayyar 1974, 109–116. In one poem, Śiva carries an axe or mace, the instrument of Kūṟṟuvāṉ, the Tamil god of Death. Śiva also seems to be associated with Death because of his role as the Destroyer of the world; see Hart and Heifetz 1999, 42–43, 260; Hart 1975, 24. In *Puṟanāṉūṟu* 7 as translated by Hart and Heifetz, there is the line "the temple of the god with three eyes whom the Brahmins worship!" The word translated as "Brahmins" here is *muṉivar*, which also means sages or ascetics. So Śiva could be worshipped

by ascetics here. However, later in the same poem the *munivar* are said to chant the four Vedas, which suggests these sages are Brahmins, who lived apart from others in Tamil society. The word translated as "temple" is *nakar*, which can mean temple, but is an ambiguous word during this period, and can also mean town. See Hart and Heifetz 1999, 6–7, 245; *Puṟanāṉūṟu* 26–27; Hart 1975, 53; Hardy 1983, 137.

18. The date of the *Cilappatikāram* continues to be contested, as well as the author; however, it is certainly a Jain text. See Parthasarathy 1993, 1–8, 332–338; Dikshitar 1997, 8–21; Vijaya Ramaswamy 1997, 50; Zvelebil 1975, 110–115; Subramanyam 1977, vi–viii.

19. Parthasarathy 1993, 6; Zvelebil 1973, 176–177. For an extended discussion of the poetics of the epic, see Parthasarathy 1993, 279–306. The associations between Ammaiyār and Nīli, as well as with the heroine Kaṇṇaki, will be explored in Chapter 3.

20. 21.50–54; see also Parthasarathy 1993, 194.

21. For this story outline I consulted the synopsis in Parthasarathy 1993, 2–5. Pattiṉi is widely worshiped by Buddhists and Hindus in Sri Lanka today; see Obeyesekere's (1984) monumental study of this cult. The worship of Pattiṉi has almost died out in South India, or has been absorbed into the cults of other goddesses such as Kālī. Many scholars believe that the Kālī-Bhagavatī temple in Koṭuṅkoḷūr (Cranganore), Kerala, is the original temple where Kaṇṇaki/Pattiṉi was installed; it seems clear that this site was originally a Pattiṉi shrine. See Obeyesekere 1984, 535–553; Hiltebeitel 1988, 149; 1991, 366–369; Vijaya Ramaswamy 1997, 49–50. The folk ballad "The Story of Kōvalaṉ" (*Kōvalaṉ katai*) is connected to the Tiruvoṟṟiyūr Tiyākarācacuvāmi/ Tyāgarāja (Somāskanda) temple near Chennai; Kaṇṇaki is worshiped at this temple as Vaṭṭappāṟaiyammaṉ, "Goddess of the Round Stone." There are also Kaṇṇaki images in the Maturai Cellattammaṉ temple; a family temple built in 1972 in Pūmpukār; and a shrine close to Idukki, Kerala. See Parthasarathy 1993, 318–319, 366, quoting Sally Noble; Ghose 1996, 289, 355. Obeyesekere argues that Pattiṉi is primarily a Jaina-Buddhist deity rather than a Hindu deity; see 1984, 511–529. See Hiltebeitel 1991, 366–369 for a counterpoint to this argument.

The publication of *Cilappatikāram* in 1891–92 brought the epic back into the public realm; Parthasarathy 1993, 346–351. Today, "[t]he *Cilappatikāram* speaks for all Tamils as no other work of Tamil literature does"; Tamils consider the text their national epic (Ibid., 1, 344). Kaṇṇaki as the ideal, chaste wife has become a secular icon, connected to ideologies and movements that protect the Tamil language and culture. There is a statue of Kaṇṇaki along the Marina beach area in Chennai; see Pandian 1982; Sumathi Ramaswamy 1997, 73–75, 116, 129, 189.

22. Parthasarathy 1993, 305.

23. From the way that Kavunti addresses Kōvalaṉ and Kaṇṇaki, it seems that they are Jains as well, but their behavior does not make that clear; Parthasarathy 1993, 335. See also Cutler 2003, 295–301 concerning Tamil and Aryan elements in the epic.

24. For a discussion of Piṉṉai as the Tamil analogue to Radha, see Hudson 1982, 1994; Hardy 1983, 169, *passim*.

25. The sixth-century text *Devī Māhātmya* is part of the *Mārkaṇḍeya* Purāṇa, and is the first text in which the Goddess is the ultimate reality of the universe (Coburn 1996, 32). In the second episode of this text, Devī or Durgā defeats Mahiṣa, the buffalo demon. Early in the text (1.58), she is praised as "the great demoness (*mahāsurī*)." One of the earliest references to Kālī is in the third episode, where she emerges from Durgā's forehead when that goddess is enraged by the demons Śumbha and Niśumbha and their armies who come to attack her. Kālī helps Durgā and the band of Mothers defeat the demons; Coburn 1991, 60–71; Kinsley 1986, 116–118. In the *Liṅga-purāṇa* (600–1000 CE), Kālī is part of Śiva's entourage when he conquers the demons of the three cities; Kinsley 1986, 118. In Canto 12 of the *Cilappatikāram* Durgā is described with several of the attributes of Śiva, including the moon, third eye, black throat, elephant skin, and serpents; see Dorai Rangaswamy 1990, 343–345. See also Caldwell 2003, 252–258 for a concise overview of ancient South Indian goddesses.

26. The peaceful goddess Umā first appears in the *Kena Upaniṣad* of approximately 700 BCE; in the *Harivaṃśa* (ca. 450 CE) Umā is praised for practicing austerities (*tapas*) and yoga (Divakaran 1984, 271, 275). Throughout the *Mahābhārata* Śiva's spouse is called Umā or Pārvatī (Coburn 1996, 39).

27. For the definition of *aṇaṅku*, see the *Tamil Lexicon* vol. I, 61. Hart discusses *aṇaṅku* extensively; see especially 1975, 13–40, 81–137; 1973, 236 ff. See also Hart and Heifetz 1999, xv–xxi, 293, 302, 314, 330, 343; Ramanujan 1985, 287; Nilakanta Sastri 1975, 104–131; Mahalakshmi R. 2000, 28–32, and Ramaswamy1997, 48–50, 129–130. Ramaswamy is critical of Hart for attaching too much importance to *aṇaṅku* in understanding Tamil women's power. Rajam (1986) also critiques Hart's treatment of this concept. Hart has also been criticized for his over-emphasis on the power of the king, and on seeing sacred power as pervasive in the Caṅkam world; see Hardy 1983, 131, n. 48.

28. Ramanujan 1999d, 234–235; 1985, 215–217, 226–228, 286–288; 1981, 109–115; Cutler 2003b, 147; Zvelebil 1975, 103–106; Kandiah 1984, 7–10, 27–30; *Tirumurukāṟṟuppaṭai*; Nilakanta Sastri 1963, 21–22. The six sacred hills in the *Tirumurukāṟṟuppaṭai* are Tirupparaṅkuṉṟam, Tiruccīralaivāy, Tiruvāviṉaṉkuṭi, Tiruvērakam, Kuṉṟutōṟāṭal, and Paḻamutircōlai. See Clothey 1978, 116–131 for a discussion of the six sacred hills of Murukaṉ in contemporary Tamilnadu. See Ghose 1996 for the history of the development of the Tyāgarāja/Somāskanda image and cult in Tiruvārūr.

29. Ramanujan 1999d, 235; Cutler 2003b, 147.

30. Ramanujan 1999d, 235–243, 255–259; 1985, 218–225, 286–292; 1981, 109–110; Hardy 1983, 202–217; Zvelebil 1975, 101–102.

31. Nilakanta Sastri refers to the Kalabhras as "evil rulers" who are the "enemy of civilization"; 1975, 3–5, 129–131; 394–396. Other scholars take a more nuanced stance: Stein, 1980, 72–86; Ahir 1992, 115–155; Peterson 1999, 166–167; Ramanujan 1981, 104–108; Monius 2001, 3–7; Hardy 1983, 122–123.

32. Dhavamony 1971, 13–23; Carman 2005, 856.

33. Biardeau in particular has traced the development of bhakti from Vedism; 1995, especially 25–40, 84–121; Dhavamony 1971, 47–67. Prentiss (1999, 13–41) includes an analysis of Biardeau's work in her detailed and thorough overview of bhakti scholarship. For the *Upaniṣads* see Olivelle 1996, 231–247; 252–265; Sharma 1987, 206–208.

34. Biardeau 1995, 84–121; Prentiss 1999, 18–20; Carman 2005, 857–858.

35. VII, 18, 19; Miller 1986, 73. Dhavamony 1971, 38–42, 77–83; Sharma 1987, 109–119; Prentiss 1999, 19–20; Hardy 1983, 25–29.

36. Prentiss 1999, 20–22; Ramanujan 1984, 212–213; Carman 2005, 856–857; Hawley 1995.

37. Ramanujan remarks that it is not surprising that the first devotional poetry was written in Tamil, since it is the only Indian mother tongue that also had a literary tradition as the bhakti tradition was beginning. The literary languages of Sanskrit and the Prakrits were not spoken as a daily language; and the regional vernaculars of North India did not have literary forms until after the tenth century; Ramanujan 1981, 126–127.

38. The other nine āḻvārs are Tiruppāṇ, Tirumaḻicai, Toṇṭaraṭippoṭī, Kulacēkaraṉ, Periyāḻvār, Āṇṭāḷ, Tirumaṅkai, Nammāḻvār, and Maturakavi. In the *antāti* form, the last syllable(s) of a verse is identical with the first syllable(s) of the next verse. Zvelebil (1975, 155) dates the three early poets ca. 700 CE, substantially later than Ammaiyār but still in the early stages of the devotional movements; Cutler (1987, 124) and Hardy (169, *passim*) date the early āḻvārs in the sixth century, making them contemporaneous with Kāraikkāl Ammaiyār. Cutler (1987, 122) notes that two important hagiographical accounts of the early Vaiṣṇava poets from the twelfth to thirteenth centuries—contemporary with Cēkkiḻār's *Periya Purāṇam*—explain that Pēy got his name because his love for Viṣṇu was so complete he acted as if he were possessed by a spirit. See also the discussion in Pechilis 2008, 28–29. We will explore this idea of being possessed by the divine in Chapters 2 and 3. Zvelebil 1975, 152–155; Cutler 1987, 1–3, 122–130; Dehejia 1988, 6–32, 182–183; Ramanujan 1999d, 243–246; Hardy, *passim*.

39. Peterson (1989, 19) places Cuntarar at the end of the seventh or early eighth century; Shulman (1990, xli–xlii) places him in the first half of the ninth century.

40. Zvelebil 1975, 130–151; 1973, 185–191; Peterson 1989, 12–21; Dehejia 1988, 6–20, 129–135, 153–181; Champakalakshmi 2004, 53–66; Prentiss 1999, 143–144; Nilakanta Sastri 1963, 35–48; Ayyar 1974, 122–284; Stein 1980, 63–89; Sivaraman 2001, 30–39; Monius 2004a, 165–166; 2004b, 116–121.

Peterson (15–16) states that Nampi Āṇṭār Nampi had to recover the lost musical modes of the hymns, which along with the story of the discovery of the *Tēvāram* manuscripts suggests that there might have been a break in the oral transmission of the hymns.

On the dating of Kāraikkāl Ammaiyār, see Nilakanta Sastri 1975, 333–334; Dorai Rangaswamy, 971–973; Karavelane 1982, 96–98 (essay by François Gros). Dorai Rangaswamy and Gros discuss the possible reference to Ammaiyār in a poem by Appar, who lived in the sixth to seventh century. Appar says to Śiva, "pēyt toḻil āṭṭiyaip-peṟṟuṭaiyīr," "you who created a woman who acted as a demon/who lived performing the activities of a demon" (*Tēvāram* V, 96.4).

41. Dorai Rangaswamy 1103–1104; Zvelebil 1973, 185–193; Dehejia 1988, 15–18; Champakalakshmi 2004, 54–62.

42. Stein 1980, 63–89; Peterson 1999, 173–177; 1989, 14; Davis 2000, 12–13; 1999, 219; Filliozat 1983.

43. Ishimatsu 1999; N.d., 51–75; Davis 2000, 3–21; 1999, 219–220; Prentiss 1999, 134–152; Peterson 1989, 16–18; Zvelebil 1975, 198–207; Dhavamony 1971, 1–7, 175–334; Monius 2004, 166–167; *Tirumantiram*, Pillai 2001, 29–31, *passim*; *Thirumandiram*, Natarajan 1999, 12–14, *passim*. The four great Śaiva Siddhānta ācāryas are Meykaṇṭar, Aruṇanti, Umāpaati, and Maṟaiñāṉacampantaṉ (Zvelebil 1975, 198).

44. Davis 2000, 22–41, 83–111; 1988, 41–44; Ishimatsu forthcoming, 60–61; Dhavamony 1971, 119–121; Sivaraman 2001, 1–31; Peterson 1989, 17–18; Sharma 1987, 223–229; Navaratnam 1963, 52–90; Devasenapathi 1966, 69–310; Schomerus 2000; Monius 2004a, 177.

45. Peterson 1999, 164; Davis 1999, 220.

46. Peterson 1999, 168–177; 1989, 19–21; Davis 1999, 215.

47. Davis 1999; Peterson 1999; Orr 1999.

48. For detailed explorations of the god Rudra-Śiva in Vedic and mythic literature, see Kramrisch 1988; Chakravarti 1986; Sivaramamurti 1984; O'Flaherty 1981; 1975, 116–174; Bhandarkar 1983, 145–164; Siddhantashastree 1975, 1–48. For the *Śatarudrīya Stotram* see Sivaramamurti 1976; Long 1983; Gonda 1980; Peterson 1989, 25–27.

49. Long 1983, 126–127.

50. Kramrisch 1988; O'Flaherty 1981; 1975, 116–149, 250–282; Chakravarti 1986; Peterson 1989, 24–27.

51. Peterson 1989, 24–32; 2003, 7–20; Miller 1984; Filliozat in Karavalene, 1–9. The eight forms of Śiva are the five elements of water, fire, ether, earth, and air; the sun and moon; and the sacrificer.

52. See Zvelebil 1974, 97–98; 1975, 135–137; Dorai Rangaswamy, 972–973; Pechilis 2008, 28–29; *Kāraikkālammaiyār Tirumuṟai*.

53. My abbreviated discussion of Tamil poetics is based on Hart 1975, 197–210, and Peterson 1989, 76– 91. All of the *veṇpā* verses in *Aṟputat Tiruvantāti* and *Tiruviraṭṭai Maṇimālai* contain a hyphen at the end of the second line, after which is just one word.

54. Ramanujan 1981, xvii; also partially quoted in Peterson 1989, 89.

55. Dorai Rangaswamy 1990, 3–18; Hardy 1983, 202–213; Prentiss 1999, 51; Ayyar 1974, 211; Krishna Murthy 1985, 6–14, 42–47; Peterson 1982, 72.

56. See Srinivasan 1984; Joshi 1984; Siddhantashastree 1975, 49–69. Dhaky 1984 discusses sculptured images of *gaṇas* and *bhūtas* in temples in north and south India beginning with the Shore Temple (ca. 700 CE) in Mahāmallapura, an ancient seaport of the Pallavas in Tamilnadu.

Notes to Chapter 2

1. See Zvelebil 1973, 199–200 for this schematization of bhakti poems, using a different Kāraikkāl Ammaiyār poem to illustrate the pattern.

2. Zvelebil 1973, 197–206; Peterson 1989, 23–33; Cutler 1987, 10–29. Cutler (19–29) diagrams and discusses the communication between poet, deity, and audience.

3. Mani, 726; O'Flaherty 1975, 274–280; Dorai Rangaswamy, 262–271; Kramrisch 1988, 145–153; Peterson 1989, 344; Chakravarti, 34–35.

4. See especially Peterson 1989 23–41, 95–141.

5. The only poem in which she does not identify herself explicitly as "Kāraikkāl Pēy" is the *Tiruviraṭṭai Maṇimālai*.

6. See Peterson 1989, 2, 203; 1982, 75–76.

7. As we saw in Chapter 1, one of the three earliest āḻvārs, who wrote devotional poetry to the god Viṣṇu, was called Pēy, and another was called Pūtam, from the Sanskrit bhūta, a synonym for *pēy*.

8. See Mahalakshmi R., 23–27; Gros 176–186; and Gros's Postface in Karavelane, 96–105. Cēkkiḻār mentions the beginning of this verse in his story about Ammaiyār in his *Periya Purāṇam*, which suggests but does not say that Ammaiyār is describing herself in this verse.

9. Mahābhārata XIII, 14, 17, 50, 58, 61, 154, 156; VII, 39, 40, 80, as cited in Sivaramamurti 1994, 74–81; 1984; 1976, 19, 39; Vatsyayan; Dorai Rangaswamy 396. On the early forms see Sivaramamurti 1994, 156–214; Srinivasan; Joshi; Zvelebil 1985, 13–23, Kaimal 4.

10. See Hart and Heifetz (3, 243, 250) for Caṅkam references to *gaṇas*. For descriptions of Śiva dancing in the *Cilappatikāram* see verses 6.38–45, 20.37–38, and 28.67–77.

11. See Dorai Rangaswamy 400–404; Mahalakshmi R.; Pechilis 2008, 28; Handelman and Shulman, 214.

12. Ammaiyār refers to demonic beings—*pēys*, *gaṇas*, *bhūtas*, *picācus*—in 24 of her poems. Some of the poems contain several references to demons, including four in which Ammaiyār describes herself as a *pēy*. See also Karavelane 144; Pechilis 2008, 28 n.44.

13. See Kramrisch 1981, 439–442 especially; Narayanan, especially 500–501; Dorai Rangaswamy 378–404.

14. I am basing this section of my discussion especially on Peterson's analysis of the *Tēvāram* poets: 1989, 23–50, 95–102, and 1982, 71–80; see also Miller 1984; Handelman and Shulman, *passim*. Hardy (284) states that the first polarized, sectarian poetry was composed by Ammaiyār to Śiva and by the early āḻvārs to Viṣṇu.

15. My analysis of these two poems is based largely on the commentary by Śri Āṟumukattatampirāṉ in *Kāraikkālammaiyār Pirapantaṅkaḷ*, 13–15; personal communications from Dr. R. Vijayalakshmy; and Peterson 1989, 17–18, 44–47, 95–102. See also the *Tamil Lexicon* vol. I, 301.

16. *Tamil Lexicon* vol. III, 1218; vol. IV, 2245. Śiva as both with and without form, *cakaḷaniṭkaḷam* is represented by the *liṅga*.

17. See Davis 2000, 22–29; Ishimatsu, N.d., 58–61; Peterson, 1989, 17–18; Suriamurthy, 37–61. See also Dhavamony; Devasenapathy; and Schomerus.

18. Kāraikkāl Ammaiyār refers to serving Śiva, being "enslaved" by him in 13 stanzas of her *Aṟputat Tiruvantāti*: 3, 4, 7, 8, 11, 12, 23, 31, 44, 69, 79, 91; and in stanzas 4 and 16 of *Tiruviraṭṭai Maṇimālai*. The Tamil word "āḷ" can be a verb that means to rule, govern, cherish, maintain, or a noun that means a servant, slave, or devotee (*Tamil Lexicon* vol. I, 254). The word "aṭimai" means slavery, servitude, servant, or devotee; "aṭiyāṉ" means slave, servant, or devotee (*Tamil Lexicon* vol. I, 50–51). Ammaiyār uses various permutations of these terms.

19. In Śaiva Siddhānta philosophy Śiva performs five cosmic activities: creation (*sṛṣṭi*), preservation (*sthiti*), dissolution (*saṃhāra*), concealment (*tirobhāva*), and grace (*anugrāha*). The act of concealment, or veiling, is one way for Śiva to push devotees toward his grace. Sivaraman 127–152; Monius 2004a, 177; Peterson 1989, 99–100; Shulman 2002, 132–134.

20. See Ramanujan 1994, 105–110. For a detailed discussion of the ascetic meanings of matted hair see Olivelle 1998, especially 23–26, 31–41.

21. *Śiva Purāṇa* vol. 1, 54–57 (Vidyeśvarasaṃhitā 7); Mani, 277; Dorai Rangaswamy, 272–280; Peterson 1989, 347–348; O'Flaherty 1973, 229–233; Chakravarti, 58–59.

22. See O'Flaherty 1981, especially 210–255, for a rich discussion of Śiva as the paradoxically erotic ascetic.

23. *Tamil Lexicon* vol. IV, 2092.

24. *Śiva Purāṇa* vol. 3, 1075–1078 (Śatarudrasaṃhitā 2–3); vol. 4, 1812–1827 (Vāyavīyasaṃhitā 12–16); Kramrisch 1988, 197–207; O'Flaherty 1973, 111–112.

25. *Śiva Purāṇa* vol. 2, 525–548 (Rudrasaṃhitā, Pārvatīkhaṇḍa, 14–19); Mani, 378–379; O'Flaherty 1973, 148–151; 1975, 154–159; Kramrisch 1988, 349–363; Dorai Rangaswamy, 337–342, 417–439; Peterson 1989, 345–346. In some versions of this story Śiva is sitting under a banyan tree in the Himalayas teaching four sages the highest knowledge of the Absolute when Kāma interrupts him; this is Śiva's form as Dakṣiṇāmūrti, the great teacher.

26. In the Tamil Śaiva tradition, Śiva performed his "Eight Heroic Deeds" in the Tamil land. The *Tēvāram* poets link the eight myths with specific places where the deeds were performed, the Aṭṭavīraṭṭāṉam or "shrines of the Eight Heroic Deeds." Kāraikkāl Ammaiyār refers to five of the eight heroic deeds: Śiva cuts off the heads of Brahmā, burns Kāma, destroys the three demon cities, flays the elephant-demon, and saves Mārkaṇḍeya by conquering death. She does not refer to Śiva destroying Dakṣa's sacrifice, killing the demon Andhaka, or killing the demon Jalandhara. See Peterson 1989, 34–35, 342.

27. Dorai Rangaswamy, 296–303; Peterson 1989, 344.

28. Mani, 488; Dorai Rangaswamy, 359–368; Peterson 1989, 347.

29. Kramrisch 1988, 158–178; Dorai Rangaswamy, 196–209; O'Flaherty 1975, 137–141; Peterson 1989, 343.

30. Peterson 1989, 101; Gros 187, in Karavelane 106–107; *Tamil Lexicon* vol. III, 1218.

31. Nilakanta Sastri 1975, 308–312; Iyengar, 463–486; Hart 1975, 51–80, 149; Pillay, 39–53; Hart and Heifetz, xxxi, *passim.*; Ayyar, 101–109.

32. Dorai Rangaswamy 380, 393, 396 especially; Sivaramamurti 1994, 5; Murugan 3–6; Zvelebil 1975, 100–101; *Tamil Lexicon* vol. II, 869.

33. O'Flaherty 1973, 123–130; 1975, 141–154; Kramrisch 1988, 250–300; Dorai Rangaswamy 1990, 372–416; Mani 1975, 115, 387, 728–729; Peterson 1989, 345; Chakravarti 1986, 49–50. In some variants of this myth, Śiva cuts off Brahmā's head because he desires his own daughter.

34. See, for instance, Appar's poem describing a "woman wast[ing] from love's disease" (II–18.1, Peterson 1989, 248).

35. Hart 1975, 51–80, 149; Hart and Heifetz 1999, xxxi, *passim.*

36. Lorenzen 1972, 13–31, 53–55, 73–95, 165–184, 219; Bhandarkar 145ff; Dorai Rangaswamy 392–393, 1265; Peterson 1989, 148, 182, 259; Murthy 42–55, 92, 219–231; Flood 196, 154–173. This more extreme asceticism may be one reason why Kāraikkāl Ammaiyār's poetry is not regularly sung in Śiva temples today, in contrast to the Tēvāram poets, whose hymns are regularly sung.

37. See Khandelwal 1–47 for a historical overview of gender and Hindu renunciation.

38. See *Kāraikkālammaiyār Tirumuṟai* 31; *Kāraikkālammaiyār Pirapantaṅkaḷ*, 75–76; and Suriamurthy, 45.

39. Gros 189; in Karavelane, 108–109. See Monius 2004a for a discussion of Śiva as heroic father in later medieval poetry and theology that illuminates the image of Śiva as heroic father as well.

40. For the Tripura myth, see *Śiva Purāṇa* vol. 2, 802–858 (Rudra-Saṃhitā, Yuddha Khaṇḍa, chapters one through twelve); Mani 1975, 793–794; O'Faherty 1975, 125–137; Dorai Rangaswamy 1990, 304–322; Kramrisch 1988, 405–412; Peterson 1989, 344; Chakravarti 1986, 46–48. Sivaramamurti discusses the connections between the Tripura myth and the evolution of the figure of dancing Śiva (1994, *passim*). See Hart and Heifetz 41–42, 259–260 for a Caṅkam reference to the three cities myth, and Dorai Rangaswamy 306–307 for a discussion of this myth in *Cilappatikāram*. Ammaiyār refers to this myth in nine of her poems: *Aṟputat Tiruvantāti* 27, 32, 34, 37, 81, 84; *Tiruviraṭṭai Maṇimālai* 5, 9, 15.

41. See the *Tamil Lexicon* vol. II, 1138 and vol. V, 2596 for definitions of these dance terms. See Dorai Rangaswamy, 304–314 especially; Sivaramamurti 1994, 22, 82–88, *passim*; Zvelebil 1985, 43–46; Parthasarathy, especially 57–64; Murugan 3–6.

42. In my translation of this poem I am following the commentator Śri Āṟumukattampirāṉ, who translates the phrase "peyarntu naṭṭam ceyyum" as "lifting the leg and dancing" (*Kāraikkālammaiyār Pirapantaṅkaḷ* 74–75). The term "peyar" has many definitions concerning movement, including dancing, most of which suggest strong or even dramatic moves (*Tamil Lexicon* vol. V, 2862–2863).

43. Vatsyayan, 193 especially; Sivaramamurti 1994, 8–16, *passim*; Rangacharya, 22–40.

44. Kaimal 1–13; Zvelebil 1985; Smith (see Chapter 2 for the Chidambaram myth); Shulman 1980, 40–43, 82–88, 213–222; Handelman and Shulman, 1–101; Younger, 163–232; Nanda; Coomaraswamy 83–95. Many scholars highlight the detailed descriptions of Śiva's dance of bliss in Tirumūlar's *Tirumantiram*, a text that remains little studied and whose date is still contested; Zvelebil favors the seventh or eighth century CE. Tirumūlar's conception of Śiva's dance is fascinating and important but is beyond the scope of this work. See especially Zvelebil 1985, 46–52. Shulman raises intriguing connections between Chidambaram and Tiruvālaṅkāṭu that we will take up in the next chapter.

45. See Smith 3, 186–188; Handelman and Shulman, 79–101; Kaimal 7–9.

46. See Smith 222–227 for a provocative reading of the dwarf and the connections between the dwarf and Śiva's *gaṇas*.

47. I am relying heavily here on the synopses of these myths from Zvelebil 1985, 5–7 and Smith 31–34, 135–152; see also Shulman 1980, 85–89, 213–223; Younger 163–189; Handelman and Shulman, 4–14, 67–79; Peterson 1989, 97–100. Evidence for locating the dance contest between Śiva and Kālī in Tiruvālaṅkāṭu will also be discussed in Chapter 4.

48. In poem 1.7 Karavelane translates the Tamil phrase *"vaṭṭaṇaiy iṭṭu"* as crossing the lifted leg above the other: "la jambe levee et croisée au-dessus de l'autre" (62).

49. For a discussion of whether the *urdhvā-tāṇḍava* pose requires the right leg, see Dorai Rangaswamy, 456. Ammaiyār does not specify which leg is raised, but in the Tiruvālaṇkāṭu temple, Śiva's left leg is raised. It is not clear specifically what posture the *uḷḷāḷam* pose is; see the *Tamil Lexicon* vol. I, 473; Ramachandran 5. Kaliyāṇacuntaraṉār glosses this term instead as *kuṇālam* (11–12), which means either "riotous dancing" or a "Warrior's shout of triumph" (*Tamil Lexicon* 984), which makes sense in the context of the poem.

50. Hart 1975, 23, 45, 142; Hart and Heifetz, 166; *Tamil Lexicon* vol. I 1963, Mahalakshmi R., 25–30; Sasivalli, 61–66.

51. The temple of Tiruvāḷaṅkāṭu will be discussed in more detail in the following two chapters.

52. *Tamil Lexicon* vol. II, 855. Hart and Heifetz 362–363. See also Gros 184, Karavelane 103–104 for a discussion of the differences in the two *patikam*.

53. See especially pages 269–280.

54. Hart and Heifetz 290.

55. Hudson 1989, 390; Monius 2004b, 123. Hudson and Monius are both discussing violent acts committed by some of the later nāyaṉmārs, but this insight applies here as well.

56. See especially Hart 1975, 31–41; also Vijaya Ramaswamy 1997, 129–130.

57. "Zizyphus Napeca has fruit the size of a pea with an acidic taste. Ziyzphus Vulgaris trees average 25 feet in height and are covered with a

rough, brown bark. They have many branches, with annual thorny branchlets bearing alternate, oval-oblong leaves of a clear green colour, with three to five strongly marked, longitudinous veins. The small flowers are pale yellow and solitary. The fruit is a blood-red drupe, the size and shape of an olive, sweet, and mucilaginous in taste, slightly astringent. The pulp becomes softer and sweeter in drying, and the taste more like wine. They have pointed, oblong stones." Grieve, Mrs. M., "Jujube Berries." *Botanical.com: A Modern Herbal.* http://www.botanical.com/botanicalj/jujube10.html.

58. "A low shrub with sharp axillary spines met with in scrubby jungles and common waste places, *Canthium parviflorum.*" *Tamil Lexicon* vol. II, 889.

59. Hart 1975: 32–33, 120–129. See also Nilakanta Sastri, 1975 118.

60. Personal communication from Dr. R. Vijayalakshmy, November 2001.

61. Hart 1975: 143.

62. Dr. R. Vijayalakshmy discussed how percussive the Tiruvāḷaṅkāṭu poems are when we worked together on the translations. She also made this same comment in a lecture she gave on Ammaiyār and Antāḷ at the University of Texas at Austin on November 29, 2004.

63. Sirissa, *Albizzia lebbek.*

64. Kaliyāṇacuntaraṉār 11.

65. Hart 1975: 43–44.

66. Hart and Heifetz, 148.

67. Ibid., 159.

68. Ibid., 149; also 202, 203, 206, 207, 212.

69. *Tamil Lexicon* vol. I, 221. See also Kaliyāṇacuntaraṉār, 11. The reference in these works comes from the *Tirumurukāṟṟuppaṭai,* "The Guide to Lord Murukan," of the two earliest devotional poems to Murukaṉ, probably written 400–650 CE. Zvelebil, 101–105.

70. Probably a species of mimosa.

71. See Dorai Rangaswamy 401–402.

72. I am basing my discussion here on Shulman, especially 193–218; Mahalakshmi R., especially 27–35; and Ramaswamy 2003, 163–171. See *Cilappatikāram* Canto 23, verses 138–169 for the story of Nīli. Shulman (194–195) translates Cēkkiḻār's version of the Nīli story. Hardy discusses Nīli's connections with the emerging Kṛṣṇa cult in Tamilnadu, 221–225. We will discuss this story in detail in the Temple chapter.

In Tiruvālaṅkāṭu today, Kālī has her own temple right by the temple to Śiva, in which she dances in her own shrine; in the Ratnasabhā or dance hall, dancing Śiva is flanked by his consort Civakāmicuntari and Kāraikkāl Ammaiyār in her *pēy* form. The temple's layout and sacred shrines graphically show that the fierce female beings of the ancient Tamil land have been subdued by Śiva.

73. Ammaiyār uses the term *aṇaṅku* twice in describing the cremation ground in her Tiruvālaṅkāṭu poems (2.2 and 2.8), a term that in Caṅkam poetry can refer to the fierce goddess Aṇaṅku or can also be an adjective

meaning terrible or threatening. Mahalakshmi R. takes the term to mean the goddess Aṇaṅku in poem 2.2, "Aṇaṅku's forest" as opposed to "terrifying forest." I translate the term in its adjectival form as it seems to better fit the context and tone of the poems.

This pure focus on Śiva is contrasted in the film about Kāraikkāl Ammaiyār in which Pārvatī tells her she must first worship the goddess in order to get to Śiva.

74. Several scholars have discussed the localization of northern, Sanskritic cultural elements in the Tamil land, but here I am drawing especially from the work of Shulman (1980) and Mahalakshmi R. Shulman sees Ammaiyār as "a multiform of the defeated Kālī" (1980, 218) as well as a form of Nīli (Ibid., 161).

75. I am basing my discussion of *Maṇimēkalai* on Richman, especially 53–100. See also Shulman 2001, 213–251. I consulted the Tamil version of *Maṇimēkalai* with the commentary by Dr. U. Vē. Cāminātaiyaravarkaḷ.

76. In addition to Richman, see Wilson for a discussion of Buddhist meditation particularly on female cadavers. See Monius 2001, 3–115 for a discussion of *Maṇimēkalai* and the construction of the Buddhist community during this period of Tamil history. See also Hudson 1997.

77. In Śaiva poetry, "others" are sometimes referred to as "the six faiths" (*akaccamayam*), which can refer to six sects of Śaiva Siddhānta, or six sectarian groups with different cultic deities. *Tamil Lexicon* vol. I, 8; Peterson 1989, 132–3, n. 52.

78. Peterson 1999, 171. On Jains and Buddhists in *Tēvāram* poetry and during this historical period, see Peterson 1989 and 1999; Shulman 1990; Davis 1999.

79. *Śiva Purāṇa* vol. 2, 1054–1060 (Rudrasaṃhitā, Yuddha Khaṇḍa, 57); Dorai Rangaswamy 1990, 343–351; Mani 1975, 725; Peterson 1989, 347.

80. Flood 2006, 126–129.

81. See *Kāraikkālammaiyār Pirapantaṅkaḷ* 58–59; *Tamil Lexicon* vol. III, 1840. Ammaiyār discusses the devotee's love of Śiva in eleven of her poems, nine from *Aṟputat Tiruvantāti* (1, 2, 3, 17, 31, 87, 93, 96, 101) and two from *Tiruviraṭṭai Maṇimālai* (16, 17). She uses both Tamil words *aṉpu* and *kātal* for "love."

82. Dorai Rangaswamy 1990, 3–18; Hardy 1983, 202–213, 289ff, 472, *passim*; Prentiss 1999, 51; Ayyar 1974, 211; Krishna Murthy 1985, 6–14, 42–47; Peterson 1982, 72.

83. See Peterson 1989, especially 149–203.

84. See Peterson 1989, 184–186.

85. See especially Peterson 1989, 323–336; Dorai Rangaswamy 1084–1098. Ammaiyār herself becomes one of Śiva's servants who is worshiped by later poets, such as Cuntarar (Ibid., 333).

86. See Peterson 1989, 40–41 for a discussion of references to the Tamil language in *Tēvāram* poetry.

87. Biardeau, especially 69–121, discusses the evolution from renunciation to *bhakti*. See also Prentiss, 3–24, including her discussion of the atemporality of *bhakti* on 19.

88. See also Bourdieu for a discussion of the importance of *habitus* or structured dispositions to act in particular ways, on social formation and power, especially 72–95 and 114–158.

89. Flood 2006, 4. Tantra is a huge category of texts and traditions. In addition to Flood, my discussion is informed by Padoux, Lorenzen 2002, Brooks, Davis 2000, and White (1996 and 2000).

Śaiva Siddhānta is a Tantric, orthodox temple tradition based on the Āgamas, the *Tantras* or liturgical texts centered on Śiva. In Śaiva Siddhānta the ultimate goal is *mokṣa*, final liberation, in which the soul is released from its bondage. The soul does not merge with Śiva but remains separate, attaining an identical form to become a Śiva. During daily worship and initiation, the male worshipers and priests ritually transform their bodies into divine bodies, making them fit to worship Śiva and contributing to their final liberation. See Davis 2000, 83, *passim*.

90. See Mahalakshmi R., especially 27–40; Ramaswamy 1997, 129–134. Both discuss the potential emancipatory character of the devotional movements without ignoring the power of hegemonic forces over people's lives.

Notes to Chapter 3

1. Peterson 1989, 14–18, 331–336; Shulman 1990, 239–248; Ramaswamy 1997, 134; Pechilis 2006, 174–176; Gros 176–180, 231–265.

2. Zvelebil 1975, 130–136; Dorai Rangaswamy 1997, 971–973; Gros, in Karavelane, 96–102; Gros, 176–182; Peterson 1989:14–17; Pechilis 2006, 173–174; Ramaswamy 1997, 134; *Periya Purāṇam enṟu Tiruttoṇṭar Purāṇam* 271–281. Dorai Rangaswamy (971) discusses the possible reference to Ammaiyār in a poem by Appar, who lived in the sixth to seventh century. Appar says to Śiva, "pēyt toḻil āṭṭiyaip-peṟṟuṭaiyīr," "you who created a woman who acted as a demon/who lived performing the activities of a demon" (*Tēvāram* V, 96.4). Gros disputes this and believes the verse refers to a frightening goddess (177). Also, it is possible that a poem by Campantar (roughly contemporaneous with Appar) refers to Ammaiyār, although it could be a reference to the local goddess Nīli, who will be discussed later (Peterson 1989, 203). The other two women saints are Īcaiñāṉiyār, the mother of Cuntarar, and Maṅkaiyarkkaraciyār, a queen in the Pāṇṭiyaṉ dynasty of Maturai.

3. I used Karavelane for Cēkkiḻār's Tamil version and French translation (74–94), and Pechilis's full English translation (2006, 180–186). The verse numbers refer to Ammaiyār's story separately from the *Periya Purāṇam;* in the full text, her story begins with verse 1722.

4. Śiva at Tiruvālaṅkāṭu is called Vaṭāṇyēśvara, and the temple is called Vaṭāṇyēśvara Swamy Tirukōyil. On the back cover of the temple's older official history is an upside-down picture of Mt. Kailāsa, which is the view Kāraikkāl Ammaiyār had as she walked down from Mt. Kailāsa to Tiruvālaṅkāṭu on her hands. Interestingly, the temple history book that is

currently sold at the temple bookstore (first published in 1998; latest edition published in 2002), contains a streamlined version of the story of Kāraikkāl Ammaiyār that takes just over a page of prose. It jumps from Paramatattan̲, leaving Pun̲itavati out of fear of her power, to Pun̲itavati taking the *pēy* form, composing the first two sets of poems, then climbing Mt. Kailāsa on her head to see Śiva, and asking for liberation from rebirth and to see his dance. She goes to Tiruvālaṅkāṭu, composes the two poem cycles set there, and remains at Śiva's feet, watching his dance, for which she is famous.

5. The first 38 distiches of the *Tirukkur̲aḷ* deal with morality, including a distich on the domestic life and one on a good wife; see for instance Zvelebil (1975, 23); Sundaram; and Vanmikanathan (532–533). The dating of the *Tirukkur̲aḷ* is still controversial. See Zvelebil (1975, 123–127); Sundaram (8).

6. Verses 55 and 56; Sundaram, 24. Also cited in Ramaswamy (1997: 90).

7. At the Kāraikkāl Ammaiyār festival at Tiruvālaṅkāṭu on March 17, 2006, the renowned orator, Dr. Ira. Selvaganapati, performed in the evening, telling the story of the two mangoes and expounding upon it. At the point in the story when Pun̲itavati is distressed over not having the second mango to give her husband, he said, "Tamil women give their husbands whatever they want to eat."

8. Pechilis (2008, 28–29) discusses Cēkkil̲ār's use of Pun̲itavati's *pēy* form as a pure consciousness of God, rather than a ghoulish form.

9. See especially Hart (1975, 93–119).

10. Hart (1975, 97); also cited in Ramaswamy (1997, 49).

11. Hart (1975, 21–22; 98–100; 133). Hart (1975) discusses *aṇaṅku* extensively; see especially Chapter 5, "The Role of Sacred Power," 81–137. See also Mahalakshmi R. (2000, 32) and Ramaswamy (1997, 48–50). Ramaswamy is critical of Hart for attaching too much importance to *aṇaṅku* in understanding Tamil women's power. Rajam (1986) also critiques Hart's treatment.

12. Canto 20, verses 34–44. Noted in Ramaswamy (1997, 50).

13. Ramaswamy (1997, 44–46); *Cilappatikāram* Canto XII, verses 20–64.

14. Monius analyzes Cēkkil̲ār's transformation of Śiva and Śaiva theology in 2004a and 2004b; the latter text analyzes the relationship between Śaivas and Jains in particular detail. See also Ryan; Peterson 1999; Davis 1999.

15. Monius 2004a, 185–188; Peterson 1989, 35, 100, 342.

16. Monius 2004a, 186. Ammaiyār refers to Śiva as the wandering beggar in seven verses of her *Ar̲putat Tiruvantāti*: 25, 43, 46, 54, 56, 57, 74.

17. See verses 3, 4, 17, 18, 19, 25, 28, 48, 50, 53, 55, 56, 59, 61–65. Pechilis (2006, 179–180) discusses the less frightening image of Śiva in Cēkkil̲ār's work.

18. Monius 2004b; Hudson 1989; Shulman 1993, 18–47.

19. Monius 2004b, 154–158 especially; Peterson 1999; Pechilis 2006, 176.

20. Monius 2004a, 188–197; 2004b, 165–166.

21. Hudson 1989, 375.

22. See Pechilis 2008; Mahalakshmi R., especially 25–30; Ramaswamy 1997, 18–21, 129–134; Chakravarty, 21–28.

23. Ramanujan (1999e) discusses how women saints defy social conventions in order to remain devoted to their god. He says that Ammaiyār terrifies her husband in order to get rid of him (274), which attributes a calculatedness to her actions that is not evident in Cēkkiḻār's story. Many female saints reject male sexual advances; Ramanujan says that Ammaiyār "turns into a skeleton before a lust-infatuated male" (275), which may be over-reading the scene in Cēkkiḻār's story but does highlight Ammaiyār's asexuality.

24. The first film of a Śaiva saint was "Siruthonda Nayanar" in 1935; see Monius 2004b, 117 n. 16.

25. I watched this film on the national television channel in Chennai on October 19, 2001. I also have a DVD distributed from Columbia Films in Kuala Lumpur, Malaysia. The actress who plays Kāriakkāl Ammiayār is K. P. Sundara Ambal.

26. This version of Ammaiyār's ascent of Mt. Kailāsa in which *liṅgas* sprout up at every step is also told in the magazine article about the Tiruvālaṅkāṭu temple, "Śakti Taricaṉam" Part Two, 125.

27. See Lakshmi, especially 16–21; Chinniah. Lakshmi and Chinniah discuss the role played by the Tamil political parties the Dravida Kazhagam (begun in 1944) and its 1949 off-shoot the Dravida Munnetra Kazhagam in shaping a sense of Tamil identity and celebrating the Tamil language. These parties operated as families, using kin relations to identify each other. Women's identities in this structure were based on chastity (*kaṟpu*) and motherhood (Lakshmi 16–17; Chinniah 32–33). See also Baskaran 28–37. Baskaran writes that perhaps the height of the trend for films celebrating Tamil culture and Tamil language is the film *Avvaiyar* (1953), "A story woven around episodes from the life of the legendary poetess Avvaiyar whose works are considered to be one of the glories of Tamil literature. Every Tamil child is initiated into the language and culture through her poems. The film is dedicated to Mother Tamil and opens with a song praising Tamilnadu. Avvaiyar herself symbolizes Mother Tamil and her deity, Murugan, is hailed as god of the Tamils" (23). K. P. Sundara Ambal, who played Kāraikkāl Ammaiyār, also played Avvaiyar.

28. Some of the Tamil texts published as inexpensive and accessible paperbacks combine theological discussions with Ammaiyār's story and poetry, such as *Kāraikkāl Ammaiyāriṉ Vāḻvum Vākkum* by Ka. Na. Vēlaṉ, who argues that the purpose of Śiva's *ūrdhva-tāṇḍava* dance is to raise the Kundalini śakti (6). In a small book published in 1977, *Kāraikkāl Ammaiyār Icai Nāṭakam*, the author has set Ammaiyār's story to music.

29. Bālakumāraṉ (23–25). The translations here are mine.

Notes to Chapter 4

1. I made the on-site visits to the temples described in this chapter and conducted the interviews with the priests, caretaker, devotees, and other individuals with my research associate, Mr. M. Thavamani. He was integral to the project at every step, from arranging visits to translating interviews.

2. A middle-aged male devotee we asked about the shrine said that Ammaiyār has seen God directly, so she is like a saint. For some people she is a goddess. According to the temple watchman/caretaker, Tirumalai, devotees think she's a goddess; nobody believes she is human. Interview, February 4, 2006.

3. According to Tirumalai, pūjā is performed for Ammaiyār twice a day. Interview, February 4, 2006.

4. See the temple book, *Kāraikkāl Talapurāṇamum, Kāraikkālammaiyār aruḷ varalāṟum*, 72. Plus, the artist signed one of the wall panels. The current temple structure dates to 1929. Ibid, 76.

5. In Tamil it is "Kayilācanāta," but since the Sanskrit form is more common I use that here.

6. This synopsis is based on the story in the temple book, 40–48, and the *Kāraikkāl Sthalapurāṇa*.

7. Gros discusses a work by "the first French master of Tamil studies," Julien Vinson, in which he claims: "For about thirty years [he writes this in 1920], . . . the festival of Puṉitavati has been celebrated with great pomp and ceremony, attracting a large number of devotees" (175–176). Mr. Kailasanathan, the editor of the temple book and an organizer of the festival from the local community, said in an interview on July 10, 2006, that thirty years ago the festival was ten days long. He also said that people worship Ammaiyār as a goddess during the festival.

8. This section is based on the description of the festival written on one of the walls of the Kailāsanātha temple, and on the description given by Tirumalai, the caretaker of the Ammaiyār temple, as well as the notes and photos of Mr. M. Thavamani, who attended the festival in July of 2006.

9. Vināyakar is Ganesh. In this festival the Kailāsanātha Temple becomes the bridegroom's house, while Ammaiyār's temple becomes her house. The Chettiārs are primarily a trading community and are the central community involved in celebrating this festival. Personal communication, Mrs. Hema Chandrasekhar, June 19, 2006.

10. Subrahmaṇya is another name for Murukaṉ or Skanda, the son of Śiva.

11. Mr. Kailasanathan, the organizer, said that Cēkkiḻār said a beggar came to the house and Ammaiyār gave him one of her husband's mangoes, but that in Kāraikkāl they say that the beggar is Śiva, which is why another mango appears automatically. He also said that different families or caste groups sponsor different parts of the festival. Interview on July 10, 2006 in Kāraikkāl.

12. Mr. Kailasanathan's list of the five *mūrtis* included Caṇḍeśvarar rather than Nandi.

13. Mangoes are thrown from the chariots, which many devotees consider a highlight of the festival. Mr. Kailasanathan said that many people come to the festival to eat the mangoes that are thrown in order to have a child. Many people, including film stars, have had children after eating the

mangoes during the festival. The belief is that Ammaiyār did not have a child, but once she received the mango she got a child—Śiva becomes her son. He gave the mango to his mother as a son. Since Śiva calls her Amma, Mother, he becomes her son. No one should tell her that she did not live well, which is why she had no child; so Śiva himself gave her a son. Interview, July 10, 2006.

14. Mr. Kailasanathan said that women know some of Ammaiyār's songs and sing them at this point, and in their daily worship as well. He said men are not so involved in the worship. He also said that people consider Ammaiyār a full goddess; since Śiva accepted her as mother, she is a goddess. Interview in Kāraikkāl on July 10, 2006.

15. In addition to temple texts *Irattiṉa Capaiyaiyuṭaiya Tiruvālaṅkāṭṭu Talavaralāṟu* and *Tiruvālaṅkāṭu Talavaralāṟum Tiruppatikaṅkaḷum* (1998 and 2002), this section is based on interviews with the Gurukkaḷ at the Tiruvālaṅkāṭu temple, Śri Sabarathina; his father, the Gurukkaḷ of the Paḻaiyaṉūr temple; and the newly appointed *Ōtuvār* or the musician trained to sing Tamil Śaiva hymns in the Tiruvālaṅkāṭu temple, Mr. K. Aruḷānantam. All these interviews were conducted on February 22, 2006.

16. See, for example, Campantar I.45.1 and 12; Appar IV.68.8.

17. *Irattiṉa Capaiyaiyuṭaiya Tiruvālaṅkāṭṭu Talavaralāṟu*, 45–48. One of the days that Thavamani and I were at the temple, the Gurukkaḷs were collecting money for more renovation work and the upcoming Mahā Kumbhabhiṣekham. This is a government-run temple, administered through the nearby Tiruttaṇi temple.

18. The other four *sabhais* are in temples in the following towns: the Kanaka (golden) Sabhai in Chidambaram; the Veḷḷi Ampalam (silver hall) in Maturai; the Tamira (copper) Sabhai in Tirunelveli; and the Cittira (painted) Sabhai in Kutralam.

19. Kāṣyapaṉ, "Śakti Taricaṉam" Part Two, 126–127.

20. As in the Kāraikkāl temple, it is traditional in Śiva temples in Tamilnadu to have the sixty-three *nāyaṉmārs* surround the main *liṅga* image.

21. See Shulman (1980, 218) concerning the Bhadrakālī temple. See Wood and De Bruijn for beautiful photographs of this temple.

22. Madhavan 15, 234. However, on a map of Tamilnadu published by Ideal Publishing House in 2008, only the name Paḻaiyaṉūr appears where Paḻaiyaṉūr/Tiruvālaṅkāṭu are located.

23. See Shulman 1980, 213.

24. Shulman 1980, 213–218; Mahalakshmi R., 17–40; 35–40.

25. My retelling of the story is based on the texts *Irattiṉa Capaiyaiyuṭaiya Tiruvālaṅkāṭṭu Talavaralāṟu*; *Tiruvālaṅkāṭṭu Talavaralāṟum Tiruppatikaṅkaḷum* (1998 and 2002); and the 1865 *Tiruvālaṅkāṭṭuppurāṇam*, as well as the version of the story told by Śri S. Sabarathina Gurukkaḷ of Tiruvālaṅkāṭu, in an interview on February 22, 2006. The current temple history book is much shorter than previous editions and contains a truncated version of Kāraikkāl Ammaiyār's story. In addition I consulted Dorai Rangaswamy 444; Kāṣyapaṉ "Śakti Taricaṉam"

Parts One and Two; Shulman's translation, 1980, 214–216; Sivaramamurty 1994, 366–367. I also consulted Mahalakshmi R.'s analysis, 35–40.

26. Kāṣyapaṉ, "Śakti Taricaṉam" Part One, 122; *Irattiṉa Capaiyaiyuṭaiya Tiruvālaṅkāṭṭu Talavaralāṟu*, 122–123.

27. For a much more extensive discussion of visual images of Kāraikkāl Ammaiyār see Dehejia, Plates 65–77, pp. 142–150; Karavelane 110–114, 153–168; Gros 190–195; Sivaramamurti 1994, 141, 234, *passim*; De Bruijn 25–38. Ammaiyār's image spread to Kerala and Sri Lanka, but apparently not to other parts of India. Images of Kāraikkāl Ammaiyār in her *pēy* form next to the dancing Śiva are apparently found as early as the ninth century in Cambodia, such as at the Banteai Srei temple; see Sivaramamurti 1994, 342–348; Gros 190–195. See Sivaramamurti 1994 and Dhaky 1984 for sculptured images of Śiva's *gaṇas* and *bhūtas* in temples in South India.

28. 1980, 213. Shulman bases his claim partly on the reference to Devī watching the dance in Tiruvālaṅkāṭu in one of Appar's poems (*Tēvāram* 666).

29. Shulman 1980, especially 193–213; see also Mahalakshmi R., especially 27–35.

30. Chapter 23, verses 138–169.

31. I.45.1, in Peterson 1989, 203.

32. Ulrich 2003, 2–3; Shulman 1980, 196–197; Ramaswamy 1997, 97–98; 2003, 163.

33. *Periya Purāṇam* 4.5.3; *Cēkkiḻār Purāṇam* v. 15; Shulman 1980, 194–195; Ramaswamy 2003, 165–166.

34. Zvelebil 1987, xi; Ramaswamy 2003, 168–171; Ram 45–46.

35. This is my retelling of the Nīli story based on the versions in two of the Tiruvālaṅkāṭu temple books (2002: 46–57; 1997: 178–196); a synopsis in Kāṣyapaṉ, "Śakti Taricaṉam" Part One, 124–125; the interview with the Tiruvālaṅkāṭu Gurukkaḷ; the versions by Cēkkiḻār (*Periya Purāṇam* 4.5.3; *Cēkkiḻar Purāṇam* v. 15); and the version in Shulman (194–195). The Tiruvālaṅkāṭu Gurukkaḷ knew the Nīli story well. The Paḻaiyaṉūr Gurukkal said that the Nīli story is not connected to Kāraikkāl Ammaiyār, but to the town where the Vēḷāḷar panchayat took place. He also said that the Nīli story is very ancient, more ancient than Kāraikkāl Ammaiyār.

36. The Nīli story in the older Tiruvālaṅkāṭu temple book says that the Vēḷāḷar's wife prayed for children at the Ratna Sabhai in Tiruvālaṅkāṭu.

37. Shulman (1980, 218) believes this to be the case.

38. The oldest temple book claims this memorial was erected 5,000 years ago (1997, 88).

39. Interview on February 22, 2006.

40. *Tamil Lexicon* vol. V, 2890. The Tiruvālaṅkāṭu Gurukkaḷ emphasized that Śiva told Pārvatī that Kāraikkāl Ammaiyār "is the mother who protects us. She is my mother." Interview, February 22, 2006.

41. The following description of this festival is based on the notes that my fieldwork associate Thavamani made on two days of the festival, April 7 and 8, 2006. He notes that during the festival, there is no electrical power in the villages, as it is all directed to the festival!

42. Mr. Ādimoolam, the Vice President of the Vaṇiyar Caṅkam that sponsors this part of the festival, said in an interview that every year community member Mr. Nambar Reddiyar gives 10,000 rupees for the car decoration alone. Then the members of the organization gather donations from the surrounding villages for the other expenses involved. The Vaṇiyar community today is at least partly connected to business and trade; in Tamil the word "vaṇikaṉ" means a merchant or trader. Cēkkiḻār describes Puṉitavati and her husband as born into the Vaṇikar community, as does the handbill describing the Kāraikkāl Ammaiyār festival. It seems that the association between the Vaṇikar community and Kāraikkāl Ammaiyār has continued for centuries.

43. Mrs. Hema Chandrasekhar communicated with me about this festival during the celebrations, and then later on May 4 and June 19, 2006.

44. One storyteller who was telling Ammaiyār's story told the audience that Tamil women give their husbands whatever they want to eat, which is why it was so distressing for Puṉitavati that her husband had asked for a second mango but she had already given it to the Śaiva devotee. While Thavamani and I were listening to the entertainment, one of the temple Gurukkaḷs explained that mangoes from this temple's festival have a lot of power; childless couples come here, receive a mango as prasād, and have children after eating the mango.

45. To my knowledge, this is the only temple in which her songs are sung; and this festival is the only time in which all of her Tiruvālaṅkāṭu songs are sung at once. The Ōtuvār, Mr. K. Aruḷānantam, said that her songs are performed at other times in the temple, but it was not clear how often they are sung. He said that they sing verses from Cēkkiḻār's *Periya Purāṇam* regularly. He sang one of Ammaiyār's Tiruvālaṅkāṭu hymns for us during the interview on February 22, 2006. Mr. Aruḷānantam had only been appointed to the temple about two months before the festival, and he was the first Ōtuvār at the Tiruvālaṅkāṭu temple. See Peterson 1989, 55–75, for a discussion of the history and training of Ōtuvārs.

46. Mrs. Hema Chandrasekhar told me that one of the reasons people do not know as much about Kāraikkāl Ammaiyār is that her poetry is very difficult to understand, even for a native Tamil speaker. Mr. K. Aruḷānantam, the devotional singer, was the temple's first Ōtuvār and had only recently been appointed, so perhaps Ammaiyār's poetry may become more integral to the temple's activities.

Notes to Chapter 5

1. This poem refers to the myth describing Śiva swallowing the world poison (*Viṣāpaharaṇamūrti*). In order to obtain *amṛta* (ambrosia), the elixir of immortality, the gods and demons churned the ocean of milk. Mount Mandara was the churning stick, supported by Viṣṇu; the snake king Ādiśeṣa or Vāsuki was the rope. The gods held one side of the rope, the demons the other. As they churned the ocean a burning black mass of poison, the terrifying Kālakūṭa, emerged. In order to save the world Śiva immediately swallowed the poison,

holding it in his throat, which turned blue-black because of the Kālakūṭa. Mani 1975, 726; O'Flaherty 1975, 274–280; Dorai Rangaswamy, 262–271; Kramrisch 1988, 145–153; Peterson 1989, 344; Chakravarti 1986, 34–35.

2. Kāraikkāl Ammaiyār sometimes uses the pronoun "we" and at other times "I." There appears to be a fluidity at play between contexts when she is speaking about her personal experience, and when she is deliberately using the plural pronoun to include others listening to show that direct experience of Śiva is possible for anyone with the right attitude.

3. The word *āḷ* means slave, servant, and devotee in old Tamil, and is a key concept used in Tamil devotional poetry to refer to the relationship between God and His true devotee, who perpetually serves Śiva as His devoted slave.

4. The Tamil sandhi here could render this word either "mother" or "father." The other nāyaṉmārs have called Śiva mother; Māṇikkavācakar, for example, says to Śiva "You are my mother and father" (37.3, Iraianban 234). Although Ammaiyār is focused on Śiva, the female divinity is always present.

5. This poem refers to the myth in which the demon Gajāsura ("Elephant-Demon") continually antagonized the gods. Śiva killed the elephant demon, flayed him, and draped the still-bloody skin around him. *Śiva Purāṇa* vol. 2, 1054–1060 (Rudra-Saṃhitā, Yuddha Khaṇḍa, 57); Dorai Rangaswamy 1990, 343–351; Mani 1975, 725; Peterson 1989, 347. *Tapas* means austerities, including renouncing the ordinary world and meditating on God. In this poem Ammaiyār emphasizes that *she* has performed these actions intentionally.

6. This poem refers to the myth of Śiva receiving Gaṅgā in his matted hair (*Gaṅgadharamūrti*). The ancestors of King Bhagīratha angered the sage Kapila by disturbing him during his meditation; the sage burned them to death with his eyes. King Bhagīratha sought to purify his ancestors' ashes with the waters of the celestial river Gaṅgā. He performed severe austerities (*tapas*) so that Gaṅgā would come down to earth; he asked Śiva to break the impact of the mighty river's fall. As Gaṅgā descended, Śiva graciously caught the river in his matted hair and cushioned her impact on earth. *Śiva Purāṇa* vol. 1, 54–57 (Vidyeśvarasaṃhitā 7); Mani 1975, 277; Dorai Rangaswamy 272–280; Peterson 1989, 347–348; O'Flaherty 1973, 229–233; Chakravarti 1986, 58–59.

7. This poem refers to Śiva in his *Ardhanārīśvara* or half-male, half-female form. See Chapter 2 for a discussion of the myth underlying this central form.

8. This poem describes Śiva's *līla*, his play, in which he has taken a body as an ornament, so that there is a concrete form for the devotee to meditate on.

9. In this poem Ammaiyār implies—as she does in other poems—that she is more devoted to Śiva than even the gods.

10. This poem contains the seeds of what will become important Śaiva Siddhānta philosophy. First of all, it expresses the more general idea that karma causes rebirth; and second, this poem describes the last stage when the soul

is about to be liberated by Śiva, when good and bad karmas are the same, when there is no distinction; karma is no longer being generated because the souls do not perform any action; karma has ripened and fallen away.

11. This poem refers to the myth of Rāvaṇa attempting to lift Mt. Kailāsa (*Rāvaṇānugrahamūrti*). Rāvaṇa, the ten-headed demon king of Laṅkā, was riding through the air in his chariot; he saw that Śiva's Himalayan abode Mt. Kailāsa was blocking his path. Śiva was sitting with Pārvatī on the mountain. Rāvaṇa began to lift the mountain up to remove it from his path; when the mountain began to tremble, Śiva pressed his big toe down and crushed Rāvaṇā underneath. The frightened demon worshiped Śiva with hymns; in return, Śiva graciously granted him boons. Dorai Rangaswamy 296–303; Peterson 1989, 344.

This poem also refers to Śiva's form as half Viṣṇu, and probably also to the myth of the fiery liṅga in the next poem.

12. This poem refers to the myth in which Śiva manifests himself as the fiery *liṅga* (*Liṅgodbhavamūrti*). In the darkness and flood before the beginning of a new cosmic age, Brahmā and Viṣṇu argued with each other over who was the supreme divine power in the universe. A massive pillar of fire, a *liṅga* of light, suddenly appeared in the darkness. Brahmā took the form of a wild goose and flew up as high as he could; Viṣṇu took the form of a boar and burrowed into the earth as far as he could go. Neither god could reach the end of the great pillar and came back to the earth's surface. Śiva showed himself inside his fiery *liṅga*; Brahmā and Viṣṇu admitted defeat, acknowledged Śiva as the supreme deity in the world, and worshiped him. Kramrisch 1988, 158–178; Dorai Rangaswamy 196–209; O'Flaherty 1975, 137–141; Peterson 1989, 343.

The three-times-seven worlds refers to seven worlds in each of the three regions: heaven, earth, and hell.

13. This poem and the following poem elucidate Śiva's nature as encompassing eight forms, or Aṣṭamūrti (Tamil *aṭṭamūrtti*): He is the five elements of earth, water, air, fire, and space; the sun and the moon; and the sacrificer. Śiva has created the elements of the cosmos and has become them himself; he is both manifest in forms (*cakaḷam*) and is beyond form (*niṭkaḷam*). See Chapter 2 for a more detailed discussion of these ideas.

14. This poem refers to Śiva as the wandering beggar; see the note to poem 56.

15. This poem refers to Śiva's destruction of the three cities of the demons (*Tripurāntakamūrti*). The demon Tāraka's three sons, Tarakāṣa, Kamalāṣa, and Vidyunmālin, practiced austerities (*tapas*) and won a boon from Brahmā. The three demons asked for immortality, but Brahmā could not give them that. So the demons asked to live for a thousand years in three fortified cities that could move around the universe; they would reunite after a thousand years and combine their three cities into one city. The three cities could only be destroyed by the god who could pierce them all with one arrow. The architect Maya built three cities, of gold, silver, and iron, in which the three demons roamed around marauding and attacking all the beings in the

world. The gods complained to Brahmā, but he said only Śiva had the power to destroy the demons because of his yogic practices. Śiva consented to the gods' request to conquer the demons' cities. When the demons reunited after one thousand years, Śiva rode out in a special chariot with a bow and arrow, all composed of divine beings and celestial and terrestrial elements. Brahmā served as his charioteer. Śiva released the fire-tipped arrow and destroyed the three cities. *Śiva Purāṇa* vol. 2, 802–858 (Rudra-Saṃhitā, Yuddha Khaṇḍa, Chapters one through twelve); Mani 1975, 793–794; O'Faherty 1975, 125–137; Dorai Rangaswamy 304–322; Kramrisch 1988, 405–412; Peterson 1989, 344; Chakravarti 1986, 46–48.

16. This poem encompasses the stock *bhakti* or devotional idea that the devotee is "without sense," or innocent, simple, nothing compared to the all-powerful, all-knowing God.

17. This poem is discussed in Chapter 2. Here I have translated *pēy* as "ghoul."

18. This poem conveys the idea that Śiva is beyond form and certainly cannot be known only through books, but only through experience. Therefore, he can appear in whatever form the devotee imagines and worships.

19. This poem again refers to Śiva's destruction of the three cities; see the note to poem 27.

20. The red-gold mountain in this poem is Mt. Meru, located in the center of the Hindu cosmos. The silvery mountain is Mt. Kailāsa, where Śiva lives with Umā in many of his myths.

21. This poem refers to the practice of worshiping the devotees of Śiva, which becomes an important part of the Śaiva tradition. Ammaiyār is also marking out a community of Śiva devotees against those who do not follow him.

22. "Māl" is another name for Viṣṇu in South India. "Measuring the world" refers to the myth in which Viṣṇu takes his form as a dwarf and defeats a demon king by measuring the universe in just three steps, signaling his control of the cosmos. Both Viṣṇu and Umā are considered part of Śiva.

23. This poem refers to Śiva as the wandering beggar; see the note to poem 56.

24. This poem refers to the idea that a devotee must make an effort to worship Śiva, despite the grace Śiva activates. This will become an important concept in Śaiva Siddhānta.

25. Himavān is the Lord of the Himalayas, the father of Pārvatī. *Koṉṟai* flowers are the usual flower offering to Śiva.

26. This poem refers to Śiva in his *Ardhanārīśvara* or half-male, half-female form, as in poem 13. See Chapter 2 for a discussion of the myth underlying this central form.

27. Tirumāl is a name for Viṣṇu, who is often described as "red-eyed." He is considered the brother of Pārvatī, and is therefore frequently shown next to Śiva.

28. This poem again refers to the myth in which Śiva becomes a liṅga of fire; see note 12. Viṣṇu, who is dark like rain clouds, is often considered

part of Śiva in Śaiva myths; from the Śaiva perspective Śiva is the supreme Lord who absorbs all other gods into Him. See Peterson, 200, n. 119, 120.

29. This poem refers to the myth of Bhairava cutting off Brahmā's head (*Brahmaśiraśchedamūrti*). Brahmā haughtily declared himself the highest reality in the universe. Śiva, in his terrifying Bhairava form, sliced off Brahmā's fifth head with his nail, incurring the sin of brahminicide. The skull stuck to his palm, so Bhairava became known as the Kāpālika, the Skull-Bearer. In order to expiate his sin he took a vow to wander naked begging for alms, holding the skull as his begging bowl. In this Bhikṣāṭana form, Śiva wandered all over the world asking for alms; women in the houses he stopped at were enchanted by him. Eventually he came to the Pine Forest where the sages were practicing austerities; they did not recognize Śiva. The ascetics' wives were infatuated by the naked beggar, which outraged the sages, who angrily demanded that Śiva make his *liṅga* fall off. He did, and vanished. There was chaos in the world, so the sages went to Brahmā, who told the sages that the beggar was the great god Śiva. The sages went back to the Pine Forest and worshiped Śiva.

Śiva continued wandering and came to Viṣṇu's abode. The gatekeeper Viṣvaksena did not recognize Śiva and blocked his entry; Śiva pierced him with his trident and carried his corpse into Viṣṇu's residence as Kaṅkāla-murti. Viṣṇu offered him gushing streams of blood from a vein in his forehead, but the blood did not fill Śiva's begging bowl. Śiva left Viṣṇu's abode and proceeded to Vārāṇāsī; when he entered the holy city, the skull fell off his hand and he was free of the sin of brahminicide. In some variants of this myth, Śiva cuts off Brahmā's head because he desires his own daughter. O'Flaherty 1973, 123–130; 1975, 141–154; Kramrisch 1988, 250–300; Dorai Rangaswamy 1990, 372–416; Mani 1975, 115, 387, 728–729; Peterson 1989, 345; Chakravarti 1986, 49–50.

In this poem Ammaiyār shows that even though some people seem to think that what Śiva is doing is wrong, she knows he has a reason for everything, even though we may not see it, so he should tell us!

30. See note to poem 7 concerning the elephant skin.

31. In many poems Kāraikkāl Ammaiyār relies on mythological references to paint a portrait of Śiva; here she confides that she hasn't seen him and is asking for a vision.

32. This poem refers to an episode in the epic *Mahābhārata* in which Arjuna meets Śiva as a hunter (*Kirātārjunamūrti*). The hero Arjuna went to the Himalayas to practice severe austerities (*tapas*) in order to receive the Pāśupata weapon from Śiva so that the Pāṇḍavas could defeat their enemies in the war. Śiva tested the hero by appearing to him as a Kirāta or hunter. At that moment a wild boar came to attack Arjuna; he and the hunter both shot arrows at it. The hunter argued with Arjuna over the dead animal and a fight ensued. The hunter was invincible and even took Arjuna's Gāṇḍiva bow, but Arjuna continued fighting with his hands. Śiva was pleased with Arjuna's courage and revealed himself to him; he then granted Arjuna the Pāśupata weapon with which he and the Pāṇḍavas won the Bhārata war.

Śiva Purāṇa, vol. 3, 1228–1253 (Śatarudrasaṃhitā 37–41); Mani 1975, 412; Dorai Rangaswamy 281–285; Kramrisch 1988, 357–359; Peterson 1989, 347.

33. This poem seems to refer to Rāhu, the planet in the Hindu cosmos that is in the form of a snake and that is always looking for the moon, and who swallows the moon during an eclipse. See Mani 171–172, 626.

34. Yama is the god of death; when one worships Śiva, there is no need to fear death.

35. This poem emphasizes Umā's modesty and shyness by telling Śiva that the moon will outshine her if it is placed near her. The implication is that Śiva also outshines Umā.

36. The seven worlds can refer to either the seven celestial or seven subterranean worlds. See the *Tamil Lexicon* vol. I, 568 for *ēḻulakam*.

37. This poem plays with part of the myth of Śiva wandering as a beggar as penance for cutting off Brahmā's fifth head. In the myth it is said that his begging bowl could not even be filled by the gods, but here Kāraikkāl Ammaiyār says that if one is truly devoted to Śiva, wanting nothing but to be his slave, then like these pure women, one can reach him. The line in the poem describes the innocent women giving alms "without thinking," which I have translated as "without wanting anything in return" to make clear that the women gave the alms out of pure love.

38. This is another poem referring to the planet Rāhu that swallows the moon during an eclipse. See the note to poem 64.

39. This poem refers to Śiva's cosmic dance of creation and construction; he is the foundation of the universe. See the discussion of this poem in Chapter 2.

40. In this poem Ammaiyār refers to herself in the third person, as "the person who thinks this way" or "such a person." The word translated here as "pride," *cerukku*, has the meaning of pride due to having achieved something, as well as a sense of joy because of the accomplishment.

41. See the note for poem 18 for the myth of Rāvaṇa. The other myth referred to here is about Śiva saving his ardent devotee Mārkaṇḍeya from death (*Kālasaṃhāramūrti*). The sage Mṛkaṇḍu was childless and performed austerities to Śiva. Śiva appeared before him to present his boon, and gave him the choice of an evil son who would live a long life, or a pious boy who would live only to the age of sixteen. Mṛkaṇḍu chose the pious boy; when he was born, he named him Mārkaṇḍeya. This boy grew up to be a wise, virtuous, ardent devotee of Śiva. When he entered his sixteenth year he was immersed in meditation before a Śiva *liṅga*; as Yama, the god of death, approached him to take him away, Mārkaṇḍeya embraced the *liṅga*. Śiva sprang out of the *liṅga* and kicked Yama to death. Mārkaṇḍeya was given the boon of immortality and remained sixteen years of age forever; Śiva revived Yama. Mani 1975, 488; Dorai Rangaswamy, 359–368; Peterson 1989, 347.

42. See the note to poem 27 for the myth of Śiva's destruction of the three cities. This poem contains an important concept in Śaiva Siddhānta. The two karmas refers to good and bad karmas. Eradicating them means

that such a soul is close to the stage of being released from all of the bonds that keep it from realizing its true, divine nature.

43. The metaphor Ammaiyār uses to describe the harsh nature of Śiva for those who do not worship him is that he is like a *koṭi* of fire, or a creeper, pole, banner of fire, none of which work in English. The implication is that the fire is not comforting and lovely like a golden flame, but menacing and dangerous.

44. Here Śiva is described as having three eyes, the sun and the moon in addition to his usual third eye in his forehead, the eye of divine knowledge. He is the universe, including the sun and moon.

45. Śiva's attendants are called *gaṇas,* and are usually demons, goblins, or ghosts. See Chapter 2 for a discussion of this poem.

46. Mataṉ is another name for Kāma, the god of desire and love. This poem refers to the myth of Śiva burning Kāma (*Kāmārimūrti, Dakṣiṇāmūrti*). The terrible demon Tāraka was terrorizing the gods and causing havoc in the world. The gods knew that only a son of Śiva was capable of killing him. The ascetic yogi Śiva was engaged in meditation in a Himalayan forest. Satī had been reborn as Pārvatī, the daughter of the mountain, Himavān, and was performing austerities (*tapas*) in order to win Śiva as her husband. The gods sent Kāma, the god of Desire, to pierce Śiva with his flower-arrow to rouse his passion and love for Pārvatī so that they could produce the son that would save the world. But when Kāma came before Śiva with his bow and arrow, Śiva opened his third eye and burned Kāma to ashes. In some versions of this story Śiva is sitting under a banyan tree in the Himalayas teaching four sages the highest knowledge of the Absolute when Kāma interrupts him; this is Śiva's form as Dakṣiṇāmūrti, the great teacher. *Śiva Purāṇa* vol. 2, 525–548 (Rudra-Saṃhitā, Pārvatī Khaṇḍa, 14–19); Mani 1975, 378–379; O'Flaherty 1973, 148–151; 1975, 154–159; Kramrisch 1988, 349–363; Dorai Rangaswamy 337–342, 417–439; Peterson 1989, 345–346.

47. Unlike the later *Tēvāram* poets, Kāraikkāl Ammaiyār does not specify other religious groups such as Jains and Buddhists. But it is clear that she is defining her path against non-Vedic groups among others. See Chapter 2 for a discussion of this poem.

48. Here Śiva is the Truth, the Real. But because He is everything, there is no separate being to know Him.

49. In the poem Ammaiyār repeats the verb *aṇi,* "to adorn," using it first to describe Śiva adorning himself with ash, then in the last line to ask which of the goddesses is adorned with his love. I have translated this word as "enjoys" his love.

50. In this poem the love of Hara or Śiva leads the devotees to try to keep him all for themselves by hiding him from others. The word Ammaiyār uses for "deception" or "illusion" is the Tamil *māyam* or Sanskrit *māyā,* which signifies an important aspect of Śaiva Siddhānta cosmology in later centuries. As part of his activity of manifesting and reabsorbing the universe, Śiva, through his Śakti or Goddess, acts upon the original pure potential

substance of the universe, *bindu* or "drop," from which emerges *māyā*; from *māyā* all the elements of the lower material universe are manifested. The cosmos is intimately linked to the degree to which Śiva is concealed. The word Ammaiyār uses to convey the special relationship Śiva has with his devotees is *tāyam*, which connotes family inheritance, share of wealth, and a paternal relationship, all suggesting that the devotee has essentially a "right" to a share of Śiva's grace since he is the divine father who responds to his worshipers' devotion. This poem is discussed in Chapter 2.

51. The fire here is the *pralāya* (Tamil *piraḷayam*), Śiva's fire of destruction that annihilates the world at the end of each cosmic period. She is asking where he keeps that fire when it is not time for the destruction of the world.

52. The word Ammaiyār uses to describe Śiva's hero's ankle bracelets, *āṭu*, means to dance, move, shake, unlike words she uses in other poems to describe the sound the ankle bracelets make. She uses this word three times to describe Śiva's dance, the fire dancing in his hand, and the ankle bracelets shaking.

53. The *antāti* is a poetic structure in which the last syllable or word of a verse is repeated as the first syllable or word of the next verse, forming a kind of chain. *Veṇpā* is a poetic meter that consists of two, three, or four lines per verse. The last line of the verse contains three feet (Tamil *cīr*); the other lines contain four feet. See Chapter 1 for a discussion of Tamil meter.

54. *Erukku* is a purple flowering shrub which grows in cemeteries because it doesn't need much water.

55. Śaṅkaraṉ is a Sanskrit epithet for Śiva that means "good deeds." This poem refers to Śiva's destruction of the three cities of the demons; see the note to *Aṟputat Tiruvantāti* 27.

56. The "moon in the red sky" refers to the moon on Śiva's red matted hair, above which is the snake that also adorns Śiva.

57. This poem also refers to the myth of Śiva as the fiery *liṅga*; see the note to *Aṟputat Tiruvantāti* 19. The commentary to this poem in *Kāraikkālammaiyār Pirapantaṅkaḷ* (69) says that this poem suggests that since even the god Viṣṇu was unable to understand the nature of Śiva's form, who will be able to know his form?

Ātirai is the sixth of the twenty-seven stars and is in the constellation Orion (*Tamil Lexicon* vol. III, 1917). Ātirai is the lunar asterism in the Tamil month of Mārkaḻi (December–January). The *Tēvāram* poet Appar describes this important festival, which suggests it is possible that Ammaiyār was also referring to a festival performed for Śiva on this day (Peterson 1989, 184–186). According to the saints' tradition on this day the darkness of ignorance rises and souls are shown the light (*Kāraikkālammaiyār Tirumuṟai* 26–27, note to poem 8).

58. The five supreme things can mean the five-syllable mantra to Śiva: Nama Śivāyaḥ; or the five ethical restraints: not harming, stealing, lying, deceiving, or being angry (*Kāraikkālammaiyār Tirumuṟai*, 27–28). Or they can refer to the Śaiva Siddhānta categories of God, Śakti or energy, soul, *tirōtam* or concealment of spiritual truths, and mala or one of the fetters (*Kāraik-*

kālammaiyār Pirapantaṅkaḷ, 70–71; *Tamil Lexicon* vol. III, 1924). For the day of Ātirai, see the previous note.

59. In the first line of the Tamil poem, the word *kaṇṭāw* is taken by some commentators as a meaningless syllable simply filling in the meter, which is common. However, this word is an emphatic that intensifies the focus on the poet's heart. Interestingly, Ammaiyār uses the generic male point of view when discussing becoming an ascetic for Śiva.

60. This poem refers to Śiva destroying the demon Rāvaṇa, who has ten heads and therefore twenty shoulders (and arms); see the note to *Aṟputat Tiruvantāti* 18.

61. *Bhūtas* are ghosts; *rākṣasas* are a kind of demon. This poem refers to Śiva's destruction of the three cities of the demons; see the note to *Aṟputat Tiruvantāti* 27.

62. In Śaiva Siddhānta, Śiva conceals himself until the individual soul is ready to reach him. Here Śiva's three forms can refer to Tirumāl and Umā in addition to his own form, or to Murukaṉ and Umā; see *Kāraikkālammaiyār Tirumuṟai* 31; *Kāraikkālammaiyār Pirapantaṅkaḷ*, 75–76; and Suriamurthi, 45. See the note to *Aṟputat Tiruvantāti* 7 for the myth of how Śiva got the elephant skin he wears.

63. This verse is an example of the poetic form *vañcappukaḻcci* in which it seems that the poet is ridiculing an object (or praising it), when in fact the poet is artfully praising it (or ridiculing it); *Tamil Lexicon* vol. VI, 3464. Note that in this poem Ammiayār specifies that it was another snake—Vāsuki—who emitted the poison that Śiva drank, not his own snake.

64. In this poem Ammaiyār artfully shows that devotees do not want to be separated from Śiva but want him to keep them as close to him as he does Umā, who shares his body as half of his form; see *Kāraikkālammaiyār Pirapantaṅkaḷ* 78. A *toṇṭai* fruit looks like a small cucumber and is blood red when ripe.

65. This poem imparts the urgency of following the path of Śiva by emphasizing the impermanence of the body and that one will be transformed and liberated by understanding and loving Śiva.

66. See Chapter 2 for a detailed discussion of the cremation ground and Śiva's dance that Kāraikkāl Ammaiyār describes in this set of poems.

67. I consulted Norman Cutler's translation of this poem, 1987, 121.

68. The *vākai* tree is where *pēys* customarily gather; *Kāraikkālammaiyār Tirumuṟai*, 10. *Iṇtu* can refer to several different plants, but most of them are species of mimosa (*Tamil Lexicon* vol. I, 289). The *āṇṭalai* is possibly a terrestrial bird such as a cock or hen, but more probably here it is a "[f]abulous bird of prey with a head like [a] man's" (*Tamil Lexicon* vol. I, 221). Flags with figures of these birds were used to frighten evil spirits away so that they would not take the offerings from the altar (Ibid).

69. The *picācu* is another kind of demon.

70. In this poem I have kept the first *pēy* in the singular untranslated, but have translated the plural of *pēykaḷ* here into English rather than using "*pēys*."

The word I have translated here as "terrifying" is *aṇaṅku,* which can also refer to a terrifying goddess; see Chapter 2 for a discussion of this term.

71. In this poem I have not translated *kaḻal* or hero's anklets to help distinguish them from the other pair of anklets, the *cilampu* worn by Kālī. Ammaiyār uses the two different sets of ankle bracelets, which each make different sounds, to show that both Śiva and Kālī are dancing.

72. The seven notes of the scale in the order in which they are played here are *tuttam, kaikkiḷai, viḷari, tāram, uḻai, iḷi, ōcai*. The instruments in this poem are difficult to identify definitively; I consulted the commentaries to the poem in *Tiruvālaṅkāṭṭu Talavaralāṟum Tiruppatikaṅkaḷum*, 38–39 and *Kāraikkālammaiyār Tirumuṟai*, 14–15. The *uṭukkai* is the small two-sided drum that Śiva plays.

73. Reaching Śiva or *civakati* here means the devotee will achieve final liberation from this world.

74. The botanical and common names of the plants in this poem are as follows: *eṭṭi* is strychnos nuxvomica; *ilavam* is eriodendron anfractuosum, or the silk cotton tree; *īkai* is a species of mimosa; *cūrai* is zizyphus hapeca; and *kārai* is webera tetrandra (Ramachandra, 13).

75. See the note to poem 6 in the first *patikam* for a discussion of the word for "terrifying."

76. The *tāḷi* palm has leaves that look shredded.

77. In classical Tamil literature there is a belief that there are pearls inside bamboo; personal communication, Dr. R. Vijayalakshmy. Māyaṉ means dark-complexioned, here an epithet of Śiva. This is another poem in which I have translated *aṇaṅku* not as a goddess but as threatening; see the note to poem 6 in the first *patikam*.

78. "The One Without Blemish" is literally the one without *mala*, the primordial stain that is one of the fetters that keep the soul in bondage in Śaiva Siddhānta.

Works Cited

Tamil Texts

Akanāṉūṟu Kaḷiṟṟiyāṉai Nirai. 1981. Poems 1–50. With commentary by Pō. Vē. Cōmacuntaraṉār. Chennai: The Tirunelveli South India Saiva Siddhanta Works Publishing Society.

Bālakumāraṉ. 1999. "Kāraikkāl Ammaiyār." In *Periya Purāṇak Kataikaḷ*. Chennai: Thirumagal Nilayam.

Cēkkiḻār. 1970. *Periya Purāṇam eṉṟu Tiruttoṇṭar Purāṇam*. Commentary by Śrimat Muttukkumāra Swami Tampirāṉ. Śri Vaikuṇṭam: Śri Kumarakuruparaṉ Caṅkam.

Cilappatikāram. 1999. Commentary by N. Mu. Vēṇkaṭacāmi Nāṭṭār. Tirunelvēli: The South India Saiva Siddhanta Works Publishing Society Tinnevelly, Limited, 1999.

Irattiṉa Capaiyaiyuṭaiya Tiruvālaṅkāṭṭu Talavaralāṟu: Ālaṅkāṭṭil Aṇṭamuṟa Nimirntāṭum Maṇiyampalakkūttaṉ. 1997. Chennai: Kavuniyan Press.

Kaṭaic Caṅkappulavaruḷ oruvrākiya Maturaik Kūlavāṇikaṉ Cīttalaic Cāttaṉar Maṇimēkalai. 1965. Commentary by Doctor. U. Vē. Cāminātaiyaravarkaḷ. Chennai: Kabeer Printing Works.

Kāraikkāl Ammaiyār. n.d. Columbia Films DVD.

Kāraikkāl Stalapurāṇam. 1895. Karikal: Intiyakāvalaṉ Printing-house.

Kāraikkālammaiyār Pirapantaṅkaḷ. 1961. Commentary by Śri Aṟumukattampirāṉ. Tiruvāvaṭuturai: Tiruvāvaṭuturai Math.

Kāraikkālammaiyār Tirumuṟai. 1994. Commentary by Tiru. Vi. Kaliyāṇacuntaraṉār. Chennai: Pāri Nilaiyam.

Kāraikkāl Talapurāṇamum Kāraikkālammaiyār Aruḷ Varalāṟum. 2005. Edited by Śiva Kailācanātaṉ. Kāraikkāl: Śri Kayilācanāta Cuvāmi Śri Nittiya Kalyāṇap Perumāḷ Vakaiyaṟā Tēvastāṉam.

Kāṣyapaṉ. 2001. "Śakti Taricaṉam," Part One. *Āṉanta Vikaṭaṉ* Vol. 76, No. 40, October 7, 2001: 120–128.

———. 2001. "Śakti Taricaṉam," Part Two. *Āṉanta Vikaṭaṉ* Vol. 76, No. 41, October 14, 2001: 120–128.

Kriyāviṉ Taṟkālat Tamiḻ Akarāti (Tamiḻ-Tamiḻ-Āṅkilam). 2001. Dictionary of Contemporary Tamil (Tamil-Tamil-English). Chennai: Cre-A.

Pāpaṉācam Civaṉ. 1977. *Kāraikkāl Ammaiyār Icai Nāṭakam*. Chennai: Grace Printers.
Periya Purāṇam eṉṟu vaḻaṅkukiṉṟa Tiruttoṇṭar Purāṇam. 1970. Edited by Cuppiramaṇiya Piḷḷai. Śri Vaikuṇṭam: Śri Kumarakuruparaṉ Caṅkam.
Puṟanāṉūṟu. 1983. Commentary by Puliyūr Kecikaṉ. Chennai: Maruti Press.
Suriamurthy, Gomathi. 2003. *Kāraikkāl Ammaiyār*. New Delhi: Sahitya Akademi.
Tirumantiram. 2001 [1942]. Edited by P. Irāmanāta Piḷḷai. Vol. 2. Chennai: The South India Saiva Siddhanta Works Publishing Society.
Tirumurukāṟṟuppaṭai. 1967. Commentary by Ti. Paṭṭucāmi Ōtuvār. Chennai: Aṉṉai Nilaiyam.
Tiruvālaṅkāṭṭuppurāṇam. 1865. Chennai: Kalviviḷakka Printing Press.
Tiruvālaṅkāṭṭu Talavaralāṟum Tiruppatikaṅkaḷum. 1998. Tiruttaṇi: Cuppiramaṇiya Cuvāmi Tirukkōyil.
Tiruvālaṅkāṭṭu Talavaralāṟum Tiruppatikaṅkaḷum. 2002. Tiruttaṇi: Cuppiramaṇiya Cuvāmi Tirukkōyil.
Vēlaṉ, Vittuvāṉ Ka. Na. 2000. *Kāraikkāl Ammaiyāriṉ Vāḻvum Vākkum*. Chennai: M. K. Enterprises.

Texts in Other Languages

Ahir, D. C. 1992. *Buddhism in South India*. Delhi: Sri Satguru Publications.
Ayyar, C. V. Narayana. 1974. *Origin and Early History of Śaivism in South India*. Madras: University of Madras.
Baskaran, S. Theodore. 1996. *The Eye of the Serpent: An Introduction to Tamil Cinema*. Madras: East West Books.
Bell, Catherine. 1992. *Ritual Theory, Ritual Practice*. New York: Oxford University Press.
Bhandarkar, Ramkrishna Gopal. 1983. *Vaiṣṇavism, Śaivism and Minor Religious Systems*. New Delhi: Asian Educational Services.
Biardeau, Madeleine. 1995. *Hinduism: The Anthropology of a Civilization*. New Delhi: Oxford.
Bourdieu, Pierre. 1977. *Outline of a Theory of Practice*. Cambridge: Cambridge University Press.
Brooks, Douglas Renfrew. 1990. *The Secret of the Three Cities: An Introduction to Hindu Śākta Tantrism*. Chicago: University of Chicago Press.
Buck, David C., and K. Paramasivam, transl. 1997. *The Study of Stolen Love: A Translation of Kaḷaviyal eṉṟa Iṟaiyaṉār Akapporuḷ with Commentary by Nakkīraṉār*. Atlanta: Scholars Press.
Bynum, Caroline Walker. 1987. *Holy Feast, Holy Fast: The Religious Significance of Food to Medieval Women*. Berkeley: University of California Press.
Caldwell, Sarah. 2003. "Margins at the Center: Tracing Kālī through Time, Space, and Culture." In *Encountering Kālī: In the Margins, At the Center,*

In the West. Edited by Rachel Fell McDermott and Jeffrey J. Kripal, 249–272. Berkeley: University of California Press.

Carman, John B. 2005 [1987]. "Bhakti." In *Encyclopedia of Religion*. 2d ed, vol. 2. Edited by Lindsay Jones, 856–860. New York: Macmillan Reference USA.

Chakravarti, Mahadev. 1986. *The Concept of Rudra-Śiva Through the Ages*. Delhi: Motilal Banarsidass.

Chakravarty, Uma. 1989. "The World of the Bhaktin in South Indian Traditions—the Body and Beyond." *Manushi* Numbers 50–51–52: 18–29.

Champakalakshmi, R. 2004. "From Devotion and Dissent to Dominance: The Bhakti of the Tamil Āḻvārs and Nāyanārs." In *Religious Movements in South Asia 600–1800*. Edited by David N. Lorenzen, 47–80. New Delhi: Oxford University Press.

Chinniah, Sathiavathi. 2008. "The Tamil Film Heroine: From a Passive Subject to a Pleasurable Object." In *Tamil Cinema: The Cultural Politics of India's Other Film Industry*. Edited by Selvaraj Velayutham. London: Routledge: 29–43.

Cilappatikaram. 1997. Trans. V. R. Ramachandra Dikshitar. Chennai: International Institute of Tamil Studies.

Clothey, Fred W. 1978. *The Many Faces of Murukaṉ: The History and Meaning of a South Indian God*. New Delhi: Munshiram Manoharalal Publishers Pvt. Ltd.

Coburn, Thomas B. 1991. *Encountering the Goddess: A Translation of the Devī-Māhātmya and a Study of Its Interpretation*. Albany: State University of New York Press.

———. 1996. "Devī: The Great Goddess." In *Devī: Goddesses of India*, Edited by John Stratton Hawley and Donna Marie Wulff, 31–48. Berkeley: University of California Press.

Coomaraswamy, Ananda. 1999 [1918]. *The Dance of Shiva*. New Delhi: Munshiram Manoharlal Publishers.

Craddock, Elaine. 2001. "Reconstructing the Split Goddess as Śakti in a Tamil Village." In *Seeking Mahādevī: Constructing the Identities of the Hindu Great Goddess*. Edited by Tracy Pintchman, 145–169. Albany: State University of New York Press.

———. 2007. "The Anatomy of Devotion: The Life and Poetry of Karaikkal Ammaiyar." In *Women's Lives, Women's Rituals in the Hindu Tradition*, Edited by Tracy Pintchman, 131–147. New York: Oxford University Press.

Cutler, Norman. 1987. *Songs of Experience: The Poetics of Tamil Devotion*. Bloomington: Indiana University Press.

———. 2003a. "Three Moments in the Genealogy of Tamil Literary Culture." In *Literary Cultures in History: Reconstructions From South Asia*. Edited by Sheldon Pollock, 271–322. Berkeley: University of California Press.

———. 2003b. "Tamil Hindu Literature." In *The Blackwell Companion to Hinduism*. Edited by Gavin Flood, 145–158. Oxford: Blackwell Publishing.

Davis, Richard H. 1988. "Cremation and Liberation: The Revision of a Hindu Ritual." *History of Religions*. 28/1 (August): 37–53.

———. 1999. "The Story of the Disappearing Jains." In *Open Boundaries: Jain Communities and Cultures in Indian History*. Edited by John E. Cort, 213–224. Delhi: Sri Satguru Publications.

———. 2000. *Ritual in an Oscillating Universe: Worshiping Śiva in Medieval India*. Delhi: Motilal Banarsidass.

De Bruijn, Peter J. J. 2007. *Kāraikkālammaiyār: Part 1: An iconographical and textual study; Part 2: Poems for Śiva*. Rotterdam: Dhyani Publications.

Dehejia, Vidya. 1988. *Slaves of the Lord: The Path of the Tamil Saints*. New Delhi: Munshiram Manoharlal Publishers.

Denton, Lynn Teskey. 1992. "Varieties of Hindu Female Asceticism." In *Roles and Rituals for Hindu Women*. Edited by Julia Leslie, 211–231. Delhi: Motilal Banarsidass.

Devasenapathy, V. A. 1983. "*Karma* and Grace in Śaiva Siddhānta." In *Experiencing Śiva: Encounters with a Hindu Deity*. Edited by Fred W. Clothey and J. Bruce Long, 7–18. Columbia, Mo: South Asia Books.

Devasenapathi, V. A. 1966 [1960]. *Śaiva Siddhānta: As Expounded in the Śivajñāna-Siddhiyār and Its Six Commentaries*. Madras: University of Madras.

Dhaky, M. A. 1984. "Bhūtas and Bhūtanāyakas: Elementals and Their Captains." In *Discourses on Śiva: Proceedings of a Symposium on the Nature of Religious Imagery*. Edited by Michael W. Meister, 240–256. Bombay: Vakils, Feffer & Simons Ltd.

Dhavamony, Mariasusai. 1971. *Love of God According to Śaiva Siddhānta*. Oxford: Clarendon Press.

Divakaran, Odile. 1984. "Durgā the Great Goddess: Meanings and Forms in the Early Period." In *Discourses on Śiva: Proceedings of a Symposium on the Nature of Religious Imagery*. Edited by Michael W. Meister, 271–288. Bombay: Vakils, Feffer & Simons Ltd.

Dorai Rangaswamy, M. A. 1990 (1958/1959). *The Religion and Philosophy of Tēvāram*. 2d ed. Madras: University of Madras.

Dowson, John. 2000. *A Classical Dictionary of Hindu Mythology and Religion: Geography, History and Literature*. Varanasi: Pilgrims Publishing House.

Filliozat, Jean. 1983. "The Role of the Śaivāgamas in the Śaiva Ritual System." In *Experiencing Śiva: Encounters With a Hindu Deity*. Edited by Fred W. Clothey and J. Bruce Long, 81–101. Columbia, MO: South Asia Books.

Flood, Gavin. 1996. *An Introduction to Hinduism*. Cambridge: Cambridge University Press.

———. 2004. *The Ascetic Self: Subjectivity, Memory and tradition*. Cambridge: Cambridge University Press.

———. 2006. *The Tantric Body: The Secret Tradition of Hindu Religion*. London: I. B. Tauris.

Ghose, Rajeswari. 1996. *The Tyāgarāja Cult in Tamilnadu: A Study in Conflict and Accommodation*. New Delhi: Motilal Banarsidass.

Gonda, J. 1980. "The Śatarudriya." In *Sanskrit and Indian Studies: Essays in Honor of Daniel H. H. Ingalls*. Edited by Masatoshi Nagatomi, B. K. Matilal, M. M. Masson, and E. C. Dimock, Jr., 75–91. Dordrecht: D. Reidel.

Grieve, Mrs. M., "Jujube Berries." *Botanical.com: A Modern Herbal*. Accessed November 10, 2003. http://www.botanical.com/botanicalj/jujube10.html.

Gros, François. 2009. *Deep Rivers: Selected Writings on Tamil Literature*. Translated from French by M. P. Boseman. Edited by Kannan M. and Jennifer Clare. Pondicherry: Institut Français de Pondichéry; Tamil Chair, Department of South and Southeast Asian Studies, University of California at Berkeley.

Handelman, Don, and David Shulman. 2004. *Śiva in the Forest of Pines: An Essay on Sorcery and Self-Knowledge*. New Delhi: Oxford University Press.

Hardy, Friedhelm. 1983. *Viraha-Bhakti: The Early History of Kṛṣṇa Devotion in South India*. New Delhi: Oxford University Press.

Harlan, Lindsey, and Paul B. Courtright. 1995. "Introduction: On Hindu Marriage and Its Margins." In *From the Margins of Hindu Marriage*. Edited by Lindsey Harlan and Paul B. Courtright, 3–18. New York: Oxford University Press.

Hart, George L., III. 1973. "Woman and the Sacred in Ancient Tamilnad." *Journal of Asian Studies*, 32/2 (February): 233–250.

———. 1975. *The Poems of Ancient Tamil*. Berkeley: University of California Press.

———. 1976. "The Relation Between Tamil and Classical Sanskrit Literature." *A History of Indian Literature*. Edited by Jan Gonda, 10/2: 317–352. Wiesbaden: Otto Harrassowitz.

———. 1979. "The Nature of Tamil Devotion." In *Aryan and Non-Aryan in India*. Edited by Madhav N. Deshpande and Peter Hook, 11–33. Ann Arbor: Michigan Papers on South and Southeast Asia, 14.

———. 1980. "The Theory of Reincarnation Among the Tamils." In *Karma and Rebirth in Classical Indian Traditions*. Edited by Wendy O'Flaherty, 116–133. Berkeley: University of California Press.

———. 1988. "Early Evidence for Caste in South India." In *Dimensions of Social Life: Essays in Honor of David G. Mandelbaum*. Edited by Paul Hockings, 467–491. Berlin: Mouton de Gruyter.

———, and Hank Heifetz, transl. and ed. 1999. *The Four Hundred Songs of War and Wisdom: An Anthology of Poems from Classical Tamil: The Puṟanāṉūṟu*. New York: Columbia University Press.

Hawley, John Stratton. 1995. "The Nirguṇ/Saguṇ Distinction in Early Manuscript Anthologies of Hindi Devotion." In *Bhakti Religion in North India: Community Identity and Political Action*. Edited by David N. Lorenzen, 160–180. Albany: State University of New York Press.

Hiltebeitel, Alf. 1988. *The Cult of Draupadī, 1: Mythologies: From Gingee to Kurukṣetra*. Chicago: University of Chicago Press.

———. 1991. *The Cult of Draupadī, 2: On Hindu Ritual and the Goddess*. Chicago: University of Chicago Press.

Hudson, D. Dennis. 1994. "Rādha and Pinnai: Diverse Manifestations of the Same Goddess?" *Journal of Vaishnava Studies*, 3, 115–153.

Hudson, D. Dennis. 1982. "Pinnai: Krishna's Cowherd Wife." In *The Divine Consort: Rādhā and the Goddesses of India*. Edited by John Stratton Hawley and Donna Marie Wulff, 238–261. Berkeley: Graduate Theological Union.

———. 1989. "Violent and Fanataical Devotion Among the Nāyanārs: A Study in the *Periya Purāṇam* of Cēkkilār." In *Criminal Gods and Demon Devotees: Essays on the Guardians of Popular Hinduism*. Edited by Alf Hiltebeitel, 373–404. Albany: State University of New York Press.

———. 1997. "The Courtesan and Her Bowl: An Esoteric Buddhist Reading of the *Maṇimēkalai*." In *A Buddhist Woman's Path to Enlightenment: Proceedings of a Workshop on the Tamil Narrative Maṇimēkalai*, Uppsala University, May 25–29, 1995. Uppsala: Academiae Ubsaliensis: 151–190.

Iraianban, Swamiji, transl. 1999. *Om Namashivaya: Tiruvasagham*. New Delhi: Abhinav Publications.

Ishimatsu, Ginette. 1999. "The Making of Tamil Shaiva Siddhānta." *Contributions to Indian Sociology*. n.s. 33/3, 571–579. New Delhi: Sage Publications.

———. N.d. "Between Text and Tradition: Hindu Ritual and Politics in South India." Unpublished manuscript.

Iyengar, P. T. Srinivasa. 1995. *History of the Tamils From the Earliest Times to 600 A.D.* New Delhi: Asian Educational Services.

Joshi, N. P. 1984. "Early Forms of Śiva." In *Discourses on Śiva: Proceedings of a Symposium on the Nature of Religious Imagery*. Edited by Michael W. Meister, 47–61. Bombay: Vakils, Feffer & Simons Ltd.

Kailasapathy, K. 1968. *Tamil Heroic Poetry*. Oxford: The Clarendon Press.

Kaimal, Padma. 1999. Shiva Nataraja: Shifting Meanings of an Icon." *Art Bulletin*. 81/3 (September): 390–419. Retrieved November 3, 2003 from Academic Search Premier Database.

Kandiah, A. 1984. *Cult and Worship of Murukan̲ as Reflected in the Paripāṭal and the Tirumurukār̲r̲uppaṭai*. Sri Lanka: Government Press.

Karavelane, trans. 1982. *Chants dévotionionnels Tamouls de Kāraikkālammaiyār*. Edited and translated by Karavelane. Introduction by Jean Filliozat; Postface by François Gros. Pondicherry: Publications de l'Institut Français d'Indologie de Pondichéry, No. 1. New Edition.

Khandelwal, Meena. 2004. *Women in Ochre Robes: Gendering Hindu Renunication*. Albany: State University of New York Press.

Kinsley, David. 1986. *Hindu Goddesses: Visions of the Divine Feminine in the Hindu Religious Tradition*. Berkeley: University of California Press.

Kramrisch, Stella. 1988. *The Presence of Śiva*. Delhi: Motilal Banarsidass.

Krishna Murthy, C. 1985. *Śaiva Art and Architecture in South India*. Delhi: Sundeep Prakashan.

Lakshmi, C. S. 2008. "A Good Woman, A Very Good Woman: Tamil Cinema's Women." In *Tamil Cinema: The Cultural Politics of India's Other Film Industry*. Edited by Selvaraj Velayutham, 16–28. London: Routledge.

Long, J. Bruce. 1983. "Rudra as an Embodiment of Divine Ambivalence in the *Śatarudrīya Stotram*." In *Experiencing Śiva: Encounters with a Hindu Deity*. Edited by Fred W. Clothey and J. Bruce Long, 103–128. New Delhi: Manohar.

Lorenzen, David N. 1972. *The Kāpālikas and Kālāmukhas: Two Lost Śaivite Sects*. Delhi: Motilal Banarsidass, 1972.

———. 2002. "Early Evidence for Tantric Religion." In *The Roots of Tantra*. Edited by Katherine Anne Harper and Robert L. Brown, 25–36. Albany: SUNY Press.

Lutgendorf, Philip. 2000. "City, Forest, and Cosmos: Ecological Perspectives from the Sanskrit Epics." In *Hinduism and Ecology: The Intersection of Earth, Sky, and Water*. Edited by Christopher Key Chapple and Mary Evelyn Tucker, 269–289. Cambridge: Harvard University Press.

Madhavan, Chithra. 2005. *History and Culture of Tamil Nadu: As Gleaned From the Sanskrit Inscriptions*, Volume I (Up to *c*. AD 1310). New Delhi: D. K. Printworld Ltd.

Mahalakshmi R. 2000. "Outside the Norm, Within the Tradition: Kāraikkāl Ammaiyār and the Ideology of Tamil Bhakti." *Studies in History*, 16, 1, n.s., 17–40. New Delhi: Sage Publications.

Mani, Vettam. 1975. *Purāṇic Encyclopaedia*. Delhi: Motilal Banarsidass.

Miller, Barabara Stoler. 1984. "Kālidāsa's Verbal Icon: Aṣṭamūrti Śiva." In *Discourses on Śiva: Proceedings of a Symposium on the Nature of Religious Imagery*. Edited by Michael W. Meister, 223–239. Bombay: Vakils, Feffer & Simons Ltd.

———, transl. 1986. *The Bhagavad-Gita: Krishna's Counsel in Time of War*. New York: Bantam Books.

Mines, Diane P. 2005. *Fierce Gods: Inequality, Ritual, and the Politics of Dignity in a South Indian Village*. Bloomington: Indiana University Press.

Monius, Anne E. 2001. *Imagining a Place for Buddhism*. Oxford: Oxford University Press.

———. 2004a. "Śiva as Heroic Father: Theology and Hagiography in Medieval South India." *The Harvard Theological Review* 97, No. 2: 165–197.

———. 2004b. "Love, Violence, and the Aesthetics of Disgust: Śaivas and Jains in Medieval South India." *Journal of Indian Philosophy* 32: 113–172.

Murugan, V. 1999. *Kalittokai in English*. Chennai: Institute of Asian Studies.

Nanda, Vivek, ed. with George Michell. 2004. *Chidambaram: Home of Nataraja*. Mumbai: Marg Publications.

Narayanan, Vasudha. 2003. "Embodied Cosmologies: Sights of Piety, Sites of Power." *Journal of the American Academy of Religion* 71, No. 3 (September): 495–520.

Natarajan, B., transl. 1999. *Thirumandiram: A Classic of Yoga and Tantra*. 3 vols. Chidambaram: Babaji's Kriya Yoga Order of Acharyas, U.S.A., Inc.

Navaratnam, Kalaipulavar K. 1963. *Studies in Hinduism*. Jaffna, Ceylon: Thirumakal Press.

Nilakanta Sastri, K. A. 1963. *Development of Religion in South India*. Bombay: Orient Longmans.

———. 1975. *A History of South India*. 4th ed. New Delhi: Oxford University Press.

Obeyesekere, Gananath. 1984. *The Cult of the Goddess Pattini*. Chicago: University of Chicago Press.

O'Flaherty, Wendy Doniger. 1981. *Śiva: The Erotic Ascetic*. London: Oxford University Press.

———, transl. 1975. *Hindu Myths*. London: Penguin Books.

Olivelle, Patrick. 1998. "Hair and Society: Social Significance of Hair in South Asian Tradition." In *Hair: Its Power and Meaning in Asian Cultures*. Edited by Alf Hiltebeitel and Barbara D. Miller, 11–49. Albany: State University of New York Press.

———, transl. 1996. *Upaniṣads*. New York: Oxford University Press.

Orr, Leslie. 1999. "Jain and Hindu 'Religious Women' In Early Medieval Tamilnadu." In *Open Boundaries: Jain Communities and Cultures in Indian History*. Edited by John E. Cort, 187–212. Delhi: Sri Satguru Publications.

Padoux, Andre. 2002. "What Do We Mean by Tantrism?" In *The Roots of Tantra*. Edited by Katherine Anne Harper and Robert L. Brown, 17–24. Albany: SUNY Press.

Pandian, Jacob. 1982. "The Goddess Kannagi: A Dominant Symbol of South Indian Tamil Society." In *Mother Worship: Themes and Variations*. Edited by James J. Preston, 177–191. Chapel Hill: University of North Carolina Press.

Parthasarathy, R., transl. 1993. *The Tale of an Anklet, An Epic of South India: The Cilappatikāram of Iḷaṅkō Aṭikaḷ*. New York: Columbia University Press.

Pechilis, Karen. 2007. "The Story of the Classical Tamil Woman Saint, Kāraikkāl Ammaiyār: A Translation of Her Story from Cēkkiḻār's *Periya Purāṇam*." *International Journal of Hindu Studies* (2006) 10:173–186; published online March 2007, Springer Science+Business Media B.V.

———. 2008. "Chosen Moments: Mediation and Direct Experience in the Life of the Classical Tamil Saint Kāraikkāl Ammaiyār." *Journal of Feminist Studies in Religion* Vol. 24, No. 1: 11–31.

Peterson, Indira V. 1982. "Singing of a Place: Pilgrimage as Metaphor and Motif in the Tevaram Songs of the Tamil Saivite Saints." *Journal of the American Oriental Society* Vol. 102, No. 1: 69–90. Accessed through JSTOR: http://www.jstor.org/journals/aos.html, on November 11, 2003.

Peterson, Indira Viswanathan. 1989. *Poems to Śiva*. Princeton: Princeton University Press.

———. 1999. "Śramaṇas Against the Tamil Way: Jains as Others in Tamil Śaiva Literature." In *Open Boundaries: Jain Communities and Cultures in Indian History*. Edited by John E. Cort, 163–185. Delhi: Sri Satguru Publications.

———. 2003. *Design and Rhetoric in a Sanskrit Court Epic*. Albany: State University of New York Press.

Pillay, K. K. 1979. *Studies in the History of India with Special Reference to Tamil Nadu*. Madras: Rathnam Press.

Prentiss, Karen Pechilis. 1999. *The Embodiment of Bhakti*. New York: Oxford University Press.

Rajam, V. S. 1986. "*Aṇaṅku*: A Notion Semantically Reduced to Signify Female Sacred Power." *Journal of the American Oriental Society*, Vol 1, No. 2: 257–272.

Ram, Kalpana. 2008. "Bringing the Amman into Presence in Tamil Cinema: Cinema Spectatorship as Sensuous Apprehension." In *Tamil Cinema: The Cultural Politics of India's Other Film Industry*. Edited by Selvaraj Velayutham, 44–58. London: Routledge.

Ramachandran, T. N., transl. 1993. *The Hymns of Kaaraikkaal Ammaiyaar*. Dharmapuram: International Institute of Savia Siddhanta Research.

Ramanujan, A. K., transl. 1981. *Hymns for the Drowning: Poems for Viṣṇu by Nammāḻvār*. Princeton, New Jersey: Princeton University Press.

———. 1985. *Poems of Love and War from the Eight Anthologies and the Ten Long Poems of Classical Tamil*. New York: Columbia University Press.

———. 1994 [1967]. *The Interior Landscape: Love Poems from a Classical Tamil Anthology*. Delhi: Oxford University Press.

Ramanujan, A. K. 1984. "The Myths of Bhakti: Images of Śiva in Śaiva Poetry." In *Discourses on Śiva: Proceedings of a Symposium on the Nature of Religious Imagery*. Edited by Michael W. Meister, 212–222. Bombay: Vakils, Feffer & Simons Ltd.

———. 1999a. "Towards an Anthology of City Images." In *The Collected Essays of A. K. Ramanujan*. Edited by Vinay Dharwadker, 52–72. New Delhi: Oxford University Press.

———. 1999b. "Classics Lost and Found." In *The Collected Essays of A. K. Ramanujan*. Edited by Vinay Dharwadker, 184–196. New Delhi: Oxford University Press.

———. 1999c. "Form in Classical Tamil Poetry." In *The Collected Essays of A. K. Ramanujan*. Edited by Vinay Dharwadker, 197–218. New Delhi: Oxford University Press.

———. 1999d. "From Classicism to *Bhakti*." In *The Collected Essays of A. K. Ramanujan*. Edited by Vinay Dharwadker, 232–259. New Delhi: Oxford University Press.

Ramaswamy, Sumathi. 1997. *Passions of the Tongue: Language Devotion in Tamil India, 1891–1970*. Berkeley: University of California Press.

———. 2004. *The Lost Land of Lemuria: Fabulous Geographies, Catastrophic Histories*. Berkeley: University of California Press.

Ramaswamy, Vijaya. 1997. *Walking Naked: Women, Society, Spirituality in South India*. Shimla: Indian Institute of Advanced Study.

———. 2003. "The Metamorphosis of Alli and Neeli: Folktales and Mythic Images of Tamil Women." In *Re-searching Indian Women*. Edited by Vijaya Ramaswamy, 149–174. New Delhi: Manohar.

Rangacharya, Adya, transl. 1996. *The Nāṭyaśāstra: English Translation with Critical Notes*. New Delhi: Munshiram Manoharlal Publishers.
Richman, Paula. 1988. *Women, Branch Stories, and Religious Rhetoric in a Tamil Buddhist Text*. Syracuse: Maxwell School of Citizenship and Public Affairs, Syracuse University.
Ryan, James. 1999. "Erotic Excess and Sexual Danger in the *Cīvakacintāmaṇi*." In *Open Boundaries: Jain Communities and Cultures in Indian History*. Edited by John E. Cort, 67–83. Delhi: Sri Satguru Publications.
Sasivalli, Dr. S. *Karaikkal Ammaiyar*. 1984. Chennai: International Institute of Tamil Studies.
Schomerus, H. W. 2000. *Śaiva Siddhānta: An Indian School of Mystical Thought*. Translated by Mary Law. Delhi: Motilal Banarsidass.
Sharma, Krishna. 1987. *Bhakti and the Bhakti Movement: A New Perspective*. New Delhi: Munshiram Manoharlal Publishers.
Shulman, David Dean. 1980. *Tamil Temple Myths: Sacrifice and Divine Marriage in the South Indian Śaiva Tradition*. Princeton: Princeton University Press.
———. 1985. *The* King *and the* Clown *in South Indian Myth and Poetry*. Princeton: Princeton University Press.
———. 1993. *The Hungry God: Hindu Tales of Filicide and Devotion*. Chicago: University of Chicago Press.
———. 2001. *The Wisdom of Poets: Studies in Tamil, Telugu, and Sanskrit*. New Delhi: Oxford University Press.
———. 2002. "*Tirukkovaiyār*: Downstream into God." In *Self and Self-Transformation in the History of Religion*. Edited by David Shulman and Guy G. Stroumsa, 131–149. Oxford: Oxford University Press.
———, transl. and annotation. 1990. *Songs of the Harsh Devotee: The Tēvāram of Cuntaramūrttināyaṉār*. Philadelphia: University of Pennsylvania, Studies on South Asia Volume 6.
Siddhantashastree, Rabindra Kumar. 1975. *Śaivism Through the Ages*. New Delhi: Munshiram Manoharlal.
The Śiva Purāṇa. 1999 [1970]. Translated by a Board of Scholars; edited by J. L. Shastri. Vol. 1. Delhi: Motilal Banarsidass.
The Śiva Purāṇa. 2000 [1970]. Translated by a Board of Scholars; edited by J. L. Shastri. Vol. 2. Delhi: Motilal Banarsidass.
The Śiva Purāṇa. 2002 [1969]. Translated by a Board of Scholars; edited by J. L. Shastri. Vol. 3. Delhi: Motilal Banarsidass.
The Śiva Purāṇa. 1998 [1970]. Translated by a Board of Scholars; edited by J. L. Shastri. Vol. 4. Delhi: Motilal Banarsidass.
Sivaramamurti, C. 1994. *Nataraja in Art, Thought and Literature*. New Delhi: Ministry of Information and Broadcasting, Government of India.
———. 1984. "Forms of Śiva in Sanskrit Sources." In *Discourses on Śiva: Proceedings of a Symposium on the Nature of Religious Imagery*. Edited by Michael W. Meister, 182–190. Bombay: Vakils, Feffer & Simons Ltd.
———. 1976. *Śatarudrīya: Vibhūti of Śiva's Iconography*. New Delhi: Abhinav Publications.

Sivaraman, K. 2001 [1973]. *Śaivism in Philosophical Perspective: A Study of the Formative Concepts, Problems and Methods of Śaiva Siddhānta*. Delhi: Motilal Banarsidass.

Smith, David. 1998. *The Dance of Śiva: Religion, Art and Poetry in South India*. Cambridge: Cambridge University Press.

Srinivasan, Doris Meth. 1984. "Significance and Scope of Pre-Kuṣāṇa Śaivite Iconography." In *Discourses on Śiva: Proceedings of a Symposium on the Nature of Religious Imagery*. Edited by Michael W. Meister, 32–46. Bombay: Vakils, Feffer & Simons Ltd.

Stein, Burton. 1980. *Peasant State and Society in Medieval South India*. New Delhi: Oxford University Press.

Subramaniam, V. 1992. "The Origins of Bhakti in Tamilnadu: A Transformation of Secular Romanticism to Emotional Identification with a Personal Deity." In *Bhakti Studies*. Edited by G. M. Bailey and I. Kesarcodi-Watson, 11–51. New Delhi: Sterling Publishers.

Subramanyam, Ka. Na., translator. 1977. *The Anklet Story*. Delhi: Agam Prakashan.

Sundaram, P. S., transl. 1990. *Tiruvalluvar: The Kural*. London: Penguin Books.

Tamil Lexicon. 1982. 6 Volumes and Supplement. Madras: University of Madras.

Thapar, Romila. 1966. *A History of India, Volume One*. Middlesex: Penguin Books.

Ulrich, Katherine. 2003. "Practical Polemics from the Main Nīlakēci." Paper delivered at the American Academy of Religion Meeting, November 20.

Vanmikanathan, G., transl. 1985. *Sekkizhaar, Periya Puranam: A Tamil Classic on the Great Saiva Saints of South India*. Condensed English Version. Madras: Sri Ramakrishna Math.

Vatsyayan, Kapila. 1984. "Śiva-Naṭeśa: Cadence and Form." In *Discourses on Śiva: Proceedings of a Symposium on the Nature of Religious Imagery*. Edited by Michael W. Meister, 191–201. Bombay: Vakils, Feffer & Simons Ltd.

White, David Gordon. 1996. *The Alchemical Body: Siddha Traditions in Medieval India*. Chicago: University of Chicago Press.

———. 2000. "Introduction." In *Tantra in Practice*. Edited by David Gordon White, 3–38. Princeton: Princeton University Press.

Wilson, Elizabeth. "The Female Body as a Source of Horror and Insight in Post-Ashokan Indian Buddhism." In *Religious Reflections on the Human Body*. Edited by Jane Marie Law, 76–99. Bloomington: Indiana University Press.

Wood, Michael. 2004. "The Temple at Tiruvalangadu and the Myth of the Dance Competition." In *Chidambaram: Home of Nataraja*. Edited by Vivek Nanda with George Michell. Photographs by Bharath Ramamrutham. Mumbai: Marg Publications, Vol. 55, No. 4: 106–117.

Younger, Paul. 1995. *The Home of Dancing Śivaṉ: The Traditions of the Hindu Temple in Citamparam*. Oxford: Oxford University Press.

Zvelebil, K. V. 1975. *Tamil Literature*. Leiden: E. J. Brill.
Zvelebil, Kamil. 1973. *The Smile of Murugan: On Tamil Literature in South India*. Leiden: E. J. Brill.
Zvelebil, Kamil V. 1985. *Ānanda-Tāṇḍava of Śiva-Sadānṛttamūrti: The Development of the Concept of Āṭavallāṉ-Kūttaperumāṉaṭikaḷ in the South Indian Textual and Iconographic Tradition*. Madras: Institute of Asian Studies.
———, transl. 1987. *Two Tamil Folktales*. New Delhi: Motilal Banarsidass.
Zvelebil, Kamil Veith. 1974. *Tamil Literature*. Wiesbaden: Otto Harrassowitz.

Index

abhiṣeka, 109, 163n17
acai (metrical element), 31–32
Āgamas, 26, 29
Agastya, 97
akam, 8–10, 13–15, 19, 20, 43, 48, 67, 83, 146n2
Āḻvārs, 24, 26, 151n38, 153n7
Ammai ("Mother"), 3, 73, 76, 78, 82, 85, 86, 98, 107, 108, 163nn13–14, 164n40
ānanda-tāṇḍava, 56, 57
aṇaṅku, 19, 79, 150n27, 157n73, 160n11
Aṇaṅku, goddess, 18, 75, 78, 79, 157n73
animals in poetry, 13, 14, 58, 63, 69, 139, 173n68
Āṇṭāḷ, 26, 82
antāti (poetic structure), 24, 31–33, 36, 172n53
Appar, 25, 26, 28, 66, 68, 96, 97, 172n57
Aṟputat Tiruvantāti, 31, 32, 35–52, 54, 55, 57, 65–69, 72, 75, 81, 85, 95, 115–34, 152n53, 154n18, 155n40, 158n81, 160n16
artha (wealth) in *Tirukkuṟaḷ*, 14
Arundhatī, 15
Aryan-Dravidian synthesis, 15
asceticism, 50, 65, 79, 81, 83, 145n3, 155n36
ascetics, 14, 18, 27, 49, 50, 63, 71, 148n17, 169n29
aṣṭamūrti (eight forms of Śiva), 31, 40, 152n51, 167n13
asuras, 52
Atikaḷ, Ilāṅkō, 15
Ātirai, lunar asterism, 68, 172n57
aṭṭavīraṭṭāṉam (Śiva's Eight Heroic Deeds), 80, 154n26
austerities. See *tapas*

Bālakumāraṉ, 86–89
Balarāma, 15
bards, 9, 11, 12, 19, 147n6
battlefield, 10, 12–14, 17, 21, 36, 53, 59, 82
Bell, Catherine, 70
Bhagavad Gītā, 23–24
bhakti, 1, 4, 22–31, 33, 35, 36, 41, 51, 67, 71, 78, 83, 151n33, 151n37, 153n1, 158n87, 168n16
Bharata, 54
Bharata Nāṭyam, 85, 86
bhūtas (ghosts), 38, 39, 53, 95, 152n56
birds in poetry, 13, 14, 61, 63, 69
bones, motif in poetry, 39, 41–44, 50–52, 66
Brahmā, 44, 46, 47, 50, 80, 92, 99
Brahman(s), 14–17, 22, 26, 29, 39, 102, 103, 148n17
Brāhmī script, 8
brahminicide, 48–50, 80, 169n29
Buddhism, 1, 2, 22, 28, 63, 148n15